# Artificial Intelligence and International Arbitration Law

The book asks whether the use of Artificial Intelligence (AI) and Generative AI (GenAI) in international arbitration represents a revolution or an evolution of the international dispute resolution landscape.

Critically engaging with the transformative impact of the Fourth Industrial Revolution (4IR), this book focuses on the integration of AI and GenAI into international commercial arbitration. Set against the backdrop of rapid technological advancement, it explores how arbitral tribunals and stakeholders are cautiously yet progressively adopting these innovations in a manner that respects and preserves the foundational principles of arbitration. Through an interdisciplinary and practice-oriented approach, the book examines the evolving role of AI in arbitration. It analyzes how AI is perceived and applied by parties, arbitral institutions, and arbitrators, as well as assesses the legal frameworks in place to govern it. Offering a balanced analysis of both the opportunities and legal and ethical dilemmas posed by emerging technologies, the book asks if a duty of disclosure is relevant in relation to AI use, and what challenges this might entail. It also covers the status of AI-generated arbitral awards under international law, as well as copyright law.

This book will be of interest to researchers in the field of international arbitration and commercial law.

**Magdalena Łągiewska**, Habilitation (postdoctoral degree) in Law (University of Gdańsk 2025), PhD in Law (University of Gdańsk 2017, East China University of Political Science and Law 2020), is Assistant Professor at the University of Gdańsk, Poland (Department of Public International Law), Research Associate in the "China, Law and Development" project at the University of Oxford, UK, Asia Global Fellow 2024 at the University of Hong Kong, Hong Kong, and Fellow of the Chartered Institute of Arbitrators (FCIArb) in London.

## Routledge Research in International Commercial Law

### Available titles in this series include:

**Jurisdiction and Arbitration Agreements in International Commercial Law**
*Zheng Sophia Tang*

**Progressive Commercialization of Airline Governance Culture**
*Jan Walulik*

**Economic and Environmental Regulation of International Aviation**
From Inter-National to Global Governance
*Steven Truxal*

**Combining Mediation and Arbitration in International Commercial Dispute Resolution**
*Dilyara Nigmatullina*

**Non-State Rules in International Commercial Law**
Contracts, Legal Authority and Application
*Johanna Hoekstra*

**Commercial Law in the South Pacific**
*Mohammed L Ahmadu and Bridget Fa'amatuainu*

**Digital Finance Law**
Common and Civil Law
*Robert Walters*

**Good Faith in International Commercial Arbitration**
*Georgios Martsekis*

**Artificial Intelligence and International Arbitration Law**
Revolution or Evolution
*Magdalena Łągiewska*

# Artificial Intelligence and International Arbitration Law

## Revolution or Evolution

**Magdalena Łągiewska**

Routledge
Taylor & Francis Group
LONDON AND NEW YORK

First published 2026
by Routledge
4 Park Square, Milton Park, Abingdon, Oxon OX14 4RN

and by Routledge
605 Third Avenue, New York, NY 10158

*Routledge is an imprint of the Taylor & Francis Group, an informa business*



The electronic version of this book was funded to publish Open Access through Taylor & Francis' Pledge to Open, a collaborative funding open access books initiative. The full list of pledging institutions can be found on the Taylor & Francis Pledge to Open webpage.



*British Library Cataloguing-in-Publication Data*
A catalogue record for this book is available from the British Library

ISBN: 978-1-041-12420-7 (hbk)
ISBN: 978-1-041-13048-2 (pbk)
ISBN: 978-1-003-66783-4 (ebk)

DOI: 10.4324/9781003667834

Typeset in Times New Roman
by Deanta Global Publishing Services, Chennai, India

**To Professor Liu Xiaohong, My Mentor, with deepest gratitude**

# Contents

# Introduction

"Information technology and business are becoming inextricably interwoven. I don't think anybody can talk meaningfully about one without talking about the other".[1] Such a statement, made by Bill Gates in 1999, is still relevant in the context of today's legal industry. In fact, technology is not only limited to lawyers, who are also experts in the field of technology, but all legal professions need to master some technological skills. As a result of the ever-changing environment, technology has also influenced the practice of law in various ways.[2]

K. Fach Gómez believes that the legal industry "is morphing from a lawyer dominated, practice-centric, labor-intensive guild to a tech-enabled, process and data-driven, multi-disciplinary global industry".[3]

In addition, tech lawyers understand the importance of technology to the legal industry and practice. In fact, they are explicit about this trend:

> With regard to tech adoption, there is no going back. Overnight, technology transformed from a tool to a lifeline, from a nicety to a necessity. Those among us who were already technologically astute took their use of technology to an even higher level. Those who were less advanced in their use of technology had no choice but to accelerate their adoption. But now having stepped up their use of technology, there will be no going back. We have all learned that technology is not merely a convenience or an efficiency tool, but something that is, literally, essential to our survival and success as legal professionals.[4]

1 K. Fach Gómez, *The Technological Competence of Arbitrators*, Special Issue, https://doi.org/10.1007/978-3-031-11681-0_1, Springer 2023, p. 1; B. Gates, *Business @ the speed of thought: using a digital nervous system*, Penguin 1999, vol 10., pp. 11–18.

2 K. Fach Gómez, *The Technological Competence*..., p. 1.

3 *Ibidem*; MA Cohen, *What's a lawyer now? Law's shift from practice to* skill, "Forbes" September 29, 2019, https://www.forbes.com/sites/markcohen1/2019/09/23/whats-a-lawyer-now-laws-shift-from-practice-to-skill/?sh=55e6159d745b.

4 K. Fach Gómez, *The Technological Competence*..., p. 2; B. Ambrogi, *The 2021 Wolters Kluwer future ready lawyer. Moving beyond the pandemic. Survey report 2021*, https://www.wolterskluwer.com/en/know/future-ready-lawyer-2021, p. 31.

DOI: 10.4324/9781003667834-1

Given that, the legal market seeks a hybrid lawyer profile that combines both a law degree with some technical background that allows them to better understand the application of new technologies in the legal industry. On the other hand, many legal professionals are rather skeptical about the use of new technologies. Therefore, they adopt an ostrich-like approach that results in considering technology in terms of a threat or unnecessary element in performing their legal work. Such an approach has had an impact on the training of lawyers. Only 21% of the respondents decided to undergo special training in new technologies to better understand their application in exercising their tasks. Interestingly, 44% of respondents believed that emerging technologies were somewhat important in their work, whereas 35% did not even recognize their significance. This survey already shows that there is a relatively low number of lawyers who want to broaden their knowledge on this topic. Such skepticism results mostly from the general perception that legal professions do not pertain to early adopters of new technologies.[5]

This book is inspired by the Fourth Industrial Revolution (4IR) and recent advances in the use of Artificial Intelligence (AI) and Generative AI (GenAI) in international commercial arbitration. These new technologies are even described as "Fourth Party" in dispute resolution. In this light, the main objective of this book is to answer the question of whether the use of Artificial Intelligence (AI) and Generative AI (GenAI) in international arbitration represents a revolution or an evolution of the international dispute resolution landscape. In this context, it is crucial to remember that:

> The real question is not where the 'Fourth Party' is today but where it is going. The 'Fourth Party' is becoming more capable all the time. As computer processors become more powerful and user experience designs more intuitive, the 'Fourth Party' expands what it is able to provide. Also, the 'Fourth Party' can operate as a service, so it can be available on the phones in the parties' pockets all day every day, which can increase accessibility and improve responsiveness. The 'Fourth Party' can do things that a third party cannot (or should not) do because of its concern that it will be perceived as partial (algorithms cannot be influenced by compliments or charisma). Parties may also react differently to suggestions from a third party as opposed to a 'Fourth Party', perhaps because the 'Fourth Party' has no feelings that will be hurt if its suggestion is rejected.[6]

Given that, this study seeks to test the following thesis. In general, technological advances in AI and GenAI can be considered the Fourth Industrial Revolution (4IR). However, in the context of international arbitration, arbitral institutions seek to balance the benefits and potential challenges of using these new technologies in

5 K. Fach Gómez, *The Technological Competence…*, p. 3.

6 L. Wing, J. Martinez, E. Katsh, C. Rule, *Designing ethical online dispute resolution systems: The rise of the fourth party*, "Negotiation Journal" 2021, vol. 37, issue 1, p. 52, https://doi.org/10.1111/nejo.12350.

order to fully respect the fundamental principles of arbitration. As a result, arbitral tribunals are cautiously embracing such innovations and implementing them gradually, opting for evolutionary change. This book also focuses on answering the following research questions:

1. How is the use of AI considered in international arbitration? How is it implemented by different actors, including parties, arbitral institutions and arbitrators?
2. What is the legal framework for the use of AI in international arbitration?
3. Is there a duty to disclose the use of AI in arbitral proceedings? What are the consequences and possible challenges?
4. What is the status of AI-generated arbitral awards under international law? What is the copyright on such awards?

The first chapter discusses the Fourth Industrial Revolution (4IR) and international commercial arbitration. International commercial arbitration is widely recognized as a neutral, efficient, and enforceable dispute resolution mechanism. The 4IR has brought advances in Artificial Intelligence (AI), Machine Learning (ML), Internet of Things (IoT), and blockchain, among others, and has significantly reshaped the dispute resolution landscape. The purpose of this chapter is to provide a brief introduction to 4IR and the legal framework of international commercial arbitration. It also aims to identify the intersection between 4IR and international arbitration. Finally, it analyzes the technical skills required of arbitrators in the digital age. This chapter provides background information on how AI-based tools have been integrated into international arbitration and what kind of new skills are needed to work as an arbitrator in such a digital environment.

The second chapter, entitled "Artificial Intelligence (AI) in International Arbitration for Different Actors", provides a comprehensive analysis of various AI-based tools used during arbitral proceedings by different actors, namely parties, arbitral institutions and arbitrators. Importantly, this part consists of examples of such AI tools, the results they provide, and their limitations. As such, this chapter aims to outline various applications of such AI-based tools, from drafting an arbitration clause to filing a case, to conducting remote hearings, to drafting arbitral awards. Finally, it also touches on two stages of AI implementation in international arbitration. Such an analysis is necessary to understand that AI is already widely used by arbitral institutions worldwide. The number of AI tools that improve the efficiency of arbitration proceedings is constantly increasing.

Third, the use of AI tools in international arbitration raises many legal challenges. The third chapter therefore seeks to address these challenges and provide solutions. It begins with a brief introduction to both "hard" and "soft" law governing the use of AI in arbitration. It then examines human rights concerns related to the use of AI in arbitration, with a particular focus on the right to a fair trial, due process (including hallucinations, bias, and discrimination of AI-generated content), and privacy issues. Importantly, it also analyzes different approaches to copyright in AI-generated output from the perspectives of the US, China, and Europe. Finally, it addresses the recognition and enforcement of AI-generated arbitral awards under the current legal framework, the existing challenges, and implications. It also provides possible solutions to this challenging problem. Therefore, this chapter touches on practical legal issues related to the use of AI-powered tools in arbitration, in addition to the generated content in the form of arbitral awards. Importantly, it provides in-depth insights into how best to benefit from AI-powered new technologies with respect to the fundamental principles of international commercial arbitration.

Last, the fourth chapter is entitled "Response of International Arbitration to AI: Revolution or Evolution?". Based on the analysis in the previous sections of the book, this chapter seeks to answer the main question of whether there is a fundamental revolution or a gradual evolution in the international dispute landscape. Therefore, it primarily analyzes different principles that should be followed when using AI tools, such as human oversight, transparency, confidentiality, and ethical issues. It also discusses how to find a "golden mean" to properly balance the challenges and benefits of using AI in international arbitration. This "golden mean" can be achieved through AI disclosure and the absence of a "black box" dilemma, the implementation of specialized multi-agent AI tools alongside human-AI hybrid models that would allow the best of AI tools to be used with human oversight. This analysis leads us to conclude that we are facing an evolutionary process in which AI tools are increasingly implemented in international arbitration. International commercial arbitration keeps pace with technological advancements. Consequently, many innovation-driven technologies are considered to be setting a new standard in international arbitration. In this context, AI-powered tools have been introduced to improve arbitral proceedings.

The book outlines the applicable legal framework as of June 30, 2025.

# 1 Fourth Industrial Revolution and international commercial arbitration

## 1.1 Fourth Industrial Revolution (4IR)

### *1.1.1 Definition of the 4IR*

The Fourth Industrial Revolution (4IR or Industry 4.0) has become a natural consequence of the previous three great industrial revolutions. The first (1760–1840) is related to the invention of the steam engine, replacing manual processes with innovations such as steam-powered automobiles, locomotives, and industrial processes. Under the second industrial revolution, which started in the late 19th century, electricity was invented and powered factories and streetlights and transportation of electricity based on cables became the new normal. Moreover, since the 1960s, the third revolution has introduced automation in factories.[1] Importantly, it is also commonly known as the computer or digital revolution, mainly due to the rapid development of semiconductors and mainframe computers in the 1960s, personal computers in the 1970s–1980s along with the Internet in the 1990s.[2] In this context, it is worthwhile to note that:

> Throughout the 1980s, the cost of computing continued to decrease, and personal computers entered most workplaces in the early to mid-1990s. The advent of the Internet led to another revolution in connecting people to information, but it wasn't enough to fundamentally transform the way people live and work until interactive capabilities ('Web 2.0') became more prevalent. The expansion of mobile devices, the introduction of mobile apps, and the increasing reliability of cloud computing led to a convergence of services. Multiple consumer touch points (phone, tax, web, tablets) gradually blended into the 'single view of costumer' that most organizations now have [...]. And now, we are on the cusp of the Fourth Industrial Revolution, one that introduces intelligent cyber-physical systems to the mix.[3]

1 P. Jindal, R.K. Sindhu, *Opportunities and Challenges of the Fourth Industrial Revolution* [in:] *Artificial Intelligence and the Fourth Industrial Revolution*, ed. U. Chakraborty, A. Banerjee et al., T Jenny Stanford Publishing (Taylor&Francis Group) 2022, p. 46.

2 K. Schwab, *The Fourth Industrial Revolution*, World Economic Forum 2016, p. 11.

3 N.M. Radziwill, *Connected, Intelligent, Automated: The Definitive Guide to Digital Transformation and Quality 4.0*, Quality Press 2020, p. 5.

DOI: 10.4324/9781003667834-2

First, even though the Internet expansion should be seen as a catalyst for innovation, the true digital revolution is happening now. There are many reasons behind this new phase of development, such as Cloud Computing, more available data, Intelligent Processing, and new modes of interacting with people and data, among others. In view of Cloud Computing, it is crucial to remember that previously organizations had to build their own IT systems from scratch. Practically, it means the purchase of hardware, configuration of servers and firewalls, and employment of technical staff to supervise the Internet's connections. Today, thanks to cloud services, many of these tasks have been replaced by outsourced specialized providers who have not only reduced the deployment times but also allowed organizations to concentrate on their own competencies. Different tools like Software as a Service (SaaS), Platform as a Service (PaaS), and Infrastructure as a Service (IaaS) focus equally on streamlining operations and boosting efficiency, increasing resilience and lowering costs.[4]

Second, the volume of data is constantly increasing, driven by human activity along with the proliferation of the Internet of Things (IoT) (discussed further). Thanks to the invention of sensors, actuators, and compact devices such as Arduino and Raspberry Pi, these technological enablers have become not only more affordable but also accessible and powerful. All these tools are pushing forward a new wave of experimentation, which results in more technological advancements.[5]

Third, the Intelligent Processing also plays a crucial role in the 4IR. Following the combination of affordable data storage together with powerful computing resources and processing power, it is possible to generate insights (which is already taking place). Cutting-edge technologies, including exoskeletons and brain-computer interfaces, aim to augment and enhance human performance as well as pave the way for future developments in innovations. Given the software reuse, many new options for intelligent processing solutions have been employed successfully. Since the high performance of software libraries in view of complex data analysis and visualization, which are commonly accessible for free, a similar pace of development is seen across industries.[6]

Fourth, due to revolutionized human-technology interaction, there are currently new modes employed, including touchscreens, voice-activated interfaces, and AI-powered personal assistants, among others. Immersive technologies, such as virtual reality (VR), augmented reality (AR) along with mixed reality (MR) are widely grouped and classified as XR. In practice, they unlock many new ways of training and interacting with data through a hybrid physical-digital environment.[7]

Given the above, it is also worth citing the words of the executive chairman of the World Economic Forum (WEF) who stated that:

4 *Ibidem*, p. 7.

5 *Ibidem*.

6 *Ibidem*, p. 8.

7 *Ibidem*.

> We have yet to grasp fully the speed and breadth of this new revolution. Consider the unlimited possibilities of having billions of people connected by mobile devices, giving rise to unprecedented processing power, storage capabilities and knowledge access. Or think about the staggering confluence of emerging technology breakthroughs, covering wide-ranging fields such as artificial intelligence (AI), robotics, the internet of things (IoT), autonomous vehicles, 3D printing, nanotechnology, biotechnology, materials science, energy storage, and quantum computing.... The changes are historic in terms of their size, speed, and scope...[8]

In this light, 4IR or Industry 4.0 is not only a result of smart and connected machines and systems. Apparently, the scope of 4IR is even broader, and thus this revolution is widely considered to be a result of increased technological developments related to Artificial Intelligence (AI), Machine Learning (ML), Internet of Things (IoT), and blockchain, among others. Currently, there is a significant advancement in technological aspects resulting from the increasing use of automation in the digital era. Importantly, there are many new types of AI-powered tools surrounding us, including, for instance, self-driving (autonomous) cars, virtual assistants, as well as accurate diagnosis of diseases. Brian Householder and Hitachi Vantara point out that:

> The concept of digitizing everything is becoming a reality. Automation, artificial intelligence, IoT, machine learning and other advanced technologies can quickly capture and analyze a wealth of data that gives us previously unimaginable amounts and types of information to work from. Our challenge becomes moving to the next phase – changing how we think, train and work using data – to create value from the findings obtained through advanced technologies.[9]

Contrary to past industrial revolutions, the Industry 4.0's sweeping transformations focus on reshaping industries, enterprises, and societies at large. Through the fusion of connectedness, intelligence, and automation, we will improve operational efficiency thanks to actions related to uncovering patterns and insights that have not been explicitly defined by humans. This process will accelerate the transition by acting on data through automation.[10] Radziwill even goes further and refers to the concept of Quality 4.0. All these initiatives, including enhancing connectedness, adding intelligence, and advancing automation, will result in the following value propositions:

8 *Ibidem*, pp. 6–7.

9 *The Fourth Industrial Revolution is here – are you ready?*, "Deloitte Insights" 2018, p. 2, https://www2.deloitte.com/content/dam/insights/us/articles/4364_Industry4-0_Are-you-ready/4364_Industry4-0_Are-you-ready_Report.pdf. Accessed on April 30, 2025.

10 *Ibidem*, p. 15.

1. Augment (or improve on) human intelligence.
2. Increase the speed and quality of decision making.
3. Improve transparency, traceability, and auditability.
4. Anticipate changes, reveal biases, and adapt to new circumstances and knowledge.
5. Reveal opportunities for continuous improvement and new business models.
6. Learn how to learn; cultivate self-awareness and other-awareness as a skill.[11]

To sum up, the sweeping advancements resulting from Industry 4.0 and Quality 4.0 will have a significant impact not only on the different types of organizations but also everyday life. What may be regarded as magical or revolutionary today, including the ability of real-time sensing and analyzing of operating environments, instant checking of supply chains and digital traceability, within the next two decades, will become a new normal and even will be regarded as granted.[12] The 4IR is thus opening a new era with many benefits and challenges ahead.

### *1.1.2 New technologies within 4IR*

#### *1.1.2.1 Artificial Intelligence (AI) and Machine Learning (ML)*

John McCarthy is widely considered a pioneer, using the term "Artificial Intelligence" (AI) since 1956.[13] Pursuant to McCarthy's standpoint, the term AI refers to "the science and engineering of making intelligent machines, especially intelligent computer programs. It is related to the similar task of using computers to understand human intelligence".[14] Indeed, the term AI includes two words, namely "artificial" and "intelligence". The first one means "human-created", whereas the latter refers to the "thinking power". As such, AI means "a man-made object with thinking power". Given the fact that intelligence is intangible, thus it means "the ability of a system to calculate, reason, perceive relationships and analogies, learn from experience, store and retrieve information from memory, solve problems, comprehend complex ideas, use natural language fluently, classify, generalize, and adapt new situations".[15] In essence, AI refers to computer systems equipped

11 *Ibidem*, pp. 16–17.

12 *Ibidem*, p. 19.

13 M. Łągiewska, *Digitalization and the Use of New Technologies in International* Arbitration, Brill 2024, p. 64.

14 M. Waqar, *The use of AI in arbitral proceedings*, "Ohio State Journal on Dispute Resolution" 2022, vol. 37, no. 3, p. 346. See more: M. Scherer, *Artificial Intelligence and legal decision-making: The wide open?*, "Journal of International Arbitration" 2019, vol. 36, issue 5, pp. 539–573; M. Gicquello, *Artificial Intelligence in International Arbitration* [in:] *The Oxford Handbook of International Arbitration*, ed. T. Schultz, F. Ortin, Oxford 2020.

15 P.K. Garg, *Overview of Artificial Intelligence* [in:] *Artificial Intelligence: Technologies, Applications, and Challenges*, ed. L. Sharma, P.K. Garg, CRC Press (Taylor & Francis Group) 2021, p. 3.

with cognitive functions which allow them to reason and act in a rational way like humans.[16]

It is worth adding, however, that there are many different understandings of AI. To name a few, Bellman described AI in 1978 as "the automation of activities that we associate with human thinking, activities such as decision making, problem solving, learning".[17] Further, in 1990, Schalkoff considered AI as "a field of study that seeks to explain and emulate intelligent behavior in terms of computational processes".[18] In addition, Kathleen Presley and Edna Sussman define AI as "a process where a large amount of data is combined with processing systems, allowing the software to learn automatically from patterns of features in the data" and "the term AI is often used loosely and encompasses many subjects including machine learning, and also natural language processing".[19]

Currently, the term "Artificial Intelligence" (AI) is widely considered a branch of computer science that aims to create machines that can behave intelligently. According to Richard R. Khan, AI is designed to enable computers to "perform tasks that would normally require human intelligence".[20]

Nonetheless, one must note that there is no uniform legal definition of AI thus far. This means that different institutions adopt their own definitions. To illustrate, in 2018, the EC High-Level Expert Group on Artificial Intelligence elaborated the updated definition of AI as follows:

> Artificial intelligence (AI) refers to systems designed by humans that, given a complex goal, act in the physical or digital world by perceiving their environment, interpreting the collected structured or unstructured data, reasoning on the knowledge derived from this data and deciding the best action(s) to take (according to pre-defined parameters) to achieve the given goal. AI systems can also be designed to learn to adapt their behaviour by analysing how the environment is affected by their previous actions. As a scientific discipline, AI includes several approaches and techniques, such as machine learning (of which deep learning and reinforcement learning are specific examples), machine reasoning (which includes planning, scheduling, knowledge representation and reasoning, search, and optimization), and robotics (which

16 *Ibidem*, p. 4.

17 *Ibidem*.

18 *Ibidem*.

19 M. Waqar, *The use of AI in arbitral proceedings*, "Ohio State Journal on Dispute Resolution" 2022, vol. 37, issue 3, p. 346. See more: P.K. Garg, *Overview of Artificial Intelligence…*; K. Paisley, E. Sussman, *Artificial Intelligence: Challenges and opportunities for international arbitration*, "Special Feature: Artificial Intelligence and New Arbitration Data Sources, NYSBA New York Dispute Resolution Lawyer" 2018, vol. 11, no. 1.

20 R.R. Khan, *The AI Glossary: Demystifying 101 Essential Artificial Intelligence Terms for Everyone*, CRC Press (Taylor&Francis Group) 2025, p. 2.

includes control, perception, sensors and actuators, as well as the integration of all other techniques into cyber-physical systems).[21]

In contrast, the OECD provides that "An AI system is a machine-based system that, for explicit or implicit objectives, infers, from the input it receives, how to generate outputs such as predictions, content, recommendations, or decisions that can influence physical or virtual environments. Different AI systems vary in their levels of autonomy and adaptiveness after deployment".[22] This definition encompasses AI system autonomy, and namely refers to the extent to which the system is equipped with abilities to learn or act, even without human interaction, because of the autonomy of this system and automated processes. Importantly, human supervision might be applied at any phase of the AI system lifecycle, particularly in the case of "AI system design, data collection and processing, development, verification, validation, deployment, or operation and monitoring".[23] It is also worthwhile to note that certain AI systems can even produce outputs that were not explicitly described in their original objectives or do not reflect any human instructions.[24] The OECD definition was further repeated within the newly adopted Council of Europe Framework Convention on Artificial Intelligence and Human Rights, Democracy and the Rule of Law.[25]

Lastly, the ISO defines AI as "a technical and scientific field devoted to the engineered system that generates outputs such as content, forecasts, recommendations or decisions for a given set of human-defined objectives".[26] In this context, it is worth remembering that the term AI is relatively difficult to define, mainly due to its fast evolution.[27]

There are four main key concepts related to AI systems, namely learning, reasoning, perception, and adaptation. In terms of learning, AI systems are intended to learn like humans, who learn from empirical data. Such data are needed to identify patterns, make necessary predictions, and constantly improve the performance of

21 *The European Commission's High-Level Expert Group on Artificial Intelligence. A Definition of AI: Main Capabilities and Scientific Disciplines*, "European Commission" 2018, p. 7, https://ec.europa.eu/futurium/en/system/files/ged/ai_hleg_definition_of_ai_18_december_1.pdf. Accessed on June 2, 2025.

22 *Explanatory memorandum on the updated OECD definition of AI system*, "OECD Artificial Intelligence Papers" 2024, no. 8, p. 4, https://www.oecd.org/content/dam/oecd/en/publications/reports/2024/03/explanatory-memorandum-on-the-updated-oecd-definition-of-an-ai-system_3c815e51/623da898-en.pdf. Accessed on June 6, 2025.

23 *Ibidem*, p. 4.

24 *Ibidem*.

25 *Council of Europe Framework Convention on Artificial Intelligence and Human Rights, Democracy and the Rule of Law*, https://rm.coe.int/1680afae3c. See also: *Explanatory Report to the Council of Europe Framework Convention on Artificial Intelligence and Human Rights, Democracy and the Rule of Law*, https://rm.coe.int/1680afae67. Accessed on May 3, 2025.

26 *Information technology – Artificial Intelligence – Artificial Intelligence concepts and terminology*, "ISO/IEC 22989" 2022, p. vii.

27 H. Sheikh, C. Prins, E. Schrijvers, *Mission AI: The New System Technology*, Springer 2023, p. 20.

AI systems. AI systems can do some reasoning, which allows them not only to make decisions but also to solve problems faster and more accurately compared to humans. This is possible by training logical reasoning on the provided information. Under the concept of perception, "AI systems can interpret the world around them by recognizing objects, speech, and text".[28] This tool is widely used in the case of voice assistants and autonomous cars. Finally, adaptation allows AI to easily adjust its behavior in response to new information or a changing environment.[29] The OECD definition elaborates on this concept, providing that AI systems based on machine learning have the ability to evolve over time since their initial development. This means the system can modify its behavior based on direct interaction with input and data, either before or after deployment. Although AI systems undergo training that can be one-time, periodic, or continuous, certain systems can develop their own abilities to perform new forms of interaction. In this light, it is crucial to remember that these performances were not initially designed by programmers.[30]

Indeed, AI was designed as a tool that can analyze a huge amount of information. Interestingly, it is also applied to evidence and legal precedents. Therefore, the AI can effortlessly tell stories or even prepare arguments within seconds. Such a function is available based on the requested viewpoint and language, including some iambic pentameter, if needed.[31]

Finally, there are different types of AI systems, including Artificial Narrow Intelligence (ANI), Artificial General Intelligence (AGI), and Artificial Super Intelligence (ASI), among others. The first one, ANI, aka Weak AI, can perform only one task. Therefore, ANI resembles "a specialist or an expert in a specific field [...]. ANI is designed to perform specific tasks or solve particular problems without processing the broad range of abilities that a human might have".[32] Given ANI's programming limitations, this AI system has a relatively narrow set of competencies.[33] This entails that ANI focuses only on a single narrow task without having a general understanding or even consciousness about the world.[34] ANI can learn and judge merely defined tasks.[35] Nowadays, voice assistants, recommendation systems, alongside email spam filters, are based on ANI.[36]

The second type of AI, namely Artificial General Intelligence (AGI), is described as Strong AI which can mimic cognitive functions of the human brain.

28 R.R. Khan, *The AI Glossary...*, p. 2.

29 *Ibidem*.

30 *Explanatory memorandum on the updated...*, p. 4.

31 J. Kirby, *International arbitration and Artificial Intelligence: Ideas to improve the written phase of arbitral proceedings*, "Journal of International Arbitration" 2023, vol. 40, issue 6, p. 660.

32 R.R. Khan, *The AI Glossary...*, p. 4.

33 P.K. Garg, *Overview of Artificial Intelligence...*, p. 12.

34 R.R. Khan, *The AI Glossary...*, p. 4.

35 D. Pyo, J. Hwang, Y. Yoon, *Tech Trends of the 4th Industrial Revolution*, Mercury Learning and Information 2021, p. 51.

36 R.R. Khan, *The AI Glossary...*, p. 4.

In practice, AGI has been designed not only to perform various tasks but also to learn and improve itself. Thanks to the ability to perceive, understand, learn and function, "the AGI systems employ fuzzy logic to apply domain knowledge and find a solution automatically to an unknown task".[37] Compared to common forms of AI systems, AGI has been equipped with the ability to adapt to different tasks and problems. Importantly, there is no need for special programming to complete such tasks.[38] In practice, AGI as a self-teaching system can be even better than humans in many different disciplines.[39] Currently, AGI still remains a theoretical concept which has not been completed thus far, but it has already shown the future direction of developing AI systems.[40]

The last type refers to Artificial Super Intelligence (ASI) which will probably be the future AI development that will change the landscape of AI systems as the most capable intelligence globally. Therefore, "the ASI will not only replicate the intelligence of human beings but also have much higher storage (i.e., memory), faster data analysis, and better decision-making powers. The capabilities of ASI are expected to supersede that of humans".[41]

Machine Learning (ML),[42] on the other hand, is a branch of AI dedicated to building systems that can not only learn from data but also make decisions based on that data. As such, ML systems are not programmed to perform a specific task. Instead, they are designed to use large amounts of data to make predictions or decisions.[43] According to the high-level definition of ML, "Machine Learning is the field of study that gives computers the ability to learn without being explicitly programmed".[44]

In short, the four key characteristics of ML can be summarized as follows: learning from data, improving over time, broad application, and different learning methods. The first feature allows ML to use past data to identify patterns and relationships needed to make future predictions. Second, as the amount of data increases, ML systems can be continuously improved, making both predictions and decisions more accurate. Third, many different sectors can benefit from ML systems, including healthcare (i.e., diagnosing diseases), finance (i.e., predicting stock changes), and technology (i.e., recommendation systems on streaming

37 P.K. Garg, *Overview of Artificial Intelligence*..., p. 12.

38 R.R. Khan, *The AI Glossary*..., p. 3.

39 P.K. Garg, *Overview of Artificial Intelligence*..., p. 12.

40 R.R. Khan, *The AI Glossary*..., p. 3.

41 P.K. Garg, *Overview of Artificial Intelligence*..., p. 12.

42 See more: A. Smola, S.V.N. Vishwanathan, *Introduction to Machine Learning*, Cambridge University Press 2008; S. Shalev-Shwartz, S. Ben-David, *Understanding Machine Learning: From Theory to Algorithms*, Cambridge University Press 2014; A.C. Müller, S. Guido, *Introduction to Machine Learning with Python: A Guide for Data Scientists*, O'Reilly 2016.

43 R.R. Khan, *The AI Glossary*..., p. 7.

44 P. Wulff, M. Kubsch, C. Krist, *Basics of Machine* Learning [in:] *Applying Machine Learning in Science Education Research: When, How, and Why?*, ed. P. Wulff, M. Kubsch, C. Krist, Springer 2025, p. 21. See more: A. Géron, *Hands-on machine learning with Scikit-Learn and TensorFlow: Concepts, Tools, and Techniques to Build Intelligent Systems*, O'Reilly 2017.

services). Finally, because there are many types of ML systems, there are different learning methods. To name a few, supervised learning is based on labeled data, unsupervised learning is learning from unlabeled data, while reinforcement learning improves through trial and error. Importantly, ML systems are already widely used in various fields, including speech recognition systems, credit scoring, medical imaging, and others.[45]

In sum, ML, which is regarded as a core discipline within the broader AI field, makes use of algorithms that power the advancement of intelligent systems along AI applications through seeking patterns in vast amounts of data. ML, as a subfield of AI, has been developed during the past few decades and provides hundreds of distinct ML algorithms. Each of these ML algorithms can be regarded as engines of discovery providing both direct and indirect insights that might have an impact on the generation of new business operations. In this light, the key challenge lies in choosing the most relevant algorithm or even algorithmic family depending on a specific task. Given that, such a decision can determine not only the effectiveness but also the value presented by the AI-powered solutions.[46]

Currently, we can distinguish three different subcategories of ML, namely supervised, unsupervised, and reinforcement learning. The first one, supervised learning, benefits from regression and classification methods. This means that

> To solve classification problem experiences in the form of data are labelled with respect to some target categorisation. The labelling process is typically accomplished by enlisting the effort of humans to examine each piece of data and to label the data. For supervised learning classification problems performance is measured by calculating the true positive rate (the ratio of the true positives over all positives, correctly labelled or not) and the false positive rate (the ratio of false positives over all negatively classified data, correctly and incorrectly labelled). The result of this machine learning process is called a classifier.[47]

Second, unsupervised learning pays attention to understanding various data patterns and relations instead of focusing on prediction. To achieve this goal, unsupervised learning employs mainly principal components analysis and clustering methods. In fact, these methods are commonly regarded as explanatory precursors to the first subcategory.[48]

The last subcategory, reinforcement learning, focuses on using feedback to label states of the world as more or less desirable for achieving a certain goal.[49]

45 R.R. Khan, *The AI Glossary...*, p. 7.

46 N.M. Radziwill, *Connected, Intelligent, Automated...*, pp. 61–62.

47 C. Bartneck, C. Lütge, A. Wagner, S. Welsh, *An Introduction to Ethics in Robotics and AI*, Springer 2021, p. 11.

48 *Ibidem.*

49 *Ibidem*, pp. 11–12.

It is also worthwhile to note that ML is based on the Large Language Models (LLMs). For humans, the LLMs are equipped with the ability not only to "speak human" but also to "understand". This impression of LLM's skills has a far-reaching consequence, mainly misleading to classify these systems in terms of human-like intelligence, comprehension, or even reasoning behind the generated output.[50] In addition, according to the UK Bar Council's "Considerations when Using ChatGPT and Generative AI Software based on the large language models" ("Considerations"), LLM:

> is not a conventional research tool, it does not analyze the content of data and it does not think for itself. It is, rather, a very sophisticated version of the sort of predictive text systems that people are familiar with from email and chat apps on smart phones, in which the algorithm predicts what the next word is likely to be. LLMs use machine learning algorithms, first to be 'trained' on text and, based on that 'training' (which involves the application of inter alia mathematical formulae), to generate sequential text. These programmes are now sufficiently sophisticated that the text often appears as if it was written by a human being, or at least by a machine which thinks for itself.[51]

In addition, the UK Bar Council's "Considerations" also provide an overview of the key risks associated with the use of LLM systems, namely anthropomorphism, hallucinations, information disorder, biases, among others (discussed more in detail further). By the term "anthropomorphism", these Considerations mean the following:

> [LLMs] are designed and marketed in such a way as to give the impression that the user is interacting with something that has human characteristics. One of the mechanisms by which this is sought to be achieved is by the use of anthropomorphic language to describe what is happening. Perhaps the most obvious example of this is the use, by OpenAI, of the word 'Chat' in the name of its LLM products (ChatGPT). As set out above, LLMs (at least at the current stage in their development) do not have human characteristics in any relevant sense.[52]

LLMs can be widely applied in international commercial arbitration.[53] João Ilhão Moreira and Zhang Jiawei believe that LLMs (i.e. ChatGPT) can change the

50 S. Nappert, *Preface* [in:] *Transforming Arbitration: Exploring the Impact of AI, Blockchain, Metaverse and Web 3*, ed. M. Piers, S. McCarthy, Radboud University Press 2025, p. 11.

51 Bar Council of England and Wales, *Considerations when using ChatGPT and generative artificial intelligence software based on large language models*, issued on January 30, 2024. Available at https://www.barcouncilethics.co.uk/wp-content/uploads/2024/01/Considerations-when-using-ChatGPT-and-Generative-AI-Software-based-on-large-language-models-January-2024.pdf, p. 2. Accessed on May 26, 2025.

52 *Ibidem*, p. 3.

53 See more: T. Tsuvina, A. Tsuvina, *Rethinking regulation: Integrating large language models in international arbitration*, "Problems of Legality" 2025, vol. 165, pp. 212–225. https://doi.org/10.21564/2414-990X.166.315451.

landscape of dispute resolution by assisting arbitrators in the arbitral proceedings by conducting legal research, providing case analysis alongside drafting decisions. In fact, these AI-powered tools could play a significant role in enhancing efficiency and providing high-quality decisions in a shorter time. However, aside from these advantages, the use of LLMs such as ChatGPT also presents many challenges, including trustworthiness and confidentiality issues, among others (discussed in detail in Chapter 4).[54]

#### *1.1.2.2 Internet of Things (IoT)*

Internet of Things (IoT) is defined as "a global, distributed network (or networks) of physical objects that are capable of sensing or acting on their environment, and able to communicate with each other, other machines and computers".[55] IoT systems are designed to create a connection between not only physical but also digital worlds through the front-end computing devices and back-end services. The former term refers to the "computer systems equipped with sensors, such as temperature sensors, RFID tags/readers, wearable devices, flame detectors, cameras, mobile phones, etc.".[56] Importantly, such devices are often left in open environments and thus remain beyond the control of system administrators.

The latter term, in turn, means a software system which has the aim to integrate, process alongside and analyze the data collected by the front-end devices. Later on, the back-end can also deliver such processed information to the users. In addition, the IoT system often consists of three layers, including IoT devices (first layer), the communication network (second layer), and the service back-end (third layer). IoT devices are widely considered to be at the foundation of the entire architecture. Under the second layer, there is a special gateway which is responsible for managing local IoT devices through their connections to the Internet. At the top, the service back-end layer offers not only data storage but also delivers higher-level application services. Importantly, the third layer also includes data processing and necessary analysis of the collected data.[57]

This kind of "smart" objects, regardless of their sizes and capacities, interact with embedded sensors, household appliances, industrial robots, cars, trains, among others. Importantly, IoT is commonly considered a technological phenomenon which allows the connection of objects to the Internet through the so-called

54 J.I. Moreira, Zhang Jiawei, *ChatGPT as a fourth arbitrator? The ethics and risks of using large language models in arbitration*, "Arbitration International" 2025, vol. 41, issue 1, pp. 71–84, https://doi.org/10.1093/arbint/aiae031.

55 *The Internet of Things: Opportunities and Challenges*, Briefing May 2015, p. 2, https://www.europarl.europa.eu/RegData/etudes/BRIE/2015/557012/EPRS_BRI. Accessed on April 15, 2025.

56 Chen Fei, Xiao Zhe et al., *Blockchain for Internet of Things applications: A review and open issues*, "Journal of Network and Computer Applications" 2020, vol. 172, p. 2.

57 Chen Fei, Xiao Zhe et al., *Blockchain for Internet...*, Ibidem, p. 2.

machine-to-machine communications (M2M).[58] As such, IoT provides a collection and transfer of data without human-to-human or human-to-computer interaction.[59] IoT has already been widely applied in modern society, including smart manufacturing, smart homes, smart cities, etc. Given the existing limitations in terms of local computing alongside storage resources, the control of IoT systems has been shifted from a single vendor control to a mainstream cloud-based control.[60]

In view of the legal industry, IoT data may be classified within the category of "electronically stored information" (ESI) which will be described further in the e-discovery section.[61]

#### *1.1.2.3 Blockchain*

Blockchain is a kind of decentralized distributed database. Importantly, blockchain technology consists of distributed data storage, point-to-point networking, consensus mechanism, and encryption algorithm. In addition, "the blockchain relies on a consensus mechanism to enable everyone to agree on newly generated data block and work together to maintain all the blocks as a unique database".[62]

Blockchain can be defined as "a distributed data structure that is replicated and shared among the nodes of a network".[63] This technology is commonly used in IoT applications given its feature of providing secure transactions between nodes.[64] According to another definition, blockchain means "a secure data structure and a protocol for establishing consensus on valuable information within a flat network without hierarchy".[65] Under the other definition:

> A blockchain is a shared, digital ledger that contains transaction data. Each transaction is joined to the sequence of prior transactions like a link in a chain, and the data structure containing them cannot be changed once a new record has been logged and verified. The algorithms used to create each

58 J. Fothergill, K.H. Lincke, *Internet of Things (IoT): Legal considerations for businesses*, "Mariscal-Abogados", https://www.mariscal-abogados.com/internet-of-things-iot-legal-considerations-for-businesses/. Accessed on April 16, 2025.

59 M. Verga, *The Internet of Things (IoT) and litigation*, "Consilio", https://www.consilio.com/resource/the-internet-of-things-iot-and-litigation. Accessed on April 17, 2025.

60 Chen Fei, Wang Jiahao et al., *TrustBuilder: A non-repudiation scheme for IoT cloud applications*, "Computer & Security" 2022, vol. 116, https://doi.org/10.1016/j.cose.2022.102664.

61 M. Verga, *The Internet of Things (IoT)...*

62 Chen Fei, Xiao Zhe et al., *Blockchain for Internet...*, p. 1.

63 C.R. Moratelli, R.T. Tiburski et al., *Privacy and security of Internet of Things devices* [in:] *In Advances in Ubiquitous Sensing Applications for Healthcare, Real-Time Data Analytics for Large Scale Sensor Data*, ed. H. Das, N. Dey, V.E. Balas, Academic Press 2020, vol. 6, pp. 183–184.

64 See more: C.R. Moratelli, R.T. Tiburski et al., *Privacy and security of Internet...*, pp. 183–214.

65 P. Blandino, *The possibility of a uniform legal language at the interplay of legal discourse, semiotics, and blockchain networks*, "International Journal for the Semiotics of Law" 2024, vol. 37, p. 2086.

> new link in a blockchain mathematically guarantee that, once accepted, the details of the transaction in the ledger cannot be altered without applying an immense (and impractical) level of computing power.[66]

In addition, every user has the so-called authoritative copy. Therefore, each person having access to the ledger simultaneously could see the same full transaction history and verify whether all records are valid.[67] Given its structure, "a blockchain is a linked list constructed by hash pointers. Each block has both data and a hash pointer directing to the previous block; it also contains a digest of the block data, which prevents any modifications of the block".[68]

In practice, the blockchain's inherent data architecture together with its specialized computational mechanisms result in ensuring that it is almost impossible to fake information or manipulate transactions. As its name suggests, blockchain refers to a structure which is composed of blocks of information that are connected in sequence and thus represents a snapshot of a particular transaction or event. The content of a block results from the nature of the transaction. To illustrate, in the case of Bitcoin, a block stores a list of transactions that have been made between digital wallets. In supply chains, blocks can be used to document different information concerning such events as arrival, departure, inspection together with linked features of the event (metadata), including timestamps, updates on the status or environmental conditions. In fact, a blockchain has been designed to hold any content represented digitally from text and audio to photographs and videos. In this light, blockchain represents an adaptable framework created for the sake of securely recording and verifying various types of digitally stored information.[69]

Overall, the benefits of blockchain technology can be summarized as follows:

> Since the individual blocks are chronologically linked using hash functions, the result is an unalterable and traceable documentation of the information in the form of a 'chain'. This chain of data ('blockchain') is not stored and managed centrally by an overarching entity, but rather de-centrally in a peer-to-peer network consisting of many distributed 'nodes' (users). Using encryption technologies and consensus mechanisms, these accounts ensure the authenticity of data on the network. Because nodes verify and validate data, blockchains do not rely on centralized, trusted third parties to ensure high system security and data integrity.[70]

Generally speaking, there are four main features of blockchain such as decentralization, immutability, transparency, and smart contracts. Under the concept of

66 N.M. Radziwill, *Connected, Intelligent, Automated...*, pp. 221–222.

67 P. Blandino, *The Possibility of a Uniform...*, p. 2086.

68 Chen Fei, Xiao Zhe et al., *Blockchain for Internet...*, p. 3.

69 N.M. Radziwill, *Connected, Intelligent, Automated...*, p. 222.

70 C. Salger, *Decentralized dispute resolution: Using blockchain technology decentralized dispute resolution: Using blockchain technology and smart contracts in arbitration*, "Pepperdine Dispute Resolution Law Journal" 2024, vol. 24, issue 1, p. 69.

decentralization, the blockchain works through a peer-to-peer network that replaces a central authority or intermediary. Second, according to the immutability feature, "once data is recorded on the blockchain, it cannot be altered or deleted without consensus from the network".[71] Third, this technology increases transparency, as all participants have access to the data on the blockchain. Finally, blockchain provides self-executing contracts that can be automatically executed and enforced once the pre-defined conditions of the agreement are met.[72]

Blockchain technology can be implemented differently because of the required levels of anonymity, trust, and control resulting from a particular network. Bearing in mind this flexibility, there are different implementations of blockchain technology that could be classified as follows: public vs. private and "permissioned" vs. "permissionless".[73]

Under the first group, in the case of public blockchains, there is no control of the blockchain itself and the maintenance responsibilities are divided between all participants. In fact, such a decentralized control provides that these networks are generally open and applied consensus mechanisms are used in order to ensure integrity. In contrast, private blockchains function differently and thus they are like companies' corporate networks. This means that both the access and governance pertain to specific entities.[74]

In the context of the second group, the "permissioned" blockchains allow that merely designated participants such as trusted stakeholders are granted access and permission to update the information or even interact with the ledger. In practice, this solution provides tighter control alongside enhanced privacy, which can be seen as an advantage in the case of business or consortium contexts. In turn, the "permissionless" blockchain can be characterized by unrestricted access, which entails that anyone is allowed to join, validate, and contribute to the ledger, and thus no prior approval is required.[75]

Principles in distributed computing and peer-to-peer (P2P) networking laid down the foundations for blockchain technology. Distributed systems function with known participants whose behaviors are well controlled. In turn, P2P networks are based on open networks, which means that anyone can join them and upload resources or files. Such networks have been designed to enable requests by numerous participants, even to be made within a single transaction, and thus provide a high level of availability. On the other hand, it is worthwhile to note that participants are exposed to cyberattacks. In addition, P2P networks are considered "permissionless". This means that they rely on the assumption that the majority of participants act honestly. Even if this model opts for broad participation,

71 P. Blandino, *The Possibility of a Uniform...*, p. 2086.

72 *Ibidem.*

73 N.M. Radziwill, *Connected, Intelligent, Automated...*, p. 222.

74 *Ibidem.*

75 *Ibidem.*

it also results in some cybersecurity vulnerabilities, most notably in terms of cyberattacks.[76]

In practice, the blockchain technology is based on "hashing", namely a cryptographic algorithm that aims to transform data into a distinct sequence comprising not only numbers but also letters. Apparently, this process has some mathematical features and should be regarded as a core component of ensuring data integrity and security.[77] Even the slightest change in data, which might go unnoticed by a human observer, leads to a completely different hash. The latter is instantly noticeable. Given the fact that every new block in a blockchain is based on the hash from the block before it, the system itself preserves a linked history of all previous records. In fact, through such chaining, any modification to previous data would result in the disruption of the continuity of the hashes. In this view, any fraudulent behavior could be easily noticed and thus alert the administrators about the inconsistencies across the certain chain.[78]

Blockchain technology is widely applied in many different areas of social life, including finance, insurance, and government services, among others. Blockchain has become famous thanks to two successful examples such as Bitcoin and Ethereum. They both make use of Proof of Work (PoW) consensus algorithm. The latter, by contrast, is moving to the Proof of Stake (PoS) algorithm.[79]

Against this background, the legal system cannot be seen as an exception. As such, blockchain technology could be widely used in three main areas that may be summarized as follows:

1. Verification and authentication of legal documentation thus replacing the notary system.
2. Contracting, using smart contracts instead of paper contracts.
3. Dispute resolution, where instead of the traditional court system or alternative dispute resolution methods such as mediation, conciliation and arbitration, a decentralized method of dispute resolution is favoured.[80]

The more in-depth analysis of the blockchain's application regarding AI-based evidence is set forth in Chapter 2.

76 *Ibidem*, pp. 222–223.
77 *Ibidem*, p. 225.
78 *Ibidem*, p. 228.
79 Chen Fei, Xiao Zhe et al., *Blockchain for Internet*..., p. 3.
80 A. Zhuk, *Applying blockchain to the modern legal system: Kleros as a decentralized dispute resolution* system, "International Cybersecurity Law Review" 2023, vol. 4, p. 352.

## 1.2 International commercial arbitration

### *1.2.1 Definition of international commercial arbitration*

Arbitration is "a consensual, private process for the submission of a dispute for a decision of a tribunal, comprising one or more independent third persons. In making its decision, the tribunal must follow certain basic requirements, such as to act fairly and impartially, allowing each party to put its case and to respond to that of its opponent".[81] Arbitration is thus a legally binding mechanism for solving commercial disputes beyond the formal judicial system. It is based upon the mutual parties' consent to arbitrate. Such consent is expressed either in the form of an arbitration clause or an arbitration agreement. If the dispute resolution mechanism has not been specified by the parties in the contract, they can freely reach such a decision if the conflict arises. In addition, the responsibility to render a legally binding arbitral award is assigned to one or more arbitrators. In this context, their authority results from the arbitration agreement. Judges in public court systems are required to abide by strict procedural rules alongside applying the laws of the state. In contrast, arbitrators are much more flexible compared to judges, and thus they can apply procedural rules and substantive laws that best comply with the specific needs of the dispute.[82]

The arbitral tribunal renders an arbitral award that is final and legally binding upon the parties. In addition, such an award can be recognized and enforced by the courts under the United Nations Convention on the Recognition and Enforcement of Foreign Arbitral Awards (1958 New York Convention).[83]

Briefly, arbitration, an alternative dispute resolution method, shows major differences from court proceedings that can be summarized as follows:

1. Arbitration is commonly seen as a consensual process based on a previously concluded arbitration agreement;
2. Arbitration is not only private but in the majority of jurisdictions also a confidential process;
3. Arbitration is much more flexible compared to traditional court proceedings, which allow the parties to freely select the arbitral tribunal (or agree on the method of its composition), including expected qualifications and expertise of arbitrators, to choose the applicable rules for the arbitral proceedings and the language of the arbitration.[84]

81 P. Capper, *International Arbitration: A Handbook*, Informa Law (Routledge) 2004, p. 2.

82 W. Mattli, *Private justice in a global economy: From litigation to arbitration*, "International Organization" 2001, vol. 55, issue 4, p. 920, https://doi.org/10.1162/002081801317193646. See more: L. Trakman, *Legal Traditions and International Commercial Arbitration*, "American Review of International Arbitration", Spring 2007, UNSW Law Research Paper no. 2007–29, Available at SSRN: https://ssrn.com/abstract=986507.

83 *United Nations Convention on the Recognition and Enforcement of Foreign Arbitral Awards (New York, 10 June 1958)*, https://www.newyorkconvention.org/english. Accessed on April 20, 2025.

84 P. Capper, *International Arbitration*..., p. 2.

One must note, however, that recently an arbitration, albeit being considered a non-legal dispute resolution method, is being considerably impacted by the litigation practice. In this light, it is worthwhile to note that this trend is contrary to the spirit of the arbitration process itself. This phenomenon is thus discussed by Vijay K. Bhatia[85] and Maurizio Gotti under the concept of "colonization of arbitration by litigation". This refers to the increasing influence of litigation processes over arbitration practice which results in undermining the integrity of the arbitration itself. Importantly, this process is seen within the discovery procedures, written testimony, witness examination and writing of arbitral awards, among others. Considering the first one, due to the involvement of legal counsels highly experienced in traditional court litigations, there is an assumption that the discovery process held within the international commercial arbitration would be equal to litigation.[86] In this context, it is thus worthwhile to note that:

> In cross-jurisdictional arbitration trials, it is expected that the parties will cooperate in the discovery of evidence either by limited examination of the witnesses through oral testimony, or by submission of written documents. Some practitioners, especially those from a common law background, believe that without some form of discovery, however limited, there is a risk that the hearing may not lead to a reasonable conclusion, because they think it important that evidence must be presented to parties before they respond to it. In most cases, however, tribunals discourage lengthy and irrelevant discovery. This and other related issues are generally addressed and negotiated at the preparatory phase of an arbitration trial.[87]

Second, written testimonies refer to the question about the courtroom examination held especially within common law jurisdictions. This concerns mainly "a general perception that defendants have no choice of their own because it is often manipulated by legal counsels".[88] Practically, it is limited to the issue of "how much of a witness testimony is presented by the witness, and how much by the counsel?".[89] In the context of international arbitration, this begs the question of the legal responsibility for the written statements. There is a common practice that witnesses present the facts to the counsel, and further he elaborates the statement based on this information.[90]

Third, considering witness examination, arbitrators originating from common law jurisdictions are familiar with cross-examination, which is just after the oral

85 See more: V.K. Bhatia, *Interdiscursive colonisation of arbitration practice*, "World Englishes" 2011, vol. 30, no. 1, pp. 76–80.

86 V.K. Bhatia, C.N. Candlin, M. Gotti, *Contested Identities in International Arbitration Practice* [in:] *Discourse and Practice in International Commercial Arbitration: Issues, Challenges and Prospects*, ed. V.K. Bhatia, C.N. Candlin, M. Gotti, Taylor & Francis 2012, pp. 306–307.

87 *Ibidem*, p. 308.

88 *Ibidem*, p. 310.

89 *Ibidem*.

90 *Ibidem*.

testimony. In this view, the written disclosures are rather narrow in scope and thus merely handled by legal counsels. Given that, there is also a limited possibility to conduct cross-examination. Although international commercial arbitration provides flexibility in choosing the most suitable procedures and processes, arbitrators often struggle to agree on a strategy that both parties find acceptable. Indeed, it results in practical challenges that could be summarized as follows:

> The real problem is in cases where you have arbitrators or legal counsels from two different jurisdictions, one preferring written testimony and the other arguing, on the contrary, for oral witness examination. Even in cases where all the parties agree to allow written testimonies followed by some witness examination and cross-examination, one is likely to observe the tension between witness examination procedures adopted by counsels and arbitrators not only from different jurisdictions, but also, and perhaps more importantly, by the counsels from the same jurisdiction, especially those from common law backgrounds.[91]

Lastly, regarding the writing of arbitral awards,[92] it seems that arbitrators who are also members of the legal community have difficulty dissociating themselves from their primary discipline, litigation. In fact, this extensive experience in litigation impacts the awards. In this light, it is thus worthwhile to mention that:

> There is sufficient evidence in the corpus of awards from well-represented international resources that arbitrators, in general, are significantly influenced by what they are quite used to doing in their litigation practice. Their discursive products are not very different from what they write in litigation, except in that they are not as detailed as in their efforts in litigation and that their elaborate arguments and reasoning – extensively supported by references to relevant and applicable legislative sections as well as precedents in the form of references to earlier judgments, which are quite typical of legal judgments – are often not so elaborate in arbitration awards.[93]

### *1.2.2 Legal framework*

#### *1.2.2.1 Past*

The international commercial arbitration has a long history. In the modern era, the Montevideo Convention was the first international treaty to focus on dispute resolution. This Convention was signed in 1889 by many Latin American states. In practice, this treaty did not achieve a satisfactory number of signatories and

91 *Ibidem.*

92 See more: T.E. Carbonneau, *Rendering arbitral awards with reasons: The elaboration of common law of international transactions*, "Columbia Journal of Transnational Law" 1985, vol. 23, pp. 579–614, https://insight.dickinsonlaw.psu.edu/cgi/viewcontent.cgi?article=1297&context=fac_works.

93 V.K. Bhatia, M. Gotti, *Contested identities in international…*, p. 310.

thus had a limited impact on settlements of commercial disputes. Despite this fact, the Montevideo Convention is widely considered a first step in introducing multilateral conventions on international commercial arbitration. In the wake of this treaty, the 1899 Hague Convention for the Pacific Settlement of Disputes and the 1907 Hague Convention for the Pacific Settlement of International Disputes were adopted. Nonetheless, the contemporary legal framework for international commercial arbitration was introduced in the 1920s.[94]

The first decades of the 20th century were marked by increasing businesses in developed states. In addition, a pro-arbitration movement was significant and thus resulted in the establishment of institutions that were responsible for international commercial arbitration.[95] As such, there was a need to lay the foundation for using arbitration as a preferred method of dispute settlement in the case of both domestic and international disputes. Indeed, the legal framework was seen as a compulsory element to speed up the process of expansion in terms of international trade and investment. In addition, the International Chamber of Commerce (ICC) was established in 1919. This institution played a crucial role in enhancing the legal framework for international arbitration. Likewise, many other institutions were set up at that time, namely the Court of Arbitration in 1923 and the American Arbitration Association (AAA) in 1926. Indeed, the creation of such institutions means that "international arbitration had entered the organizational and expansive phase".[96]

It is noteworthy that the Age of Institutionalization (between around 1920–1950) is considered a seminal period in terms of development of the legal framework for international commercial arbitration.[97] Throughout the increasing number of legal and economic circles, it was necessary to adopt an international instrument for the sake of ensuring that the arbitration clauses remain valid. Brachet even describes this period by saying that "international arbitration was enjoying ever increasing favor… But the full development of this arbitration depends on solving two big problems: the international validity of arbitration clauses and the international enforcement of arbiral awards".[98] As a result, the most significant trade nations at that time reached a consensus on the Geneva Protocol on Arbitration Clauses in Commercial Matters (widely known as the "Geneva Protocol")[99] in 1923. This Protocol laid down a foundation for the development of international commercial arbitration. One of the most important features refers to the requirement for the

94 G.B. Born, *International Commercial Arbitration*, Kluwer Law International 2024, p. 27.

95 M. Schinazi, *The Three Ages of International Commercial Arbitration. Cambridge*, Cambridge University Press 2022, p. 89.

96 *Ibidem*, p. 89.

97 *Ibidem*.

98 *Ibidem*, p. 117; P. Brachet, *De l'exécution internationale des sentences (étude de droit comparé et de droit international privé*, Paris: Rousseau 1928, p. 2.

99 *Protocol on Arbitration Clauses*, Geneva, 24 September 1923, https://treaties.un.org/pages/LONViewDetails.aspx?src=LON&id=555&chapter=30&clang=_en. Accessed on 27 June 2025.

Contracting States to recognize the enforceability of both arbitration agreements and arbitral awards.[100]

In addition, the Geneva Protocol is widely seen as a background for many principles applicable in international arbitration proceedings, namely

> the presumptive validity of agreements to arbitrate future (as well as existing) disputes, the obligation of national courts to enforce arbitration agreements by referring parties to arbitration, the concept of arbitrating 'commercial' disputes and disputes 'capable of settlement by arbitration', and the obligation to recognize international agreements on an equal footing with domestic arbitration agreements.[101]

Interestingly, these principles were repeated in both international conventions and national legal acts on commercial arbitration. Therefore, this Protocol created a legal framework for the functioning of international commercial arbitration throughout the standards that allow for international arbitration agreements to be more enforceable compared to domestic ones. Indeed, such a trend played a significant role in promoting international arbitration as a preferred method of solving commercial disputes.[102]

Lastly, the Geneva Protocol also made a reference to the recognition of international arbitral awards. Under Article 3, "Each Contracting State undertakes to ensure the execution by its authorities and in accordance with the provisions of its national laws of arbitral awards made in its own territory". It is worth adding, however, that provision had a relatively limited scope of application. This entails that only the Contracting States could enforce an arbitral award that was made on their own territory. Given that, any "foreign" awards rendered in different countries did not meet the requirement to be enforceable. Furthermore, such enforcement was possible merely according to local law (the so-called "provisions of its national law"). Therefore, it relied upon the individual state's arbitration legislation. Similarly, the concept of party autonomy to establish the arbitral procedures was not perfect in the Geneva Protocol. In fact, it allowed applying both the procedures provided by the parties' arbitration agreement and the law of the seat. In practice, the lack of priority between these two sources created a certain level of ambiguity.[103]

In the wake of the Geneva Protocol, the 1927 Geneva Convention for the Execution of Foreign Arbitral Awards (Geneva Convention) was adopted. Indeed, this Convention aimed to address the deficiencies of the previous legislation. Given that, the Geneva Convention took a more pro-arbitration stance by expanding the enforceability of arbitral awards that were rendered in line with the arbitration agreements. This entails that it required both the recognition and enforcement of

100 G.B. Born, *International Commercial Arbitration*, Kluwer Law International 2024, p. 27.

101 *Ibidem*, pp. 27–28.

102 *Ibidem*, p. 28.

103 *Ibidem*.

"foreign" arbitral awards that were issued within any Contracting State. In addition, the Geneva Convention also forbade national courts to substantially review the merits of arbitral awards during the recognition proceedings. Despite these positive changes compared to the Geneva Protocol, the Geneva Convention also had some pitfalls. One of the most important drawbacks refers to the burden of proof that was put on the award-creditor. As such, the award-creditor was responsible for demonstrating that there was a valid arbitration agreement covering the arbitrable subject matter and that the arbitral proceedings were handled pursuant to the parties' agreement. In addition, the award-creditor had to prove that the arbitral award was final in the place of arbitration and did not violate the public policy in the recognizing state. Such an approach laid down the foundation for the concept of "double exequatur" requirement. Given that, it is possible to recognize abroad an arbitral award once it has been confirmed by the court of the place of arbitration. Indeed, such a provision created a certain level of difficulty in terms of establishing the finality of the arbitral award.[104]

Even if both the Geneva Protocol and Geneva Convention were not perfect and had some shortcomings, they are widely considered a cornerstone in shaping the legal framework of international commercial arbitration. Indeed, both instruments introduced the most fundamental principles such as "the presumptive validity of international arbitration agreements and arbitral awards, and the enforceability of arbitration agreements by specific performance, as well as recognition of the parties' autonomy to select the substantive law governing their relations and to determine the arbitral procedures".[105]

#### *1.2.2.2 Today*

Fully up-to-date, international commercial arbitration is based on two main legal foundations, including the United Nations Convention on the Recognition and Enforcement of Foreign Arbitral Awards (1958 New York Convention) and the United Nations Commission for International Trade Law (UNCITRAL) Model Law on International Commercial Arbitration (UNCITRAL Model Law).[106]

The 1958 New York Convention marked a significant turning point in the development of international commercial arbitration. Under the New York Convention, the contracting states are obliged to uphold valid arbitration agreements alongside applying a streamlined method for securing the recognition and enforcement of arbitral awards internationally. Currently, 173 countries[107] have ratified this Convention, thus admitting its extensive framework regarding the enforcement of arbitral awards.[108]

104 *Ibidem.*

105 *Ibidem.*

106 P. Capper, *International Arbitration…*, p. 3.

107 *Contracting States of the New York Convention*, https://www.newyorkconvention.org/contracting-states. Accessed on 23.04.2025.

108 P. Capper, *International Arbitration…*, p. 3.

Importantly, the New York Convention distinguishes two terms, namely recognition and enforcement of an arbitral award. In practice, an award cannot be enforced without prior recognition. On the other hand, "an arbitral award can be recognized without being enforced".[109] Given that, these two terms are widely considered two different stages. The first one, namely recognition, refers to a defensive process. A winning party is willing to recognize an arbitral award to prove that an arbitral tribunal has determined the subject matter in the disputed case. As such, this matter cannot be litigated, and thus the willing party is seeking enforcement to receive the amount granted by the arbitral award. To achieve this goal, it is necessary to present such an award to the court alongside a request the recognition of this award as both valid and legally binding on the parties concerned. By contrast, enforcement refers to the judicial process that is handled after the recognition of an arbitral award for the sake of forcing the losing party to execute the award. Given that, the enforcement process includes an element of compulsion as a further step in carrying out this arbitral award. Redfern and Hunter described this process as follows: "while recognition is a shield, enforcement is used as a sword".[110] In practice, enforcement takes place if the losing party is not interested in carrying out the arbitral award voluntarily. Therefore, the court plays an active role in executing the binding arbitral award against the losing party.[111]

In addition, the New York Convention clearly stipulated the grounds which may result in refusing recognition and enforcement of arbitral award. According to Article V(1), the competent authority may deny the recognition and enforcement of an arbitral award, based on the application of the opposing party, if that party sets forth evidence demonstrating one of the following circumstances:

(a) The parties to the agreement referred to in article II were, under the law applicable to them, under some incapacity, or the said agreement is not valid under the law to which the parties have subjected it or, failing any indication thereon, under the law of the country where the award was made; or
(b) The party against whom the award is invoked was not given proper notice of the appointment of the arbitrator or of the arbitration proceedings or was otherwise unable to present his case; or
(c) The award deals with a difference not contemplated by or not falling within the terms of the submission to arbitration, or it contains decisions on matters beyond the scope of the submission to arbitration, provided that, if the decisions on matters submitted to arbitration can be separated from those not so submitted, that part of the award which contains decisions on matters submitted to arbitration may be recognized and enforced; or

109 M. Fahim Nia, *Enforcement of Foreign Arbitral Awards: A Closer Look at the New York Convention*, Nova Science Publishers 2017, p. 6.

110 *Ibidem*, p. 7.

111 *Ibidem*.

(d) The composition of the arbitral authority or the arbitral procedure was not in accordance with the agreement of the parties, or, failing such agreement, was not in accordance with the law of the country where the arbitration took place; or
(e) The award has not yet become binding on the parties, or has been set aside or suspended by a competent authority of the country in which, or under the law of which, that award was made.[112]

In addition, paragraph 2 of this Article provides two more grounds upon which the arbitral award may be refused recognition and enforcement, namely:

(a) The subject matter of the difference is not capable of settlement by arbitration under the law of that country; or
(b) The recognition or enforcement of the award would be contrary to the public policy of that country.[113]

UNCITRAL Model Law was adopted in 1985 as a guideline for both legislation and judicial decisions. In fact, it was introduced for the sake of harmonizing international commercial arbitration laws across jurisdictions. The last revision in 2006 aimed to improve and adjust the legal framework to comply with the new features, including juridical conceptions regarding the writing requirement alongside the role of interim measures, among others.[114]

From scratch, the UNCITRAL Model Law was designed as a flexible tool. Therefore, it cannot be classified as a Convention and thus it does not impose any obligations to enact national legislation reflecting strict conformity with it. By contrast,

> The Model Law provides a set of provisions for the management of international commercial arbitration which each country may choose to accept, subject to those modifications or additions which its national legislature considers appropriate. Naturally, however, harmonisation is best promoted (and the interest of international arbitration best served) by the Law's close implementation.[115]

112 *United Nations Convention on the Recognition and Enforcement of Foreign Arbitral Awards, Article V(1)...*

113 *Ibidem, Article V(2).*

114 H.M. Holtzmann et al., *A Guide to the 2006 Amendments to the UNCITRAL Model Law on International Commercial Arbitration: Legislative History and Commentary*, Wolters Kluwer 2015.

115 *UNCITRAL Model Law on International Commercial Arbitration: Explanatory Documentation prepared for Commonwealth Jurisdictions*, "Commonwealth Secretariat" 1991, p. 3, https://uncitral.un.org/sites/uncitral.un.org/files/media-documents/uncitral/en/model-law-arbitration-commonwealth.pdf. Accessed on June 11, 2025.

In other words, the UNCITRAL Model Law represents a "soft law"[116] in international commercial arbitration. According to the UNCITRAL Secretariat, it was assumed to be "in the interest for international commercial arbitration if UNCITRAL would initiate steps leading to the establishment of uniform standards of arbitral procedure. It was considered that the preparation of a model law on arbitration would be the most appropriate way to achieve the desired uniformity".[117]

## 1.3 Intersection between 4IR and international commercial arbitration

The innovation-driven technologies developed by the 4IR have a significant influence on the legal industry, including international commercial arbitration. To name a few examples, Artificial Intelligence (AI), Machine Learning (ML), and blockchain have changed the landscape of dispute resolution. Importantly, the 4IR impacted many different "stakeholders" of the arbitration, such as disputed parties, their lawyers, arbitral institutions, arbitrators' assistants, and arbitrators as well.[118]

As a result of such fast advancement in the ODR's expansion, the technology itself, which is acknowledged as the "Fourth Party" in dispute resolution, has been introduced to provide necessary support to the third-party mediator, arbitrator, or judge.[119] In fact, this term was introduced by Katsh and Rifkin in 2001. They believed that the digital environment is highly influencing the way parties interact and how dispute resolution unfolds. Many different features of the ODR platforms, including design, interface, and developed functionalities, indicate the boundaries of real actions that can be undertaken therein. As such, the concept of

116 See more: G. Kaufmann-Kohler, *Soft law in international arbitration: Codification and normativity*, "Journal of International Dispute Settlement" 2010, pp. 283–299; L.A. DiMatteo, *Soft law and the principle of fair and equitable decision making in international commercial arbitration*, "The Chinese Journal of Comparative Law" 2013, pp. 221–255, https://doi.org/10.1093/cjcl/cxt013; H. Deeb Gabriel, *The Advantages of Soft Law in International Commercial Law: The Role of UNIDROIT, UNCITRAL, and the Hague Conference*, "Brooklyn Journal of International Law" 2009, vol. 34, issue 3, pp. 655–672, https://brooklynworks.brooklaw.edu/cgi/viewcontent.cgi?article=1172&context=bjil; S. Ali, S.K. Neuhaus, *The Emergence of Soft Law as an Applicable Source of Procedural and Substantive Law* [in:] *Cambridge Compendium of International Commercial and Investment Arbitration*, ed. S. Kröll, A.K. Bjorklund, F. Ferrari, Cambridge University Press 2023, pp. 537–562.

117 *Note by the Secretariat: further work in respect of international commercial arbitration (A/CN.9/169)*, "United Nations Commission on International Trade Law. Yearbook" 1981, vol. X: 1979, p. 109, https://uncitral.un.org/sites/uncitral.un.org/files/media-documents/uncitral/en/yb_1979_e.pdf. Accessed on June 14, 2025.

118 Wu Pijan, *A Book Review on Katia Fach Gómez "The Technological Competence of Arbitrators: A Comparative and International Legal Study" (Springer, Cham, 2023)*, "Contemporary Asia Arbitration Journal" 2024, vol. 17, no. 1, p. 119.

119 M. Łągiewska, *New technologies in international arbitration: A game-changer in the dispute resolution?*, "International Journal for the Semiotics of Law" 2024, vol. 37, p. 853; see: D. Protopsaltou, T. Schultz, N. Magnenat-Thalmann, *Taking the fourth party further? Considering a shared virtual workspace for arbitration*, "Information & Communications Technology Law" 2006, vol. 15(2), p. 157.

"Fourth Party" in dispute resolution concerns a broader socio-technical and legal dynamic and thus refers to Lawrence Lessig's standpoint that "code is law". Given this idea, digital systems should not be seen as impartial and neutral. Instead, they are designed to reveal many different values and assumptions that may result in shaping not only users' behavior but also procedural outcomes.[120]

In this light, it is worthwhile to remember that:

> The 'Fourth Party' now regularly takes a seat at the table along with party one and party two (the disputants) and the third party (the human neutral, such as a mediator or arbitrator). 'Fourth Parties' are foundational to the practice of ODR, and the concept undergirds our understanding of how algorithmic and machine learning tools fit appropriately into dispute resolution processes. In ODR trainings, third parties are encouraged to regard 'Fourth Parties' as partners in the resolution process. The same can be said for disputants utilizing technology for negotiation. 'Fourth Parties' are already leveraging rule-based systems to generate settlement offers, diagnose problems, and issue decisions, especially in low-value, high-volume caseloads. These tools are currently lightening the administrative load on parties and neutrals, saving time and money, and enhancing the performance and credibility of the ODR process, but they represent only the beginning of what the fourth party can offer.[121]

There are different approaches to "Fourth Party", namely simple and complex technological tools alongside instrumental and principal ODR systems. Under the first classification, on the one hand, there are various simple tools, including red flags, emoticons, images, or sounds that are commonly applied for the sake of attracting the attention of different stakeholders or reminding them about the approaching deadlines. In fact, these tools replace traditionally used pens and flipcharts in offline proceedings. On the other hand, aside from such simple tools, there are also complex technological tools and platforms well developed. In this context, the proper use of such technologies also requires specific technological skills (discussed further). To name a few examples, extranets, virtual case-rooms, case management websites, and videoconferencing tools became a new normal during arbitral proceedings.[122] In this light, given the rapid technological development in terms of new innovations and machine learning, the "Fourth Party" is constantly improving its skills and encompassing a broader scope of their application in arbitral proceedings. In the future, the "Fourth Party" instead of completing additional tasks, may, in some situations play many different roles in arbitral proceedings presented in detail in Chapter 2.

120 A. Sela, *Can computers be fair? How automated and human-powered online dispute resolution affect procedural justice in mediation and arbitration*, "Ohio State Journal on Dispute Resolution" 2018, vol. 33, issue 1, pp. 98–99.

121 L. Wing, J. Martinez, E. Katsh, C. Rule, *Designing Ethical Online*..., pp. 51–52.

122 D. Protopsaltou, T. Schultz, N. Magnenat-Thalmann, *Taking the Fourth Party*..., p. 159.

The second classification refers to the distinction between instrumental and principal ODR systems. Therefore, it considers the degree of autonomy in view of the decision-making capabilities of software. The first system, namely instrumental ODR platforms, is commonly regarded as the conventional "Fourth Party" in dispute resolution. Such platforms function mainly as digital facilitators, which mean that they support communication and coordination between different participants and a human arbitrator. In practice, such systems reflect virtual venues and thus allow dispute resolution to be handled online. Given that, these platforms are helpful in collecting and delivering information as well as interacting with other parties. Importantly, the entire decision-making process is controlled by the human parties. This means that the instrumental ODR systems facilitate the process online, but a human third party is needed to supervise them. Despite being equipped with intelligent features, the instrumental systems still remain subordinate to human judgments and therefore do not have any power in handling the autonomous decision-making process. [123]

In contrast, the so-called principal ODR systems are recognized to be a step forward. In this context, they are not only responsible for facilitating the proceedings online but also substituting the human third party. This means that these systems are going far beyond their role as communication platforms by taking more proactive actions. In this view, they are not only guiding but also managing dispute resolution processes. In practice, these systems are very advanced and powered by Artificial Intelligence (AI). Following this feature, they both replicate and automate functions that are usually performed by human third parties. For example, they identify interests, clarify goals, inform users about different solutions, prioritize preferences, interpret rules, classify cases, propose final decisions, among others. Compared to instrumental systems, they fulfill their role through assisting human decision-makers. In addition, they can fully autonomously navigate complex disputes and thus reduce costly human expertise. Thanks to the application of advanced technology, including human-like interaction, such systems represent well-developed and sophisticated capabilities compared to traditional ways of handling disputes. In this context, such an evolution represents a paradigm shift in terms of introducing new standards of dispute resolution in terms of enhanced efficiency, accessibility alongside procedural intelligence. Even though Katsh and Rifkin's concept of the "Fourth Party"[124] in dispute resolution has seen technology merely as a supportive tool, the principal ODR systems are reshaping this concept and thus introducing better quantitative features to be applied in the dispute resolution practice.[125]

123 A. Sela, *Can Computers Be Fair?...*, pp. 99–100.

124 See also: J. Zeleznikow, *Using Artificial Intelligence to provide intelligent dispute resolution support*, "Group Decision and Negotiation" 2021, vol. 30, pp. 789–812; K. Buhuri, *Arbitration in the era of e-commerce: A comprehensive overview*, "World Journal of Advanced Research and Reviews" 2024, vol. 23, issue 3, pp. 89–103.

125 A. Sela, *Can Computers Be Fair?...*, pp. 100–101.

In sum, this perspective considers the importance of ODR mechanisms in terms of enhancing both the communication and information flow. Even though in-person or face-to-face meetings have many advantages, they are not always necessary. In contrast, the fast development and advancements in new technologies, including software and AI, will introduce a new paradigm of dispute resolution. ODR would become increasingly capable of handling complex disputes as well.[126]

The "Fourth Party" also provides many benefits compared to traditional ways of handling arbitral proceedings. Through the implementation of AI-supported tools, there is a significant reduction of administrative burdens along with the enhanced cost- and time-effectiveness. Within this context,

> The real question is not where the fourth party is today but where it is going. The fourth party is becoming more capable all the time. As computer processors become more powerful and user experience designs more intuitive, the fourth party expands what it is able to provide. Also, the fourth party can operate as a service, so it can be available on the phones in the parties' pockets all day every day, which can increase accessibility and improve responsiveness. The fourth party can do things that a third party cannot (or should not) do because of its concern that it will be perceived as partial (algorithms cannot be influenced by compliments or charisma). Parties may also react differently to suggestions from a third party as opposed to a fourth party, perhaps because the fourth party has no feelings that will be hurt if its suggestion is rejected.[127]

This approach already confirms that "Fourth Party" is a game-changer in dispute resolution landscape and introduces new standards therein.[128]

## 1.4 Technological competence of arbitrators

There is no doubt that nowadays new technologies are much more present in arbitration than ever before. As a result of such technological advancement, arbitrators are forced to have direct contact with such technology, including, for example remote hearings or AI-powered tools. Apparently, arbitrators make use of many different types of technologies while dealing with conflict checks.[129]

In addition, the so-called intersection between technology and legal practice has become a new normal. Such a relation also plays a crucial role in arbitration, most notably in view of cybersecurity and data protection issues. In short, a

126 L. Wing, J. Martinez, E. Katsh, C. Rule, *Designing Ethical Online...*, p. 51.

127 *Ibidem*, p. 52.

128 See more: Y. Pathak, *Pioneering Innovations In Digital Jurisprudence: Evaluating ODR Systems And AI In Shaping The Future Of Conflict Resolution* (November 01, 2024). Available at SSRN: https://ssrn.com/abstract=5110555 or http://dx.doi.org/10.2139/ssrn.5110555. Accessed on 05/23/2025.

129 K. Fach Gómez, *The Technological Competence...*, p. 101.

certain level of technological knowledge is needed to avoid the leakage either of case-related data or even sensitive data. In practice, the proper consciousness and understanding of possible cyberattacks might result in a lawyer's breach of confidentiality. Therefore, arbitrators should be well-equipped with knowledge of new technologies to properly address even potential cybersecurity threats. This entails that arbitrators cannot ignore such situations and justify any possible compromises of confidentiality because of not sufficient technological knowledge. Instead, they are deemed, like the other lawyers, to fulfill their duties with respect to the Latin paremia "*ignorantia legis neminem excusat*".[130] In fact, if an arbitrator lacks proper technological skills,[131] it may lead to challenges and even problems regarding proceedings and the awards. In addition, it would be difficult to comprise the required capabilities in view of technology and thus lead to frustration of parties' expectations.[132]

Katia Fach Gómez, in her book, analyzes the technological competence of arbitrators. First of all, "she defines this competence as the ability to perform tasks efficiently and highlights the need for arbitrators to have technological skills in addition to legal expertise. Gómez distinguishes between basic competence, a fundamental expectation for all arbitrators, and premium competence, which offers a competitive edge for handling complex cases".[133]

In addition, she undergoes the "5 Ws" test, namely What, Why, Who, Where, and When. To address these issues, she raises many detailed questions such as:

> Should an arbitrator know how to accept changes, turn the feature off, or eliminate metadata from a document created in an arbitration? What should happen – if anything – in a remote hearing if arbitrator does not react to regular Zoom-bombing? Is there a problem if an arbitrator uses a hologram to chair an arbitration hearing? Do arbitrators put their clients' data and their own work at risk by using outdated technology, e.g., drafting the final award with an operating system that is no longer supported by the manufacturer? What about an arbitrator who is working on an award and connects to the public Wi-Fi of an airport or coffee shop, or sends the document to the hotel printer? If an arbitrator's legal assistant uses her/his personal laptop to review a procedural order draft, is it preferable to store the document locally on her/his device or on a cloud storage site? Can arbitrators deliberate remotely by

130 A. Dehdashti, *The technological competence of arbitrators: a comparative and international legal study: by Katia Fach Gómez, Switzerland, Springer, 2023, 186 pp.*, "International Review of Law, Computers & Technology" 2024, vol. 38(3), pp. 476–477, https://doi.org/10.1080/13600869.2024.2324595.

131 See more: S.I. Strong, *Research in International Commercial Arbitration: Special Skills, Special Sources*" The American Review of International Arbitration" 2009, vol. 20, University of Missouri School of Law Legal Studies Research Paper No. 2010-15, Available at SSRN: https://ssrn.com/abstract=1650263. Accessed on May 24, 2025.

132 Wu Pijan, *A Book Review...*, p. 119.

133 A.G. Cardoso et al., *Generative Artificial Intelligence and legal decision-making*, "Global Trade and Customs Journal" 2024, p. 722, DOI: 10.54648/GTCJ2024081.

sharing their opinions via their Gmail or Yahoo email accounts? If an arbitrator wants to use an AI application, is she or he required to understand the workings of the algorithms? Should an arbitrator inform the parties on the use of algorithmic decision-making? Should the parties tolerate an arbitrator making comments about the case under arbitration on social media? What should arbitrators do if they sense that voice manipulation has occurred in a remote witness examination? Can or should arbitrators collaborate with non-legal professionals with the aim of adequately managing the multiple technological challenges that may arise in the course of an arbitration? Do arbitrators suffer from technological Dunning-Kruger effect[134]?[135]

Even though currently there are no fully comprehensive rules of ethics referring to the technological competence of arbitrators, Katia Fach Gómez offers a fresh insight into how to fill this gap. She suggests reinterpreting "classic duties" such as "competence, ability, availability, diligence, qualification, and/or continuous training". Further, she makes some expectations that a new category of duties may arise in the future, namely "a next-generation duties". This term would refer to "maintaining cyber-security, reporting cyber intrusions, fostering technological cooperation and supervision, and the duty to automate certain legal tasks, albeit not yet expressly codified, may reinforce the need to address the future of arbitrators' duty of technological competence in a more structured and general way".[136]

In addition, although neither hard law nor soft law regulations and rules deal with the technological competence of arbitrators, even nowadays, there are many examples confirming that arbitrators must be equipped with such new skills. Importantly, since the preliminary meeting or case management conference, through technology-driven remote hearings to rendering an arbitral award, they should pay attention to both cybersecurity and data protection issues.[137]

On the other hand, it is worth remembering that technology itself has a significant impact on the reduction of costs, and arbitral proceedings cannot be seen as an exception in this regard. Indeed, this perspective should also be considered while dealing with the possible use of information technologies to boost both efficiency and transparency in international arbitration.[138] Furthermore, the proper application of technology may improve legal productivity, minimize mistakes, provide better and fairer client service and even protect and enhance the good reputation of arbitrators. Against this background, technology may even reduce the cultural isolation of arbitrators and increase diversity among them.[139]

134 See more: L.A. Frase, *When strategies go awry: Part 5 in a series on cognitive biases and their impact*, "MEALEY'S Emerging Toxic Torts" 2018, vol. 26, pp. 1–11.

135 K. Fach Gómez, *The technological competence*..., p. 8.

136 *Ibidem*, p. 165.

137 Wu Pijan, *A Book Review*..., pp. 124–125.

138 A. Dehdashti, *The technological competence*..., p. 477.

139 Wu Pijan, *A Book Review*..., p. 122.

Nowadays, an arbitrator is required to develop his technological skills on how to properly use properly digital tools and platforms for the sake of conducting remote hearings. In practice, it involves proficiency in videoconferencing platforms and various innovation-driven communication technologies.[140]

In conclusion, there are indeed many practical challenges associated with the use of new technologies, not only in the arbitral proceedings but also in the drafting of arbitral awards. It seems that arbitrators are at the forefront of such technological changes, and they need to adopt many different tools carefully and cautiously with respect to the fundamental principles of international commercial arbitration. Therefore, both due process and confidentiality should be fully respected and maintained in order to avoid possible challenges or even annulment of an arbitral award. This is particularly important in the case of sole arbitrators who have even a limited access to well-specialized AI tools that have been designed specifically for legal professionals.[141]

In this light, although there is currently no comprehensive legal framework covering these issues and providing explicit answers to all these questions, many different jurisdictions, in addition to arbitral institutions, have already recognized the importance of the technological competence of arbitrators in dispute resolution. Arbitrators would need to enhance their technological literacy to keep pace with new innovations in the field. Such skills may have an impact on the selection process of arbitrators, who may even be asked about such skills during the appointment process. The ongoing integration of technology into international arbitration will continue to deepen and become a new standard for resolving cross-border disputes.

140 Chen Lei, *Will virtual hearings remain in post-pandemic international arbitration?,* "International Journal for the Semiotics of Law" 2024, vol. 37, p. 837, https://doi.org/10.1007/s11196-023-10054-7.

141 See more: A.G. Cardoso et al., *Generative Artificial Intelligence...*, p. 722.

# 2 Artificial Intelligence (AI) in international arbitration for different actors

Artificial Intelligence (AI) in general and Generative AI (GenAI)[1] in particular may be useful in different areas of lawyers' work, including document drafting and reviewing, legal research, advisory, among others. In fact, many different AI-powered tools have already played an important role in the context of international arbitration, even far before the emergence of GenAI. In this light, it is noteworthy to recall earlier AI tools that have enhanced workflow efficiency and strategic decision-making processes and thus have led to the reduction of operational expenses. Importantly, these AI-driven technologies benefited from "Machine Learning, Natural Language Processing (NLP), text mining, predictive modeling, pattern and speech recognition along with Optical Character Recognition (OCR)".[2]

ML algorithms take advantage of various learning techniques such as supervised, unsupervised, and reinforcement learning. In fact, these techniques are commonly employed for the sake of proper training of models on historical data, including legal datasets, for instance. Through such training, ML algorithms execute multifarious tasks related to the classification of documents, sentiment analysis alongside predictive assessments. Supervised learning is based on labeled datasets which are crucial in teaching models how make a distinction between different categories of legal documents. In practice, it relates to the process of differentiating contracts from court opinions, among others. Unsupervised learning is designed to detect hidden structures along with thematic patterns in unlabeled data. This feature improves the process of identifying common topics within a large set of documents. The last, reinforcement learning, focuses on the interaction and reward-based training. This means that a model is learning the most persuasive legal arguments by simulating trial proceedings, courtroom dynamics and thus optimizing the successful outcomes.[3]

NLP plays a crucial role in translating legal documents, generating concise summaries of the case law, and extracting the most important information from

1 See more: M.J. Broyde, Mei Yiyang, *Don't kill the baby! The case for AI in arbitration*, "New York University Journal of Law & Business" 2024, vol. 21, no. 1, pp. 119-173.

2 E. Chan, K.N. Gore, E. Jiang, *Harnessing Artificial Intelligence in International Arbitration Practice*, Contemporary Asia Arbitration Journal, 2023, vol. 16, issue 2, p. 267.

3 *Ibidem*.

DOI: 10.4324/9781003667834-3

the complex legal texts. From the perspective of international arbitration, which involves a diverse linguistic and cultural background of the parties, AI-driven translation systems play a crucial role in overcoming language barriers. In practice, these tools are necessary for facilitating communication and effective cooperation between different stakeholders of arbitral proceedings, such as arbitrators, legal representatives, and parties stemming from different jurisdictions.[4]

Text mining refers to the process of analyzing and extracting meaningful information from unstructured legal texts. It is based upon the identification of critical elements, including key terminology, named entities such as parties and arbitrators, along with case-specific facts in legal documents. Once extracted, such information is further organized and categorized, which result in enhancing the accessibility of legal datasets. Thanks to both data retrieval and analysis, text mining is commonly recognized as empowering arbitration professionals in handling large volumes of legal content with better efficiency. Given that, text mining is thus crucial for facilitating legal research, case preparation, and management of documents.[5]

Predictive analytics draw on historical records in order to forecast probable future outcomes. In the context of international arbitration, these advanced algorithms are used to examine previous case data alongside arbitrator decisions. Such analysis is necessary for the sake of generating projections in view of the likelihood of a favorable judgment or potential settlement terms. In addition, "this technique can help find relevant case law, detect conflicts of interest among arbitrators, or assess the consistency of awards and decisions".[6]

Pattern recognition algorithms play a crucial role in scrutinizing individual cases to uncover both similarities and differences within court decisions and arbitral awards. These algorithms are used to find relevant case law, reveal potential conflicts of interest between arbitrators, and assess both the coherence and uniformity of arbitral awards and decisions.[7]

Speech recognition technology can change verbal exchanges made by the parties, their legal counsels, witnesses into written transcripts. Therefore, thanks to this technology, the content becomes more accessible in terms of analysis. In fact, it relies on the capacity to transform spoken dialogue into well-structured and searchable text. This feature increases its role in enhancing efficiency, improving accuracy and streamlining the review process. From the perspective of legal professionals and arbitrators, speech recognition serves as a valuable resource in terms of reviewing and referencing discussions throughout the arbitral proceedings[8] (discussed further in detail).

Finally, the OCR combines machine learning algorithms with computer vision and thus converts scanned images and paper-based documents into not only

4 *Ibidem*, p. 267.

5 *Ibidem*, pp. 267–268.

6 *Ibidem*, p. 268.

7 *Ibidem*.

8 *Ibidem*.

editable but also machine-readable text. Importantly, the OCR has a pivotal role in the process of digitizing hard copies of documents which can be easily searched, indexed, and even integrated into online legal research databases. The latter allows streamlined access and analysis.[9]

One must note, however, that the quality of a conversion of scanned documents into readable and searchable digital documents is of key significance. It might occur that OCR software misinterprets characters, unpopular fonts, or even less frequently used languages. This might result in some inaccuracies in view of the produced digital texts. Therefore, it is worthwhile to remember that the use of OCR may also lead to real issues within the context of dispute resolution. To illustrate, in 2015, the High Court of England and Wales imposed a sanction of one of the parties "for failing to meet its disclosure duties due to relying on defective OCR"[10] in the Smailes v McNally case.[11] In this particular dispute, the claimant used the OCR to scan physical documents that were further sent to a special platform dedicated to handling disputes. Nonetheless, the quality of scanned documents was not good enough and resulted in many inaccuracies. In consequence, the claimant did not submit the complete set of documents. In contrast, these scanned documents did not comply with the relevance feature, most notably in terms of applying the keyword searches. In conclusion, "the court deemed this a serious and significant failure to carry out a reasonable search, therefore emphasising the importance of ensuring the accuracy of OCR-generated text in legal proceedings".[12]

The following sections present various AI-powered tools from the perspectives of the parties, the arbitral institution, and the arbitrators.

## 2.1 Perspective of the parties

### *2.1.1 Clause Builder AI*

The American Arbitration Association (AAA) launched the so-called ClauseBuilder AI Tool. ClauseBuilder is widely recognized as "an online arbitration and mediation clause-drafting tool that assists individuals and organizations in creating clear, effective arbitration and mediation agreements".[13] Indeed, the ClauseBuilder is a GenAI-powered tool that was introduced to streamline the entire process of

9 *Ibidem.*

10 M. Apostol, *Arbitration Tech Toolbox: Blind Spots in Arbitration – When Technology Distorts Evidence Without Direct Human Intervention*, "Kluwer Arbitration Blog" February 1, 2025, https://arbitrationblog.kluwerarbitration.com/2025/02/01/arbitration-tech-toolbox-blind-spots-in-arbitration-when-technology-distorts-evidence-without-direct-human-intervention/. Accessed on June 11, 2025.

11 See more: *Smailes and another v McNally and another* [2015] EWHC 1755 (Ch), https://www.bailii.org/ew/cases/EWHC/Ch/2015/1755.html. Accessed on June 14, 2025.

12 M. Apostol, *Arbitration Tech Toolbox...*

13 *Alternative Dispute Resolution ClauseBuilder Tool for Employment Contracts,* "American Arbitration Association", https://go.adr.org/SHRM. Accessed on January 6, 2025.

drafting arbitration and mediation clauses. This tool is based on OpenAI's GPT-4.0 platform.[14]

This tool was designed to create customized dispute resolution clauses based on the needs of clients. Indeed, it incorporates the AAA's time- and court-tested Employment Arbitration Rules and Mediation Procedures. The AI-powered ClauseBuilder allows the parties to freely input their parameters and specific requirements and thus decide on the number of arbitrators, method of selecting arbitrators in the proceedings, their qualifications, governing law, process of discovery, the duration of arbitral proceedings, remedies, among others. Importantly, this tool was introduced free of charge to attract more parties to benefit from such new technologies. ClauseBuilder was designed to provide necessary assistance while drafting both commercial and construction contracts. It is worth adding, however, that the AAA already plans to further develop this tool to embrace international contracts in the future.[15] According to the AAA, the ClauseBuilder was introduced merely for the sake of providing informational and educational purposes. This means that it does not offer any legal advice nor create an attorney-client relationship.[16] Likewise, it does not have the aim to replace legal professionals. By contrast, it focuses on enhancing both the efficiency and effectiveness of legal drafting processes. Given this tool, it is easy to generate draft clauses alongside suggestions regarding optional clause language. Nevertheless, the final review and decision on the clause should be made by a professional lawyer.[17]

Aside from the positive aspects such as speeding up the process of drafting an arbitral clause, some practical issues related to confidentiality may arise. Indeed, the AAA also pays attention to these aspects. Therefore, the "ClauseBuilder AI does not conduct any analysis on generated clauses and does not use any user prompts to train the AI language learning model".[18]

Another practical question relates to the possibilities of such an AI-powered tool to adjust its outputs under specific legal jurisdictions, when needed. Accordingly, it is worthwhile to remember that the ClauseBuilder has not been designed to meet requirements resulting from any specific jurisdiction. In turn, it aims to provide generally applicable clauses. This means that this AI tool cannot verify that a certain clause fulfills the requirements under a certain jurisdiction.[19] Therefore, the verification made by a human being based on his or her knowledge, experience, and expertise is highly needed and recommended.

Lastly, one must ask the question of whether both legal information and databases are regularly updated in the case of ClauseBuilder. Indeed, the AAA plays a

14 *ClauseBuilder AI Q&A*, "American Arbitration Association", https://www.adr.org/sites/default/files/document_repository/ClauseBuilder_AI_Q-and-A.pdf, p. 1. Accessed on January 10, 2025.

15 *Ibidem.*

16 Alternative Dispute Resolution ClauseBuilder Tool, American Arbitration Association, https://www.clausebuilder.org. Accessed on January 10, 2025.

17 ClauseBuilder AI Q&A…, p. 1.

18 *Ibidem.*

19 *Ibidem.*

crucial role in providing up-to-date databases to this AI-powered tool. It influences the generated content by the ClauseBuilder, which is based on the recent legal precedents, statutory changes, alongside arbitration rules.[20]

ClauseBuilder AI seems to be a very interesting and cutting-edge new technology launched by the AAA. On the one hand, it embraces the recent developments and advancements in terms of new technologies, including GenAI in the field of international commercial arbitration with respect to fundamental principles such as confidentiality or autonomy of the parties, among others. On the other hand, it also considers some limitations of such AI-powered tools regarding challenges to meet the requirements of a particular jurisdiction. Therefore, the AAA highlights that the outputs of the ClauseBuilder AI should be carefully verified by qualified lawyers. Such an approach strikes the right balance between incorporating new technologies into the daily lives of the arbitration community and exercising the utmost caution and awareness of their limitations and risks.

#### *2.1.2 Legal research and analysis of the case precedents*

The term Legal AI was introduced as a relatively broad category that includes expert legal systems and a theoretical framework related to Computational Law. In fact, Legal AI is part in the broader industry, commonly known as “Legal Tech” (the composition of ‘Legal’ and ‘Technology’).[21]

Considering document drafting, there is no doubt that GenAI may be a useful tool in the lengthy process of changing the content and structure of the documents. Therefore, it can easily help to improve the process and assist in such repetitive and meticulous work. To name a few examples, Spellbook and Juro may play a crucial role in generating initial draft documents according to predefined templates with respect to the clients’ requirements. In the wake of such technological advancements, lawyers would be much more focused on the complexity of the case and strategic issues within the contracts.[22]

Importantly, GenAI also influenced legal research, which was deemed to be rather a laborious process in the legal profession. Apparently, the legal research was based upon reviews of case law, statutes alongside legal literature, which was not only time-consuming but also overwhelming. The GenAI provides interesting solutions to these challenging problems. It can quickly analyze extensive datasets, identify the relevant legal precedents, and even summarize the critical information once needed. On the one hand, this GenAI may be crucial in terms of reducing time on searching for relevant case studies and laws. On the other hand, it would also allow lawyers to access relevant data and thus enhance the quality of their legal

20 *Ibidem.*

21 Y-Y. Rhim, KB Park, *The applicability of Artificial Intelligence in international law*, “Journal of East Asia and International Law” 2019, vol. 12, issue 1, p. 13.

22 B. Liu, *How is generative artificial intelligence changing the legal profession?*, “Economics Observatory”, https://www.economicsobservatory.com/how-is-generative-artificial-intelligence-changing-the-legal-profession. Accessed on January 10, 2025.

services and advice. Nowadays, lawyers eagerly benefit from Westlaw Edge and Lexis+ services, which already provide predictive research suggestions along with advanced analysis. These features significantly reduce the time spent by lawyers on their research tasks.[23]

The GenAI also provides advisory capabilities in the legal field. Accordingly, it can offer sophisticated, nuanced advice and arguments that resemble those of very well-experienced lawyers and practitioners. Importantly, it is worth remembering that such advice and arguments very often require specific knowledge and expertise in the field. This means that GenAI may speed up the process and provide innovative and convincing arguments through fine-tuning and custom training. Indeed, Harvey is one of the generative AI platforms that have been developed in cooperation with OpenAI. Thanks to large datasets of case law, Harvey analyzes complex litigation scenarios within a short time.[24]

Likewise, GenAI also impacts the international arbitration landscape. The parties are familiar with the subject matter of their dispute and relevant evidence even prior to submitting the Request for Arbitration. Likewise, they also know both the place of arbitration and the governing law. Instead, it is noteworthy that ChatGPT has no access to this kind of information. This means that ChatGPT has not been trained on such data. On the other hand, the claimant's counsel may use ChatGPT to write a Statement of Claim and even a draft of a Statement of Defense before the filing of a case for arbitration.[25] AI may be widely used within arbitral proceedings from the very beginning of the disputed case. Nowadays, the parties prefer to fill a modest Request and Answer. By contrast, while using AI tools, arbitral cases could be more front-loaded. As such, parties would be eager to submit full-fledged Statements of Claim and Statements of Defense even prior to the constitution of the arbitral tribunal. Jennifer Kirby believes that this solution would improve the arbitral proceedings by speeding up the process of the first round of submissions instead of the Request/Answer phase. In addition, the arbitral tribunal would focus much more on the merits of the case. If the parties use AI during the document disclosure phase, such as the exchange of written submissions, they would be quickly prepared for the second round of such submissions. In practice, once the first phase is sped up, the hearings would be conducted much sooner. Likewise, in the case of post-hearing submissions, if the hearing transcripts are available to the parties, they could easily make their post-hearing briefs or even post-hearing draft awards.[26]

This kind of solution provided by the AI-supported tools would significantly increase the efficiency of the arbitral proceedings and decrease the time of submitting documents for the parties. Nonetheless, it is worth remembering after Maxi Scherer that "AI is not (at present) a substitute for human expertise and judgment.

23 *Ibidem*.
24 B. Liu, *How is generative artificial...*
25 *Ibidem*, p. 661.
26 *Ibidem*, p. 662.

It is rather a tool that promises to augment human abilities and allow legal teams and arbitrators to work more efficiently and effectively".[27]

### *2.1.3 ROSS Intelligence*

Legal representatives have various choices in using AI-powered tools in international arbitration, even more than the parties themselves. Importantly, this new trend in the increasing implementation of AI tools becomes more popular in conducting legal research, drafting documents, analyzing arbitral clauses, providing case summaries, and precedent decisions.[28]

ROSS Intelligence is widely considered one of the most high-profile developments in the Legal Tech industry. It is even described as the first AI attorney which was developed by IBM. One must note, however, that "this machine was initially designed to help doctors read, analyse, and summarise exceptionally large medical journals in order to help them diagnose a certain medical condition and provide solutions or treatment. Subsequently, it became used in law".[29] In the context of the legal industry, this machine has been designed to read and analyze large volumes of data in order to provide comprehensive summaries. In addition, it is noteworthy that ROSS Intelligence is equipped with very high-tech features, namely voice recognition. This is particularly important given its features to provide accurate answers to legal questions once asked, and drafting both memos and materials for the proceedings.[30]

Briefly, ROSS Intelligence represents an AI-powered legal research tool that has been introduced for the sake of enhancing legal analysis, precedent retrieval along with the decision-making process. Even if ROSS was originally designed to be a legal assistant in US case law, its comprehensive application has been perceived by the international community and thus has become a widely applied tool in this field as well. ROSS was programmed to process unstructured legal data in a short time, identify relevant precedents, and assist arbitrators in the case analysis, most notably in terms of cross-jurisdictional disputes.

Nonetheless, it is also noteworthy to refer to the Thomson Reuters (Westlaw) v ROSS Intelligence case in 2025. Accordingly,

> ROSS a new competitor to Westlaw, made a legal-research search engine that uses artificial intelligence. To train its AI search tool, Ross needed a database of legal questions and answers. So Ross asked to license Westlaw's content. But because Ross was its competitor, Thomson Reuters refused. So to train its AI, Ross made a deal with LegalEase to get training data in the form of 'Bulk Memos'. Bulk Memos are lawyers' compilations of legal

27 *Ibidem*, p. 663; M. Scherer, *Artificial Intelligence and legal decision-making: the wide open?*, "Journal of International Arbitration" 2019, vol. 36, p. 539.

28 A.O. Onyefulu-Kingston, *AI-based technologies in international...*, p. 653.

29 *Ibidem*.

30 *Ibidem*.

> questions with good and bad answers. LegalEase gave those lawyers a guide explaining how to create those questions using Westlaw headnotes, while clarifying that the lawyers should not just copy and paste headnotes directly into the questions.[31]

Overall, the court decided to grant a summary judgment for Thomson Reuters. In this light, the court recognized the infringement of copyrights by ROSS Intelligence. Equally important is to mention that the judge rejected ROSS's defenses such as "claims of innocent infringement, copyright misuse, the merger doctrine, scenes à faire, and fair use".[32] As a consequence of this ruling, ROSS Intelligence stopped being available on the market.

### *2.1.4 Westlaw Edge*

Westlaw Edge introduced the AI-Assisted Research, which is based on Large Language Models (LLMs). This tool was designed to analyze content provided on Westlaw to produce answers needed by the user. The database under analysis consists of cases, statutes, along with regulations. Importantly, these LLMs work jointly with the Retrieval Augmented Generation (RAG) engine, and thus the users can follow the process of generating a response. Given that, they can easily understand how a certain answer was reached. In addition, the legal researchers can always refer to primary sources through the linked documents. As such, they can check the accuracy of the generated content and validate such a response. In this context, Westlaw AI-Assisted Research is commonly seen as a time-saver. It is helpful in accelerating the reading of multiple documents and generating syntheses. It is equally important to note that OpenAI, including ChatGPT, benefits from all sources, and thus, their produced outcomes may be inaccurate. In this context, seemingly plausible responses may actually be false. To address these concerns, the Westlaw tool is based on trusted content. Moreover, it is built on the principle of checks and balances to ensure the reliability of the content, which is grounded in correct law.[33]

In short, this AI-powered tool was designed carefully to address challenges relating to possible hallucinations. Given that, it provides reliable information based on existing and binding laws. Despite this fact, the human oversight of the AI-produced content is still recommended.

31 *Thomson Reuters Enterprise Centre GmbH v. Ross Intelligence Inc.*, No. 1:20-CV-613-SB (D. Del. Feb. 11, 2025), p. 3, https://www.ded.uscourts.gov/sites/ded/files/opinions/20-613_5.pdf. Accessed on June 14, 2025.

32 *Ibidem*, p. 23.

33 *Introducing AI-Assisted Research: Legal research meets generative AI*, "Thomson Reuters" 11/15/2023, https://legal.thomsonreuters.com/blog/legal-research-meets-generative-ai/. Accessed on June 15, 2025.

### *2.1.5 E-discovery*

E-discovery,[34] also known as electronic discovery, is understood as a "process of pre-trial discovery in legal proceedings".[35] Under this concept, each party has the right not only to request but also to receive evidence from the opposing party. Therefore, the production of Electronically Stored Information (ESI) prevails in international commercial arbitration. There is an increasing amount of information which can be not only transmitted but also stored in both electronic and technological form. In this light, it is worthwhile to note that:

> This has led arbitration practitioners to seek, and tribunals to order, substantial amounts of e-disclosure. The availability and prevalence of e-disclosure in international arbitration has been both confirmed and perhaps encouraged by the International Bar Association's Rules on the Taking of Evidence in International Arbitration (the IBA Rules), which, starting in 2010, have made express reference to the production of 'documents maintained in electronic form'.[36]

Within the context of international arbitration, both document review and production are commonly considered an unavoidable but laborious task. In fact, these tasks are time-consuming and represent low-value strategic work to be completed. In addition, they are often straining the dynamic among external counsels and clients, most notably in terms of clients' reluctant attitude towards paying premium legal fees for such work. Bearing in mind these factors, AI-powered tools are seen as a solution that could result in reviewing documents quickly. These new technologies could significantly reduce not only time but also costs of completing these tasks.[37]

The e-discovery landscape is constantly changing due to rapid advances in AI. Importantly, AI is having a significant impact on the document review process. The so-called Technology-Assisted Review (TAR),[38] aka Predictive Coding, was launched to address these issues. According to the Grossman-Cormack Glossary of Technology-Assisted Review, TAR is understood as:

34 See more: S.C. Bennett, *"Hard" Tools for Controlling Discovery Burdens in Arbitration*, "Dispute Resolution Journal" 2018, vol. 73, no. 4, pp. 1-30, https://go.adr.org/rs/294-SFS-516/images/DRJ%20Vol%2073%20No%204-03-Bennett%20%28002%29.pdf. Accessed on June 3, 2025.

35 J.C. Scholtes, H.J. van den Herik, *Big data analytics for e-discovery* [in:] *Research Handbook on Big Data Law Research (Handbooks in Information Law series)*, ed. R. Vogl, Edward Elgar Publishing 2021, p. 255.

36 *The Guide to Evidence in International Arbitration – Second Edition: Using Technology and e-Disclosure*, "Global Arbitration Review" 2024, p. 4.

37 E. Chan, K.N. Gore, E. Jiang, *Harnessing Artificial Intelligence...*, pp. 268-269.

38 See more: M.R. Grossman, G.V. Cormack, *Technology-assisted review in e-discovery can be more effective and more efficient than exhaustive manual review*, "Richmond Journal of Law and Technology" 2011, vol. 17, issue 3, pp. 1–48, https://scholarship.richmond.edu/cgi/viewcontent.cgi?article=1344&context=jolt.

> A process for Prioritizing or Coding a Collection of Documents using a computerized system that harnesses human judgments of one or more Subject Matter Expert(s) on a smaller set of Documents and then extrapolates those judgments to the remaining Document Collection. Some TAR methods use Machine Learning Algorithms[39] to distinguish Relevant from Non-Relevant Documents, based on Training Examples Coded as Relevant or Non-Relevant by the Subject Matter Experts(s), while other TAR methods derive systematic Rules that emulate the expert(s)' decision-making process. TAR processes generally incorporate Statistical Models and/or Sampling techniques to guide the process and to measure overall system effectiveness.[40]

This means that AI tools make it possible to undergo the process of analysis, categorization, and prioritization of vast amounts of data with unprecedented speed and accuracy. Continuous Active Learning (CAL), as a subfield of TAR, is revolutionizing the legal workflow. CAL uses machine learning algorithms to accelerate the review of large volumes of electronically stored information (ESI). In addition, it provides many benefits compared to traditional ways of reviewing documents that can be summarized as follows: enhanced efficiency, improved accuracy, and cost-effectiveness, among others.[41]

Various e-discovery platforms have been introduced in international arbitration to address these pitfalls, including Relativity, Luminance, EverLaw, and CS Disco, among others. They are based on machine learning mechanisms that allow streamlining the process of categorization, extraction, and analysis of extensive amounts of documents. These e-discovery platforms employ advanced AI capabilities, namely conceptual search which represents a step forward compared to basic keyword queries, document clustering alongside data visualization. Together, these features help professionals to pinpoint relevant information in a short time and thus accelerate the process of reviewing documents. In this light, these AI-powered tools lead to the enhanced efficiency of the e-discovery process.[42]

The term "conceptual search" refers to a more advanced method of retrieving information in view of standard keyword-based searches. Instead of relying on precise word matches, conceptual search harnesses both AI and NLP to grasp not only the meaning but also context within documents. Therefore, conceptual search plays a crucial role in the e-discovery process by providing legal professionals with the tools necessary to identify relevant documents, even if specific keywords

39 See more: G.V. Cormack, M.R. Grossman, *Evaluation of Machine-Learning Protocols for Technology-Assisted Review in Electronic Discovery*, "The 37th International ACM SIGIR Conference on Research and Development in Information Retrieval, SIGIR" 2014, pp. 153–162, https://dl.acm.org/doi/pdf/10.1145/2600428.2609601.

40 *The Grossman-Cormack glossary of technology-assisted review with foreword by John M. Facciola, U.S. Magistrate Judge*, "Federal Courts Law Review" 2013, vol. 7, issue 1, p. 32, https://www.fclr.org/fclr/articles/html/2010/grossman.pdf. Accessed on June 10, 2025.

41 G.V. Cormack, M.R. Grossman, *Autonomy and reliability of continuous active learning for technology-assisted review*, "arXiv" 2015, https://arxiv.org/pdf/1504.06868.

42 E. Chan, K.N. Gore, E. Jiang, *Harnessing Artificial Intelligence…*, p. 269.

or phrases are not used. This search application significantly lowers the chances of missing critical information during the document review process.[43]

In contrast, the concept of data visualization refers to the interconnected documents that provide a graphical representation of data. Therefore, they set forth relationships, patterns, along with key insights stemming from a document set in a visual story. In fact, this approach, which transforms complex information into a more comprehensible form, allows legal teams to fully understand both the structure and dynamics of the data. Thanks to visualization, they can easily capture the significant trends and identify crucial documents. In addition, data visualization may also be helpful in developing stronger case strategies through the process of uncovering hidden linkages. This might be seen as an advantage compared to more conventional and text-based reviews.[44]

Overall, e-discovery platforms have been designed to organize interconnected documents into clusters depending on their content or themes. This feature allows reviewers to examine groups of documents relevant for completing specific tasks or issues during arbitral proceedings. The idea of clustering data can be helpful in identifying different patterns, trends, or even shared elements within the document collection. Importantly, it may be pivotal in forming a coherent legal strategy or even revealing unnoticed insights. A key advantage of clustering also stems from its ability to shape strategic and uniform decisions across the entire document collection. In practice, it can ensure the equal treatment of sensitive materials, namely privileged or confidential information.[45]

In addition, fully up-to-date there are new AI-powered tools dedicated to handling the e-discovery process. In this context, eDiscovery AI pertains to the forefront of legal technology that facilitates legal discovery because of enhanced accuracy and cost-effectiveness. eDiscovery AI pays attention to security issues and thus it is based on strong encryption. Importantly, it does not rely on any model learning and does not store data. This AI-powered tool can analyze large files, images, audio alongside foreign languages.[46]

## 2.2 Perspective of the arbitral institution

### *2.2.1 Document reviews and contract analysis*

AI becomes more commonly used in repetitive administrative tasks, including the process of reviewing clauses, cross-referencing terms, and providing compliance. AI has also been designed to review legal contracts through the analysis, summaries, and identification of key clauses within legal documents. These features have been introduced for the sake of accelerating speed and accuracy. In this light, under the current status of development, AI is equipped to identify clauses, assess risks,

43 *Ibidem.*

44 *Ibidem.*

45 *Ibidem.*

46 *Why eDiscovery AI*, https://ediscoveryai.com. Accessed on April 28, 2025.

summarize contracts, check compliance, and compare different versions of documents. First, through clause identification, AI can make such analyses based on the key clauses, including confidentiality agreements, termination conditions, alongside dispute resolution mechanisms. In the case of non-disclosure agreements, AI can verify whether the confidentiality obligations are reflected in the form of mutual or one-sided obligations. Second, in view of risk assessment, AI can identify either risky or unusual terms. To illustrate, considering a supplier agreement, the AI tool can even "alert legal teams to uncapped indemnity clauses".[47] Third, AI is trained to produce concise summaries of documents such as a 50-page agreement to be shortened to one page, including payment terms, obligations, along with warranties. Fourth, AI is helpful in checking compliance with regulations. It might be crucial in terms of ensuring that GDPR-compliant clauses are part of data processing agreements. Finally, through the option of comparing different versions, the AI may track any changes or discrepancies existing in various contract versions.[48]

Legalfly has been designed as an AI agent dedicated to the legal environment. It provides the analysis of contracts. Importantly, Legalfly pays attention to confidentiality and thus all sensitive information is first anonymized prior to any processing. This approach has been implemented in order to prevent potential misuse of such personal information. In this light, Legalfly limits access risks and ensures ethical data sharing with respect to privacy concerns.[49]

### *2.2.2 Appointment of arbitrators*

The AI tools can also be widely applied in case of appointing an arbitrator. Some scholars consider such a possibility a threat, whereas others assess it in a very positive way. Apparently, once AI is used to select arbitrators, it may result in the establishment of the so-called "fourth generation of arbitrators". In addition, "this development could give rise to the belief that technological competence is one of the qualifications to be taken into account with regard to this new generation of arbitrators".[50]

In view of the advantages, AI tools can be useful in compiling information about arbitrators by collecting details that were disclosed by arbitral institutions within their transparency initiatives. Accordingly, these efforts are introduced for the sake of increasing openness in the arbitral proceedings. In this context, AI plays a crucial role in streamlining the necessary analysis of the provided data. Through such analysis, it offers not only faster but also more efficient results compared to manual review. Therefore, AI can be a helpful tool in verifying an arbitrator's record regarding his impartiality, independence, and professional standing. This might be

47 G. Macsweeney, *The 9 best AI contract review software tools for 2025*, "Legalfly" January 22, 2025, https://www.legalfly.com/post/9-best-ai-contract-review-software-tools-for-2025. Accessed on May 21, /2025.

48 *Ibidem.*

49 *Legalfly*, https://www.legalfly.com/security. Accessed on April 28, 2025.

50 K. Fach Gómez, *The Technological Competence*..., p. 102.

of significant importance from the perspective of the disputing parties. On the other hand, through the implementation of AI-powered tools, it is possible to minimize conflicts of interest and thus promote greater diversity in the arbitration process. In this light, parties could have the chance to select arbitrators within a broader and more merit-based group based on both objective and refined criteria. Given that, any subjective biases or personal prejudices would not be involved in the selection process. In compliance with this approach, initiatives such as the Equal Representation in Arbitration Pledge and ArbitralWomen support more unbiased, data-driven appointments within arbitral panels.[51]

One of the major concerns regarding the use of AI in appointing arbitrators relates to the possibility of reinforcing the existing biases and slowing diversity in this process. In this light, international arbitration has been criticized for appointing arbitrators who do not sufficiently reflect the ethnic, racial, and gender diversity of the entire arbitral community.[52] In addition, it is noteworthy to recall that arbitral panels which comply with the:

> 'male, pale and stale' stereotype "will, over time, come to be seen as defective, as they do not reflect the composition of society in a broad sense. Where appointments are being made by arbitral institutions of prospective arbitrators, they should propose a more diverse list of arbitrators. Co-arbitrators engaged in choosing a presiding arbitrator should likewise broaden the pool of arbitrators that they consider for selection".[53]

Currently, there are various AI-powered tools that assist parties in properly appointing the arbitrators in view of their skills and qualifications. To name a few, the Kira system, ClauseBuilder, and EBRAM have already provided many solutions for the parties. Importantly, these tools have been designed to evaluate and analyze vast amounts of micro data. Indeed, such an analysis is needed to develop proper algorithms for the sake of determining the best fit arbitrator for a particular dispute. In this context, it is worthwhile to explain that these tools are dedicated to processing millions of micro data, including not only the specialization of the arbitrator himself but also the feedback and reviews provided by the parties. In fact,

51 M. Łągiewska, *Does Artificial Intelligence help women in international arbitration? A few remarks on diversity in arbitral tribunals*, "International Journal of Law in Changing World: Special Issue on Women's Research in Law and Digital Technologies" 2025, p. 78.

52 J. Brian Johns, *Artificial Intelligence in the selection of arbitrators: whether to trust the machine*, "ITA in Review", vol. 6, issue 3, https://itainreview.org/articles/2024/vol6/Issue3/artificial-intelligence-in-the-selection-of-arbitrators-whether-to-trust-the-machine.html. Accessed on April 19, 2025.

53 K. Duggal, A. Lee, *A 360-Degree, Kaleidoscopic View of Diversity and Inclusion (or Lack Thereof) in International Arbitration*, "The American Review of International Arbitration" 2022, vol. 33, no. 1, https://aria.law.columbia.edu/issues/33-1/a-360-degree-kaleidoscopic-view-of-diversity-and-inclusion-or-lack-thereof-in-international-arbitration-vol-33-no-1/. Accessed on June 28, 2025.

this AI-supported mechanism has many advantages, mainly related to the cost- and time-effectiveness in searching for the appropriate arbitrator to be appointed.[54]

According to the statistics, in 2018,

> the London Court of International Arbitration (LCIA) appointed only 13% of first-time arbitrators, and in 2017, only 17% of first-time arbitrators were appointed. In 2019, Stockholm Chamber of Commerce (SCC) published that only 23% of appointed arbitrators were women. In addition, scholars have stated that race bias is also a major issue as 45% of ICSID cases were determined by Anglo-European Arbitrators and 4% (11 cases) were determined by persons of different races. This goes to show that gender and ethnic bias are major issues in the field of arbitration and if such data are fed to algorithms the outcome will be catastrophic as the cycle of appointing known faces, as well as other known vices will persist.[55]

On 10 October 2024, the AAA-ICDR decided to adopt AAAi Panelist Search as "a new generative artificial intelligence (GenAI)-powered panelist selection tool".[56] Moreover,

> AAAi Panelist Search is designed to mine the comprehensive AAA-ICDR Roster to identify the most suitable matches for arbitration and mediation cases. Case managers will use this tool to supplement their traditional roster searches, aiming to build a list of arbitrators or mediators tailored to the specific parameters of each case.[57]

The AAAi Panelist Search is designed to accomplish broader and deeper searches to find the most suitable candidate for a particular case. Such a key feature of this AI-powered tool is advantageous not only for the parties of the dispute but also for panelists. The implementation of this tool was divided into two phases. First, the AAA-ICDR case managers gained access to the AAAi Panelist Search. Second, such an option is also available to the parties via a special link sent by the case manager. Importantly, "the tool integrates AI-enabled semantic search with traditional search options and includes advanced features that allow parties to manage and compare panelists' profiles side-by-side, giving them greater control over the arbitrator selection process".[58] Simultaneously, along with the implementation of such AI-driven technologies by the AAA-ICDR, a special resource center for

54 A.O. Onyefulu-Kingston, *AI-Based Technologies in International Arbitration: An Explanatory Study on the Practicability of Applying AI Tools on International Arbitration*, "World Academy of Science, Engineering and Technology. International Journal of Computer and Information Engineering" 2024, vol. 18, no. 10, p. 652.

55 A.O. Onyefulu-Kingston, *AI-Based Technologies in International...*,Ibidem, p. 652.

56 *AAA-ICDR Launches New AAAi Panelist Search to Enhance Panelist Selection with AI Technology*, p. 1, https://www.adr.org/sites/default/files/document_repository/Press-Release_AAA_Launches_AAAi%20Panelist_Search_AI_Technology.pdf. Accessed on April 30, 2025.

57 *Ibidem*.

58 *Ibidem*.

advocates has been launched in order to offer practical training on how to prepare and present arbitrations to be handled in the AAA-ICDR.[59]

#### *2.2.3 Case management*

Currently, AI-powered solutions are useful in case management[60] of arbitral proceedings. Using AI tools increases the efficiency of case management. Therefore, AI is helpful for completing administrative tasks related to arbitration case management. This can be achieved by automating administrative tasks such as managing documents for arbitral proceedings and scheduling preliminary meetings/case management conferences and hearings, and tracking submission deadlines according to the agreed-upon schedule. Thanks to these AI-supported tools, the arbitral institution can handle the entire process smoothly. Additionally, arbitrators can focus on the substantive issues of the dispute. Overall, implementing such solutions speeds up the arbitration process.[61]

### 2.3 Perspective of the arbitrators

There is no uniform approach to AI-based technology in international arbitration. Given that, many different ideas arise, including a distinction between data collection and data interpretation that could be supported by AI-powered tools during the decision-making process of arbitrators. It is worth noting that the process of data collection fueled by AI is commonly accepted within the international community, whereas data interpretation made by AI is more reluctant. This entails that once technology is deemed to support arbitrators in their daily work, it is acceptable and beneficial. On the other hand, when technology has the aim to replace arbitrators, there is no consent for such a change and thus this type of technology is considered dangerous and somehow harmful to the arbitration itself.[62]

This standpoint stems from the current state of Large Language Model (LLM) development and raises the question of whether LLMs can apply the law. This is a complex issue mainly concerning the legal reasoning abilities of these systems. Nonetheless, the question of capability also has further ramifications in terms of appropriateness. If LLMs are unable to effectively apply the law, that becomes a strong argument against allowing them to decide legal cases. In addition, Henrique Marcos distinguishes twofold interpretations of the question of "can" as follows:

59 *Ibidem.*

60 See also: A.C. Yıldırım, *The use of technology in case management in international investment arbitration: a realistic approach*, "Arbitration International" 2024, Vol. 40, issue 2, pp. 233–250, https://doi.org/10.1093/arbint/aiae010.

61 A.J. Schmitz, *Picking the Proper Technological Tool for Problem-Solving in Arbitration* [in:] *Transforming Arbitration: Exploring the Impact of AI, Blockchain, Metaverse and Web 3*, ed. M. Piers, S. McCarthy, Radboud University Press 2025, p. 140.

62 K. Fach Gómez, *The Technological Competence*..., p. 36.

> (1) Can LLMs apply the law to a case like ordinary people often do when discussing whether a particular action aligns with legal statutes? (2) Can LLMs apply the law to a case and, by doing so, bind legal subjects to their application in the same way as verdicts issued by judges?.[63]

In this light, it is worthwhile to remember that a positive answer to the first question is needed to answer the second one. This entails that "We can only seriously consider the matter of an LLM acting like a judge by answering whether LLMs can subsume the law to cases".[64] To address these questions, the two kinds of law application proposed by D'Almeida in "What is it to Apply the Law?" have been analyzed, such as inferential and pragmatic law application. The former refers to the mental act of reasoning for the sake of reaching a conclusion without giving any argument, whereas the latter concerns an external and non-exclusively mental act. In other words, it applies to "the act of performing an external action that is legally obliged or permitted, which is intended to settle a particular question or matter authoritatively".[65] In addition,

> Pragmatic law application is the act of a judge or court performing an action, they take to be legally justified by reference to a provision. This means that the court believes it is either legally required or legally allowed to perform the action and that the provision supports the action normatively.[66]

Importantly, this idea has been further developed in the form of the concept for understanding the communication practices which are commonly considered in terms of the "game of giving and asking for reasons" (the so-called GOGAR). In this light,

> GOGAR refers to the dialogical process through which individuals justify their actions and beliefs by providing reasons that others within the community can accept or challenge. GOGAR also helps highlight how legal reasoning functions within a community. Legal actors do not merely apply rules in isolation; they engage in a broader social practice where reasons for legal actions and interpretations are continuously exchanged, scrutinized, and validated by others. This process ensures that the application of law remains an adaptive practice, responsive to the behavior and expectations of the community.[67]

63 H. Marcos, *Can large language models apply the law?*, "AI & Society" 2024, p. 1, https://doi.org/10.1007/s00146-024-02105-9.

64 *Ibidem*.

65 *Ibidem*, p. 2.

66 *Ibidem*.

67 H. Marcos, *Can large language...*, p. 4. See also: L. Tvrdíková, *Interpretation of law as language game: the game of giving and asking for reasons in the courtroom*, "International Journal for the Semiotics of Law - Revue Internationale de Sémiotique Juridique" 2025, vol. 38, pp. 549–565, https://doi.org/10.1007/s11196-024-10177-5.

Following this perspective, Henrique Marcos explains why the current LLMs are not capable of applying the law in the context of inferential sense, mainly due to the fact of having the so-called syntactic interaction with the law instead of a semantic one. It is crucial to understand that the LLMs "cannot apply the law in the pragmatic sense, not even indirectly, as they are not members of the linguistic community that sets the standards for rule application".[68] Furthermore, the LLMs are using the so-called "two-ply account of observation", a theory introduced by Brandom. Under this concept, the first ply refers to the ability to reply differently to stimuli, whereas the second ply means the ability to participate in a linguistic practice. In this context, a system replying differently to stimuli is called "a reactive system". It means that this system can not only "read" but also "write". The ability to "read" is understood in terms of being able to discriminate between various input types. In contrast, the ability to "write" is reflected by generating different output types. It might occur, however, that both reading and writing are combined in the form of a "read/write cycle". According to this cycle, the system is allowed "to produce a token of a specific type and then read it as the type of token it is. In this sense, reactive systems that read/write can have 'reliable differential responsive dispositions' (RDRDs)".[69]

Importantly, the second ply is widely associated with the ability to take part in the social dimension of the GOGAR. Practically, once a participant is willing to be treated within a social practice, "an agent must be able to produce specific performances under certain circumstances even if they do not always do so perfectly".[70]

Given that Henrique Marcos points out that LLMs are equipped with RDRD, but they lack GOGAR. In fact, the LLMs' functioning is based upon examining datasets for the sake of identifying patterns and thus generating responses. Nonetheless, this method of operation does not overcome the key issue related to the fact that the LLMs' outputs are associated with statistical correlations instead of a genuine comprehension of the meaning.[71]

This discussion is also elaborated by Marcus, who stresses that compared to human thought processes, the LLMs lack this ability. In this context, humans use causal reasoning, abstract thinking, and the ability to make general statements within various situations. In contrast, the LLMs operate in both a limited and fragmented way. In practice, this means that LLMs are not capable of truly understanding the meaning, and thus they rely on superficial statistical datasets. This operation is thus far from flexible and contextual understanding akin to human cognition.[72]

Overall, even if the LLMs develop rapidly, they still do not possess the capacity to apply the law in a pragmatic way. It is thus crucial to distinguish twofold situations that could be summarized as follows:

68 H. Marcos, *Can large language...*, p. 5.

69 *Ibidem.*

70 *Ibidem.*

71 *Ibidem*, p. 6.

72 *Ibidem*. See more: G. Marcus, *The next decade in AI: four steps towards robust artificial intelligence*, "arXiv", 2020.https://doi.org/10.48550/arXiv.2002.06177.

> First, pragmatic law application is not directly dependent on a single agent, whether that agent is a judge, an ordinary citizen, or a non-human entity. Second, although pragmatic law application is indirectly dependent on individual agents because their collective practice in the linguistic community helps set the standards that determine rule application, LLMs are not (currently) members of the linguistic community and thus cannot contribute to these standards.[73]

Apparently, the application of legal rules pertains to a communal activity that requires both mutual understanding and practice. This entails that the process is far from isolated judgments achieved by agents. In contrast, the criteria concerning the application of legal norms stem from collective interactions. Therefore, legal reasoning is commonly considered a fundamentally social process. In addition, "deciding legal standards is not simply a matter of unilateral decision-making; it involves collective engagement".[74]

In conclusion, it is worth noting that LLMs currently are not capable of applying the law in a pragmatic sense. They are unable to impact the legal interpretation, even indirectly, due to their lack of involvement in shaping the normative standards crucial for applying legal rules. Nonetheless, LLMs might become more integrated within the social practices' framework. In this view, the recognition of LLMs as participants in the legal reasoning process may be enhanced as they become members of the linguistic community. Therefore, their acceptance as a part of the linguistic community may result from the intentions designed by human agents rather than intrinsic function.[75]

Considering the inferential application of the law, the LLMs are rather manipulating syntax instead of representing a true semantic understanding. Even if they are already designed to generate legally relevant and even context-sensitive outputs, they do not have the ability to genuinely understand the meaning of this response, which is the key element within inferential legal reasoning. This means that the simple rearrangement of symbols without their proper understanding cannot equal the process of applying the law. Furthermore, regarding the second idea, namely the pragmatic law application, the LLMs also have many shortcomings. The pragmatic application cannot be reduced merely to reaching a legal outcome. In contrast, it requires engaging in a shared and even normative practice associated with a legal and linguistic community. Given that, the LLMs cannot form the legal standards as they are not part of such a community. In the context of the current development of LLM systems, they are nowadays incapable of applying the law in both inferential and pragmatic ways. Therefore, "Their outputs, though often correct, do not contribute to the collective setting of standards that is central to

73 H. Marcos, *Can large language*..., p. 7.

74 *Ibidem*.

75 *Ibidem*.

pragmatic law application. Yet, their membership status can change in the future as humans may ascribe intentionality to AI systems".[76]

### *2.3.1 Legal analysis and case summaries*

AI is widely considered a valuable tool in terms of providing document summaries shortly. Nonetheless, we should also bear in mind some concerns related to over-reliance on AI-generated outputs, most notably in the form of memory blindness. This concept focuses on:

> the inability of individuals to detect alterations and mistakes in reports and summaries of texts prepared by other people. Memory blindness can lead to the incorporation of misinformation into their memories. This phenomenon is closely related to the concepts of choice blindness and the misinformation effect. Choice blindness occurs when individuals fail to notice changes in their choices and subsequently justify these altered choices as their own. The misinformation effect, on the other hand, involves the incorporation of misleading information into one's memory of an event.[77]

Even if this concept seems not to have direct correlation with the use of AI, in fact, it can have far-reaching implications within the framework of the legal field. To illustrate, the current development of AI tools has already provided many solutions dedicated to summarizing documents based on the extracts of key information from vast volumes of data. These tools are chiefly based on Natural Language Processing (NLP) algorithms that are designed to identify the most important content and further summarize it. Even though this solution is, without any doubt, timesaving, it might also lead to the risk of memory blindness, which is reflected by being exposed to either altered or even incomplete information provided by the AI without the notice of a user.[78]

In practice, this memory blindness may be based on various reasons, including misinterpretation of the context and overreliance on AI-generated outputs. The former concerns not accurate interpretation of the context of legal documents which might have an impact on the generated summary. In this light, the AI tools may either omit the most significant details or misrepresent the content. One must note, however, that the legal context plays a crucial role in understanding the overall situation. The latter, in turn, describes too much trust in the AI-produced summaries without the verification of their accuracy. This might result in accepting the

76 *Ibidem*, p. 8.

77 R. Harbst, *The effects of memory blindness when using AI for summarizing documents*, "Global Arbitration News" April 28, 2025, https://www.globalarbitrationnews.com/2025/04/28/the-effects-of-memory-blindness-when-using-ai-for-summarizing-documents/#_ftnref1. Accessed on June 6, 2025.

78 *Ibidem*.

misinformation if the discrepancies between the original document and AI-provided output were not identified.[79]

To address these concerns, it is thus important to verify and cross-check the AI-generated information with the original documents in order to uncover any inconsistencies or errors.

#### *2.3.1.1 Jus Mundi's AI research assistant*

Jus Mundi, widely known as the legal tech pioneer, introduced the so-called Jus AI Assistant which is recognized as the first international legal assistant supported by generative AI. Interestingly, this tool comprises not only multiple large language models (LLMs), namely GPT-4, but also the largest global case law database provided by Jus Mundi. Once launched, this AI-powered tool provides a top-tier security level alongside the confidentiality of legal data. Given its features, Jus AI Assistant has been created for the sake of increasing lawyers' productivity thanks to the access to reliable and well-contextualized legal answers which are available in any language. In addition, this tool provides simultaneously the proper level of both confidentiality and security. It is worth noting the opinion of Marina Weiss, who is a Partner of International Arbitration at Bredin Prat, who said that:

> We see this AI product as a game-changer for arbitration practices, offering the promise of streamlining complex case analysis and fostering a deeper quantitative understanding of legal precedents. By enhancing decision-making with AI-driven insights, we anticipate Jus AI will significantly benefit the arbitration community, setting a new standard for legal research and analysis.[80]

In practice, Jus AI Assistant can easily search for needed information within its database, case law, treaties, and even expert commentary stemming from a certain jurisdiction. As such, this tool plays a crucial role in dealing with legal nuances alongside finding a winning strategy for the clients. Therefore, it provides the possibility to easily draft legal documents in accordance with the requirements provided by the specific jurisdictions; prepare necessary precedents and arguments for the upcoming arbitral proceedings; conduct legal research regarding relatively niche topics; translate parts or even summaries throughout the proper understanding of the most important arguments without the need of translating the entire document. Indeed, the Jus AI Assistant is widely recognized as enhancing human expertise. This means that professionals who are dealing with international arbitration cases

79 *Ibidem.*

80 L-C. Bouttier, F. Yattara, *Jus Mundo launches the first international legal AI assistant*, "Daily Jus" February 13, 2024, https://dailyjus.com/news/2024/02/jus-mundi-launches-the-first-international-legal-ai-assistant-en. Accessed on September 30, 2024.

may concentrate on the process of applying judgments and making use of their experience and strategic thinking.[81]

Furthermore, it is worth stressing that the Jus AI Assistant has been designed in collaboration with Microsoft to ensure advanced security features and thus data privacy. Therefore, since the beginning, both accuracy and reliability have played a significant role in decreasing the possibility of biases and preventing AI hallucinations. To achieve these goals, the designers decided to base all information on exclusive and curated data stemming from Jus Mundi's extensive database. In addition, this AI-powered tool provides a double-layered scrutiny that is based upon twofold criteria. On the one hand, it applies the so-called specialized AI models to check any inconsistencies and thus guarantee the correctness of facts. On the other hand, in-house legal experts hired by Jus Mundi also provide their input regarding the proper understanding of legal nuances. Finally, Jus Mundi makes use of new techniques that have been introduced for the sake of minimizing the risk of AI hallucinations and biases. Therefore, the state-of-the-art data retrieval is necessary to ensure that all information is not only objective but also unfabricated.[82]

Jus Mundi entered into cooperation with many world-known arbitration institutions, including the Hong Kong International Arbitration Centre (HKIAC). According to Sarah Grimmer, the Secretary General of the HKIAC, "Jus Mundi is an invaluable research source for international arbitration practitioners. HKIAC is delighted to partner with Jus Mundi to provide users with insights into HKIAC's procedural decision-making".[83] In addition, it is worth recalling the CEO of Jus Mundi, Jean-Rémi de Maistre, who stressed that Hong Kong is widely considered one of the most attractive seats for international arbitration, mostly due to the HKIAC. Further, he added that:

> Jus Mundi is honored to form this unique partnership with HKIAC, facilitating global access to legal resources in Asia and, most importantly, highlighting the work of China's arbitration sector. The sharing of institutional materials by HKIAC is the next important milestone in the trend of global transparency and enhanced use of international arbitration.[84]

#### 2.3.1.2 *Thomson Reuters' CoCounsel*

CoCounsel was designed as a GenAI model that functions as an AI legal assistant. First, it was trained to understand not only the queries but also the context. Therefore, CoCounsel can make nuances through the analysis of different products

81 H. Maïo, *Meet the Minds Behind Jus AI Assistant: Legal Tech Pioneers on a Mission*, "Daily Jus" February 29, 2024, https://dailyjus.com/news/2024/02/meet-the-minds-behind-jus-ai-assistant-legal-tech-pioneers-on-a-mission. Accessed on September 9, 2024.

82 *Ibidem.*

83 *HKIAC partners with Jus Mundi*, "HKIAC" April 28, 2022, https://www.hkiac.org/news/hkiac-partners-jus-mundi. Accessed on September 30, 2024.

84 *Ibidem.*

and workflows. Based on this feature, it can provide more in-depth insights compared to simple AI-powered tools. Second, CoCounsel is linked to the most innovative Large Language Models (LLMs) that are associated with trusted and reliable content. Third, it is also integrated with industry-leading platforms, including Westlaw, Practical Law, Checkpoint, and Microsoft 365.[85]

Compared to other tools available on the legal market, the CoCounsel addresses the data privacy challenges. This means that it offers service with respect to the protection of sensitive data that is not only secure but also private. Importantly, this GenAI assistant also safeguards data through industry-standard protocols and encryption. This applies to both transit and storage of the sensitive data.[86]

CoCounsel also ensures that these data are not further used for training their AI models. In addition, this GenAI assistant also represents the so-called trustworthy AI. Through the reliance on trusted content, CoCounsel could limit both the inaccuracies of the generated content alongside algorithmic bias.[87]

CoCounsel also pays attention to privacy issues which are automatically turned on. This means that CoCounsel "never used to train the AI model. The model is accessed through dedicated, secure servers. Data is encrypted in transit and at rest and never stored by our AI partner. Clients retain all rights to their data. Your data is only used by Casetext to serve the product to your users".[88]

In the context of international arbitration, CoCounsel's "Summarize Skill" offers an interesting solution for speeding up arbitrators' daily work. Depending on the current need, CoCounsel offers three levels of detail: Brief Summary, Detailed Summary, and Comprehensive Summary. The first option summarizes content including a short piece of text, such as one to three paragraphs. The second option produces a summary based on multiple pages, combining all the necessary information from the uploaded documents. The third option produces a page-by-page summary of all submitted documents.[89]

#### *2.3.1.3 Claude Opus 4*

Anthropic introduced Claude Opus 4, a new hybrid reasoning Large Language Model (LLM). It was designed to provide advanced reasoning capabilities, visual analysis, and computer and tool use. Importantly, this AI-powered solution can perform complex computer coding tasks autonomously over time. Regarding the training data, it is worth noting that Claude benefited from public information available on the internet as of March 2025 and non-public data from third parties.

85 *CoCounsel: The industry-leading GenAI assistant for professionals*, "Thomson Reuters", https://www.thomsonreuters.com/en/cocounsel. Accessed on June15, 2025.

86 *Ibidem*.

87 *Ibidem*.

88 D.L. Evans, S. Guillon, R. Losey, V. Washington, L.G. Yancey, *Dispute Resolution Journal 2024,* vol. 78, issue 1, pp. 57–92, available at: https://go.adr.org/rs/294-SFS-516/images/DRJ%20Journal%20Article%202024.pdf, p. 14.

89 *Ibidem*, p. 4.

In summary, the data underwent a series of cleansing and filtration procedures within the framework of the training process. Accordingly, the data was subjected to a process of deduplication and classification.[90]

From the perspective of international arbitration, it is crucial to stress that Claude Opus 4 was equipped with "extended thinking mode". This entails that "they can expend more time reasoning through problems, as well as a default, standard thinking mode for faster responses. Users can toggle between these two modes as is required for their particular task".[91] This GenAI legal assistant complies with the safety and security standards as well.[92]

Given the daily work of arbitrators, the Claude Opus 4 is similar to the Anthropic Claude Pro. It allows you to produce a one-and-a-half-page summary based on the provided content.[93]

#### *2.3.1.4 Guangzhou AI assistant*

The China's arbitral institution, namely the Guangzhou Arbitration Commission (GAC) launched an AI arbitration assistant to enhance not only the efficiency of handling disputes but also to ensure the respect of procedure. In September 2023, this AI-powered tool could resolve disputes between two private companies within a very short time. Zhong Xiaowen, which is the AI assistant, even stressed that "today's hearing has come to an end. I am currently analyzing the trial data, and the ruling opinion will be sent to the arbitration tribunal via email in 5 minutes".[94] Indeed, this AI tool may be useful in terms of improving the work of arbitral institutions. According to GAC, such an AI assistant has the potential to increase the efficiency of handling disputes by four times. It can be achieved through the acceleration of procedural tasks in the arbitral proceedings, namely intelligent acceptance of cases, multilingual translation in real-time, blockchain-based recognition of evidence alongside the process of inputting viewpoints and statements. In addition, Weng Jian, who is an arbitrator in the GAC, even mentioned that "the AI assistant can provide pre-court information guidance for identity recognition, written records during the trial processes and similar cases".[95]

90 *System Card: Claude Opus & Claude Sonnet 4*, "Antropic" May 2025, p. 3, https://www-cdn.anthropic.com/4263b940cabb546aa0e3283f35b686f4f3b2ff47.pdf. Accessed on June 20, 2025.

91 *Ibidem*. p. 4.

92 See more: *System Card: Claude Opus*...

93 D.L. Evans, S. Guillon, R. Losey, V. Washington, L.G. Yancey, *Dispute Resolution Enhanced*..., p. 14.

94 *AI arbitration used for dispute in Guangzhou*, "Guangzhou International" 01.09.2023, https://www.gz.gov.cn/guangzhouinternational/home/citynews/content/post_9190081.html. Accessed on October 1, 2024. See: M. Łągiewska, *New Technologies in International Arbitration*..., p. 860.

95 *AI arbitration used for dispute*...; *AI arbitration used for dispute in Guangzhou*, "China Daily" 01.09.2023, http://epaper.chinadaily.com.cn/a/202309/01/WS64f109d2a31020d7c67bc47d.html. Accessed on October 1, 2024.

Fan Mingchao and Gary Gao point out that Zhong Xiaowen conducted arbitral hearings in 2023, and a human arbitral secretary was not present in the proceedings. Therefore, this AI assistant was designed to:

> register cases, perform multi-lingual translation in real time, identify evidence, precisely record the views of the parties stated during the hearings and produce arbitration hearing records and other procedural work, which helps to improve the efficiency of arbitration by nearly 400 per cent. Moreover, for some cases with clear facts and minor disputes, Zhong Xiaowen can produce the initial draft of arbitration awards right away by making use of its intelligent voice transcription system.[96]

There are many advantages that can result from the proper application of such an AI-powered tool. Liu Tao, who is currently the vice president of the Guangdong Lawyers Association, believes that the introduction of such an AI may be useful in terms of improving not only the efficiency of the arbitral proceedings but also ensuring procedural fairness. This entails that arbitrators may focus on the quality of arbitral awards. It is certainly important in view of the foreign-related arbitration cases, which require a more advanced level of extraterritorial laws and cases. Indeed, this AI tool may speed up the process of cross-border disputes when specialized knowledge is necessary. Given that, the arbitrators may focus on the merits of the case, which would also enhance the reliability of the arbitral institution itself. The introduction of such an AI-powered tool during the arbitral proceedings should be seen as a catalyst in improving the overall quality of arbitral proceedings. If a technology is properly designed to assist arbitrators in their daily work, it should be allowed and encouraged. On the other hand, arbitrators should also bear in mind the proper use of such innovation-driven technologies in terms of ethical issues and due process. Once a technological innovation leads to any biases, it should not be applied due to a violation, even potential, of fundamental principles of arbitral proceedings.

### *2.3.2 AI-assisted hearings*

#### *2.3.2.1 AI-powered transcription tools*

AI-powered tools can also be implemented to assist in hearings. In this light, the proper application of speech-to-text machine technology would allow for the hearing transcripts to be produced automatically. This solution is time- and cost-effective.[97] Even though this concept was first analyzed theoretically, there are already

96 Fan Mingchao, G. Gao, *A brief discussion on the implications, regulation and prospects of AI in dispute resolution practice with a focus on china*, "Dispute Resolution International" 2023, vol. 17, issue 2, pp. 118–119.

97 *Artificial Intelligence Strategy*, "Court of Justice of the European Union", p. 11, https://curia.europa.eu/jcms/upload/docs/application/pdf/2023-11/cjeu_ai_strategy.pdf. Accessed on June 11, 2025.

achievements and further steps undertaken in this respect which resulted in the implementation of this project.

To illustrate, the World Intellectual Property Organization (WIPO) launched the WIPO Speech-to-Text tool, which represents an advanced speech recognition service designed by the ATAC team of WIPO. Thanks to this technology, it is possible to convert spoken language into written text. Importantly, both the accuracy and speed are maintained. This transcription tool is widely applied during meetings and interviews, among others. Currently, it provides service in six languages of the UN, namely English, French, Spanish, Russian, Chinese, and Arabic. From scratch, this tool was developed as a state-of-the-art machine learning algorithm and thus provides accurate outcomes in its transcription despite various accents, languages, and even background noise. Importantly, WIPO also pays attention to data privacy and security issues, and this tool complies with the highest standards to safeguard not only confidentiality but also the integrity of the transcribed content. WIPO ensures that all data are well protected during the transcription process, which remains crucial for the parties involved. One must note, however, that this tool is still in the process of improvement by further enhancing accuracy in terms of specific speakers, domain-specific terminology, and vocabulary. Overall, these actions aim to provide more accurate transcriptions. This tool has already been appreciated by many organizations, including UNOG, WTO, the Court of Justice of the European Union (CJEU), etc.[98]

Another example is the AAA-ICDR, which has developed various AI-supported tools, including AI-powered transcription, for use in arbitral proceedings. Importantly, this solution reduces the cost of the traditional court reporting. Thanks to AI technology, it is possible to produce transcripts that undergo human checking in view of compliance. Such AI-supported transcription is allowed under the AAA-ICDR rules and is widely considered an interesting alternative to traditional transcripts in hearings and depositions, among others. The product developed and provided by the AAA-ICDR performs with 99% word accuracy. It completes transcription tasks due to powerful AI voice recognition with human editing. In consequence, the outcome provided by this AI-powered transcription tool is similar to the best human stenographers, and the entire text is delivered within three business days. This AI-powered transcript can be used not only in virtual but also in hybrid and fully in-person events.[99]

The next example refers to a commercial service provided by Verbit. This tool offers live transcription. It is based on automatic speech recognition (ASR) technology, commonly known as Captivate™, which was developed to provide better outcomes. Accordingly, this solution focuses on more customer-centric service

98 *WIPO Speech-to-TEXT – The Power of Transcription*, "WIPO", https://www.wipo.int/en/web/ai-tools-services/speech-to-text. Accessed on June 11, 2025.

99 *New Service: AI-Powered Transcription*, "AAA-ICDR" 2022, https://go.adr.org/rs/294-SFS-516/images/AAA402_AAA_ICDR_OptimaJuris_AI_Powered%20Transcription.pdf. Accessed on June 11, 2025.

rather than one-size-fits-all ASR. It pays close attention to all names, niche subject matters, accents, and background noise, among others. Further, it also provides an additional service such as post-production transcription supported by AI. The so-called Gen.V™ tool is powered by GenAI and delivers not only insights but also summaries, keywords, and titles which are generated accordingly to increase the efficiency of work. The Verbit service is dedicated to functioning within legal proceedings as well.[100]

The last example concerns Otter.AI, which is an AI meeting agent providing not only transcription of meetings but also automated summaries, action items, and chats with Otter to get the accurate information about the meeting itself. Currently, this tool works with 95% accuracy.[101] Overall, it is a more developed tool supported by AI to better organize the transcripts and adjust them to the needs of the user.

#### *2.3.2.2 Emotion AI*

Emotion AI is also commonly known as affective computing (AC) and concerns a special field of artificial intelligence under which machines can not only recognize but also analyze, interpret, and respond to human emotions. This is possible through different inputs, including choice of words, speech (voice patterns), facial expressions, and physiological signals. From the legal perspective, emotion AI has already been applied in Walmart's negotiation and mediation processes.[102]

One must note that both verbal and nonverbal information complement each other, and they are even necessary to properly interpret the message. To address these needs, the AI-powered tools have been designed and developed in order to analyze the emotional state of a person following "gestures (body movements and postures), facial expressions, acoustic characteristics and emotions expressed in the text".[103]

Apparently, emotion AI can be explained thanks to Facial Emotion Recognition (FER), which is considered a multidisciplinary field of research in affective computing. Therefore, it has been developed to make predictions on how to interpret human emotions and states of mind through computer technology. Thomas Gremsl and Elisabeth Hödl point out that:

100 *Video & audio transcription services*, "Verbit.AI", https://verbit.ai/solutions-transcription/. Accessed on June 12, 2025.

101 *The #1 AI meeting agent*, "Otter.AI", https://otter.ai. Accessed on June 11, 2025.

102 D. De Meulemeester, m. Lam-Khoundborind, *Arbitration Tech Toolbox: Emotion AI: A Game-Changer for Efficiency and Due Process in International Arbitration?*, "Kluwer Arbitration Blog" 04.09.2024, https://arbitrationblog.kluwerarbitration.com/2024/09/04/arbitration-tech-toolbox-emotion-ai-a-game-changer-for-efficiency-and-due-process-in-international-arbitration/. Accessed on June 11, 2025.

103 C. Marechal et al., *Survey on AI-Based Multimodal Methods for Emotion Detection* [in:] *High-Performance Modelling and Simulation for Big Data Applications: Selected Results of the COST Action IC1406 cHiPSet*, ed. J. Kołodziej, H. González-Vélez, Springer 2019, p. 308.

> Facial expressions, as forms of non-verbal communication and their interpretation by means of technologies, are the subject of research in psychology, specifically in the field of human computer interaction. Roughly speaking, an FER analysis is carried out in three steps: (1) Face Detection, (2) Facial Expression Detection, (3) Expression Classification to Emotional State. Depending on the respective algorithm, these facial expressions can be classified into categories. These are, for example, anger, disgust, fear, joy, sadness, surprise. It can also be classified into compound emotions such as happily sad, happily surprised, happily disgusted, sadly fearful, sadly angry, sadly surprised. Or it can be assigned to physiological or mental states, such as tiredness or boredom. In addition, combinations with biometric identifications are possible, i.e. with similar analyses of voice, text or health data.[104]

It is also worth recalling Ekman, who is one of the pioneers in studying both facial expressions and emotions. He elaborated six features stemming from posed facial expressions that are crucial in determining emotion recognition. They include morphology, symmetry, duration, speed of onset, coordination of apexes, alongside ballistic trajectory. Nonetheless, both eyes and mouth play a key role in identifying emotions. Through their actions, it is possible to group expressions in a continuous space, which is crucial to detect sadness and fear (based on the eyes) or disgust and happiness (based on the mouth). Further, the computer algorithm is designed to encode the chief characteristics of the face (i.e., eyebrows, mouth) and identify even a slight movement, shape, and texture. Through such analysis, tiny movements of facial muscles are well perceived, and they can be easily translated into the most common facial expressions, such as happiness, surprise, anger, among others.[105]

In addition, it is also possible to recognize emotions through voice. Therefore, the so-called human speech recognition (HSR) and automatic speech recognition (ASR) are widely applied for this purpose. Apparently, these tools are dedicated to identifying various emotional states. Considering emotion recognition through research on human speech, there are two approaches worth mentioning. The first one is commonly known as the synthetic approach and enables the generation of artificial speech samples that include specific emotions. The second, in turn, refers to the acknowledgment of the speaker's emotion through machine recognition.[106]

Considering the international arbitration environment, emotion AI could be a useful tool for parties and arbitrators in terms of enhancing both the efficiency of the entire arbitral proceedings and due process. The enthusiasts of this solution stress that it might be helpful in the course of preliminary meetings or case management conferences and hearings when emotion AI could monitor and assess in real-time the attentiveness, engagement, confusion, or anxiety of different

104 T. Gremsl, E. Hödl, *Emotional AI: Legal and ethical challenges*, "Information Polity" 2022, vol. 27, p. 165.

105 C. Marechal et al., *Survey on AI-Based...*, p. 315.

106 *Ibidem*, p. 312.

participants. Given this perspective, the arbitrators would get immediate feedback and could detect potential weaknesses or contentious points. Likewise, this tool could also assist in analyzing the witness testimonies and thus assess their credibility based on their responses.[107] Furthermore, each of the parties could also gain insights considering the other's position, including not only procedural but also substantive issues. In this context, the arbitrator could also get a chance to assess whether both parties are willing to settle their dispute. Even though the arbitrator is not deemed to adopt an active role akin to mediation, he could determine whether there are shared interests and thus a chance to reach a mutually agreeable resolution.[108] It might play a significant role in arb-med-arb procedures where such slight and difficult-to-perceive tiny observations made by emotion AI could support the arbitrator in his work.

Equally important is to mention that such interpersonal sensitivity and thus developed soft skills aimed at noticing unspoken signals and reacting to them become essential. From this perspective, "By considering the parties' emotions, an arbitrator can better facilitate the problem-solving nature of the process, guiding discussions constructively rather than allowing them to become confrontational".[109]

Nonetheless, the critics of this solution pay attention to using AI in the form of profiling and scoring. In this light,

> Profiling (Art 22 GDPR) enables the analysis and prediction of certain personal areas of people's lives. By means of systematic procedures – mathematical-statistical analysis of empirical values – the future behaviour of groups of people and individuals with certain characteristics is to be predicted. Scoring is based on the consideration that if certain comparable characteristics of an individual are present, similar future behaviour is likely.[110]

Despite the ongoing debate on the use of emotional AI in international arbitration, it is also worth stressing that an attentive arbitrator is required to comply with the due process standards. To illustrate, the High Court of the Hong Kong Special Administrative Region ("HK Court") in the dispute Song Lihua v Lee Chee Hon refused to enforce an arbitral award rendered by the Chengdu Arbitration Commission on the grounds of the arbitrator's lack of attention. Through the careful review of the hearings video, the HK Court admitted that:

> The Video clearly showed the background of Q's [arbitrator's] various locations, and it could be observed that he had moved from one room of the premises to another, at times talking to and/or gesturing to others in the

107 *Ibidem*.

108 *Ibidem*.

109 *Ibidem*.

110 T. Gremsl, E. Hödl, *Emotional AI: Legal...*, p. 168.

> room. Q could also be seen to be looking into the distance frequently, instead of watching the screen and the video of the proceedings.[111]

Therefore, the implementation of emotion AI could be regarded as a response to these challenging issues in order to mitigate potential risks of due process violations. As such,

> An emotion AI system could potentially reveal if a member of the arbitral tribunal was not paying attention during part of the hearing, thereby indicating a potential lapse in due process. By detecting signs of inattention, such as insufficient engagement or distraction, emotion AI could promptly alert the tribunal to address these concerns. This proactive approach may involve granting the parties an opportunity for supplementary submissions or revisiting specific segments of the hearing to ensure thorough consideration of all evidence and arguments. Implementing such measures would then serve to uphold the integrity of the arbitral process without resorting to the extreme actions of challenging the arbitrator or setting aside the award.[112]

In sum, emotion AI analyzes human emotions by interpreting facial expressions, focusing on intonations in speech and interpreting body language, mainly posture, gestures, and eye contact. Through proper training, emotion AI is thus able to capture subtle, involuntary facial cues that reflect authentic and very often hidden emotions. Therefore, the analysis of micro-expressions, including micro-muscle movement close to the eyes, mouth, and forehead, helps emotion AI to identify differences between spoken words and true emotions of a speaking person. Importantly, these discrepancies are usually not even perceived by human observers.[113]

To illustrate, MorphCast Facial Emotion AI was developed as an AI agent that is equipped with real-time emotion analysis. It was trained to identify more than 130 emotions and micro-expressions.[114]

In turn, the EmotionTrac Legal is currently providing such services for law firms. It stresses that 93% of communication is classified as non-verbal communication and thus emotions drive all the decisions that are undertaken by humans.[115] Even if this tool has not been implemented in arbitral proceedings so far, it has the potential to contribute significantly to the arbitration itself.

111 *Song Lihua v Lee Chee Hon (2023) HKCFI 2540*, https://legalref.judiciary.hk/lrs/common/ju/loadPdf.jsp?url=https://legalref.judiciary.hk/doc/judg/word/vetted/other/en/2022/HCCT000111A_2022.doc&mobile=N, p. 14. Accessed on June 12, 2025.

112 D. De Meulemeester, m. Lam-Khoundborind, *Arbitration Tech Toolbox*...

113 *Ibidem.*

114 *Empowering digital interactions with server-free Emotion AI*, "MorphCast Emotion AI", https://www.morphcast.com/#:~:text=MorphCast%20Emotion%20AI%2C%20with%20130,like%20interactions%20across%20diverse%20industries.. Accessed on June 11, 2025.

115 *Analyze reactions and improve your chances of winning*, "EmotionTrac Legal", https://legal.emotiontrac.com/#testimonials. Accessed on June 11, 2025.

### *2.3.3 Multilingual support and translations*

Along with the fast advancement in new technologies, legal translation becomes more dominated by machines, and artificial intelligence (AI) is of key importance in this regard. At the outset, it is worth adding, however, that legal translation based on AI should be carried out carefully due to its impact and repercussions alongside potential risks, including biases enhancing both mis- and disinformation. In this context, it is also crucial to note that the common use of online machine translation tools might generate new risks, most notably in terms of confidentiality. This concern is particularly important within the context of international arbitration.[116]

One must note that machine translation (MT) represents an automatic translation of the provided text into a target text. The entire process is handled without human intervention.[117] In other words, MT means:

> a computer-based process where translations are performed automatically via a platform or an interface. Automatic translations can also be carried out by AI-driven solutions, such as chatbots. Although chatbots were originally conceived to only interact (i. e., chat) with Internet surfers, they are now increasingly used to perform legal and translation tasks.[118]

At the outset, some scholars undermined the reliability of chatbot-based translations by demonstrating their limitations and drawbacks based on their generated outputs.[119] Despite these pitfalls, the AI-driven and MT have become much more popular within the legal field, and international arbitration is no exception in this regard. In the wake of these challenges, more advanced technologies have been developed to address the above concerns, including the State-of-the-Art (SOTA) large language models (LLMs) such as GPT-4. Given the available data, these models produce contextually more adequate and fluent translations.[120]

Nonetheless, despite the above matters, the development of Multilingual & Automatic Conversational Artificial Intelligence (MAC AI) is commonly

116 A. Panezi, J. O'Shea, *How can we manage the risks and liabilities associated with legal translation in the age of machine translation and generative AI?*, 2023, pp. 1-2. Available at SSRN: https://ssrn.com/abstract=4707819 or http://dx.doi.org/10.2139/ssrn.4707819. Accessed on June 12, 2025.

117 See also: Kai Jiang, Lu Xi, *Integrating Machine Translation with Human Translation in the Age of Artificial Intelligence: Challenges and Opportunities* [in:] *Big Data Analytics for Cyber-Physical System in Smart City*, ed. M. Atiquzzaman, N. Yen, Xu Zhen, BDCPS Advances in Intelligent Systems and Computing, Springer 2020. vol. 1303, pp. 1397-1405, https://doi.org/10.1007/978-981-33-4572-0_202.

118 P. Giampieri, *The use of AI in the translation of legal documents: A critical analysis*, "Trans-kom" 2024, vol. 17, issue 2, p. 345.

119 *Ibidem.*

120 V. Briva-Iglesia, J.L. Cavalheiro Camargo, G. Dogru, *Large language models "ad referendum": how good are they at machine translation in the legal domain?*, "MonTI. Monografías de Traducción e Interpretación" 2024, no. 16. Repensar la (des)globalización y su impacto en la traducción: desafíos y oportunidades en la práctica de la traducción jurídica, p. 75, https://doi.org/10.6035/MonTI.2024.16.02.

considered a cutting-edge technology that provides benefits for the arbitral proceedings. This chatbot has been introduced for the sake of transforming global communication. Through the implementation of language translation handled in real-time with speech-to-text capacities, MAC AI tackles linguistic barriers thanks to advanced Natural Language Processing (NLP) techniques. In this context, the integration of this tool focused on speech recognition is helpful in ensuring both the seamless processing and translation of spoken language that is converted into the target one. In addition, the MAC AI is developed on sophisticated NLP algorithms that play a key role in providing contextually accurate interactions.[121]

### *2.3.4 AI-based evidence*

The increasing number of records and information generated by AI will have an impact on the rules of evidence, most notably in respect to both the admissibility and relevance of evidence. One must note, however, that rules of evidence have been designed far before the advancement in new technologies. Given that, they are widely considered agnostic and malleable. In fact, the application of these rules to AI-produced evidence requires a better understanding of the intersection between both the technical and engineering features of AI.[122]

To start with, it is worthwhile to define the AI evidence which is acknowledged to be a form of electronic evidence. It can be defined as:

> data (comprising the output of analogue devices or data in digital form) that is generated, processed, stored or communicated by any digital device, computer or computer system or conveyed over a digital transmission system, that has the potential to make the factual account of either party more probable or less probable than it would be without the evidence.[123]

Considering AI evidence, they can refer to records, reports, tests, images, and videos that have been generated by AI tools. Importantly, in this light, it is important to note that AI evidence is linked to software processes. The non-AI algorithmics and systems that are dedicated to rendering electronic evidence are commonly seen as deterministic. This means that they make use of manually inputted rules alongside logic in order to cover various types of situations. In contrast, the AI systems differ significantly from non-AI algorithmics and systems. In fact, they operate thanks to such algorithms that are necessary to enhance their knowledge or performance based on the acquired experience. Therefore, such experience results

121 S. Imam Sheik et al., *MAC AI – Multilingual & Automatic Conversational AI*, "IEEE Xplore" 2024, International Conference on Power, Energy, Control and Transmission Systems (ICPECTS), Chennai (India) 2024, p. 1, doi: 10.1109/ICPECTS62210.2024.10780001.

122 D. Seng Kiat Boon, *'To Admit or Not to Admit: That is the Question for AI Evidence'*, https://papers.ssrn.com/sol3/papers.cfm?abstract_id=5184567. Accessed on June 24, 2025.

123 *Ibidem*, p. 2. See more: S. Murdoch, D. Seng, B. Schafer, The Sources and Characteristics of Electronic Evidence [in:] *Electronic Evidence and Electronic* Signatures, ed. S. Mason, D. Seng, University of London Press 2021, p. 41.

from data that has been uploaded to the system. In practice, this AI system is thus trained on the provided data, and the chosen machine learning (ML) algorithm is used for the sake of identifying the patterns in the data. This step is needed prior to making generalizations from the selected patterns to determine amongst multiple solutions that one which is possible. Overall, "the development of an AI system centres around building an 'accurate' statistical model of the training data, whereupon it can 'predict' or render decisions – generate 'interferences' – based on the model".[124]

Therefore, given the ubiquitous nature of the AI itself, there are various types of evidence that can be generated. Daniel Seng Kiat Boon distinguishes recordative, descriptive, predictive, and generative AI evidence.

The first type, commonly known as recordative evidence, refers to evidence either including or bearing a record, or representing a memory or reminiscence of a particular event. To illustrate, the Amazon Echo's records of conversations or Ring doorbell's records concerning the surveillance of different activities along with images and sound records stemming from phones or security robots pertain to this type of evidence. Given that, the recordative AI evidence could be thus classified as real evidence that demonstrates the objective existence of the perceived event alongside the properly maintained records. Therefore, it reflects the relevant circumstances and surrounding activities that are pertinent to a particular case. In view of these features, this type of evidence is admissible due to its autoptic preference. In addition, it is also worthwhile to remember that the recordative AI evidence can be used for the sake of showing the testimonial content of the human output. Accordingly, in this case, "the human testimony would be digitised, transcribed, indexed and processed in some way before being stored on the device or some other platform".[125] In this context, the AI processing is limited to recordation devices.[126]

The second, descriptive evidence, concerns a synthesis of records or information necessary in view of properly presenting particular characteristics of the evidence itself. This type of evidence is also widely known as analytical or prescriptive AI due to its reliance on "statistics and knowledge representation, statistical, probabilistic and other methodologies [that] can be applied to uncover patterns and relationships within the data, offering new insights, interpretations and justifications for data, including the detection of anomalies, and the recommendation of consequential actions".[127] Within international arbitration, the descriptive AI evidence could be applied in the case of electronic discovery that aims to identify the relevant elements and give an overview. One must note, however, that although the descriptive AI-generated evidence is considered demonstratively relevant evidence, in fact, it

124 D. Seng Kiat Boon, *'To Admit or Not to Admit...*, p. 3. See more: K.P. Murphy, *Machine Learning: A Probabilistic Perspective*, MIT Press 2012, p. 2.

125 *Ibidem,* p. 12.

126 *Ibidem*, pp. 12–13.

127 *Ibidem*, p. 13.

might be challenged on the grounds of involving AI algorithms that change the original data to the extent that it does not reflect the same or sufficiently similar content. Importantly, this approach should not be interpreted in a way that all autoptic or 'real' evidence should be far from any processing. In practice, there is a common acceptance of using a microscope or magnifying glasses which are helpful for the tribunal to properly assess or interpret the evidence.[128]

On the other hand, it is also worth recalling Wigmore's standpoint. He:

> noted that there could be instances where access to the raw, unprocessed record or information prior to its synthesis (for instance, via descriptive AI) would be preferable, not only because the synthesised evidence is not sufficiently similar to the original, but also because the synthesis may introduce exogenous elements that could not be easily reviewed as well as elements of hearsay. For AI and electronic evidence, this could take the form of unsworn choices made vicariously by unknown programmers through their selection of various curation criteria that would affect the tribunal's assessment of the received autoptic evidence.[129]

The third, predictive AI evidence, refers to a model dedicated to making not only predictions but also forecasts or inference in view of behaviors, characteristics, and attributes alongside actions. Compared to descriptive AI, which is focused on past events, predictive AI looks into future predictions or unknown events. Considering the accuracy of predictive AI, it highly relies on the quality of the training data, most notably in terms of reliable and unbiased data. Further, both the reliability and trustworthiness of AI systems and their generated results are mainly related to their interpretability and explainability.[130]

The last, generative AI evidence reflects a new type of evidence that results from using generative models in order to produce new text, images, videos, or other forms of data. Currently, due to the highly pervasive nature of generative AI evidence, there are some concerns related to its admissibility. Accordingly,

> Key among its concerns is the fact that many generative AI content, especially those produced through the use of large language models (LLMs), contain a mixture of memorised content and counterfactual or logically-flawed statements. Also known as hallucinations, which has been described as the 'propensity to yield erroneous or fabricated details about real-world subjects … [generating] references that are inaccurate or completely unfounded',[131] this has led many commentators to focus on the problems associated with the

128 *Ibidem*, p. 14.

129 *Ibidem*.

130 *Ibidem*, pp. 15–16.

131 S.M. Towhidul, I. Tonmy et al., *A comprehensive survey of hallucination mitigation techniques in large language models*, "Cornell University" January 8, 2024) https://arxiv.org/pdf/2401.01313.

> use of generative AI systems, particularly when they are used as intermediaries to supply information to end users.[132]

Considering the admissibility of this type of evidence, it remains crucial to determine whether the content was produced and thus the output itself is classified as "real evidence". To illustrate, in the case Moffatt v Air Canada[133], the court accepted such evidence. This case refers to the ruling of a Canadian tribunal regarding liability for misrepresentation resulting from the chatbot providing inaccurate information. In this case, the claimant, namely Jake Moffatt (Mr. Moffatt), decided to book a flight from Vancouver to Toronto with Air Canada after his grandmother's death (11 November 2022). To find the relevant flight, Mr. Moffatt decided to use a chatbot that was available on the website of this airline. The chatbot suggested that:

> Air Canada offers reduced bereavement fares if you need to travel because of an imminent death or a death in your immediate family. [...] If you need to travel immediately or have already travelled and would like to submit your ticket for a reduced bereavement rate, kindly do so within 90 days of the date your ticket was issued by completing our Ticket Refund Application form.[134]

One must note that Air Canada, in fact, provides this type of reduced fare for those passengers who are traveling because of a family member's death. In addition, Mr. Moffatt also talked to an Air Canada representative who confirmed that the fare for each flight was around $380. Therefore, in the wake of this information, Mr. Moffatt booked his flight from Toronto to Vancouver on 18 November 2022 for $845.38. The first application for the bereavement fare was submitted on 17 November 2022, which felled within the scope of the 90-day period mentioned by the chatbot. Due to the lack of a partial refund, Mr. Moffatt contacted Air Canada by email and attached screenshots of the information given by the chatbot. He also confirmed that he complies with the other requirements concerning the prescribed time to claim the bereavement rate. Just three days later, Mr. Moffatt received a reply from the airline assuming that he was misled by the chatbot. Both parties could not reach a consensus over the fare, and Mr. Moffatt filed a case before the Canadian tribunal. This court recognized that a claimant raises the question of negligent misrepresentation by Air Canada. To rule on this issue, it was crucial to determine whether "Air Canada owed him a duty of care, that its representation was untrue, inaccurate or misleading, that Air Canada had made that representation negligently, and that he had relied on that misrepresentation and suffered loss".[135]

The Tribunal confirmed the existence of duty of care and the obligation of Air Canada to ensure that the information given by its chatbot is correct. Equally, the

132 D. Seng Kiat Boon, *'To Admit or Not to Admit...*, p. 22.

133 *Moffatt v Air Canada 2024 BCCRT 149*, https://www.canlii.org/en/bc/bccrt/doc/2024/2024bccrt149/2024bccrt149.pdf. Accessed on June 5,.2025.

134 *Ibidem*, p. 4.

135 K.P. Soh, V. Ng, *Chatbots and liability for negligent misrepresentation: Moffatt v Air Canada 2024 BCCRT 149*, "SAL Practitioner" 2025, vol. 16, p. 3.

Tribunal rejected Air Canada's standpoint that this chatbot should be regarded as a separate legal entity. Likewise, the Tribunal did not accept the argument that Mr. Moffatt could have found the necessary information on another airline's website. In fact, the claimant took actions to confirm the reliability of the information provided by the chatbot with the representative of Air Canada. This led the Tribunal to reject Air Canada's claims of lack of liability. Mr. Moffatt was awarded $812,02.[136]

In fact, this case relates to Air Canada's attempt to avoid responsibility under the established rules of attribution at law which are "deployed to deem one's actions (or liability) as another's".[137] Under this concept, "artificially-intelligent (AI) system's actions and their potentially harmful consequences cannot easily be attributed to the system's developers or operators because the system acts autonomously. Nor can the system, which has no legal personality, be liable on its own account".[138]

Air Canada sought to defend its standpoint following two premises. The first one assumes that the chatbot was fueled by AI. One must note, however, that it is not so obvious. Currently, there are two different types of chatbots. The first type includes rule-based or pre-programmed chatbots that operate under "decision-trees". They function in a way that once a user inputs "X", he will get the response "Y". Therefore, these chatbots are based on "deterministic" algorithms, which means that they will generate the same outputs regardless of changing conditions. If the chatbot offered by Air Canada was "deterministic" in nature, it would be difficult, if not impossible, to avoid liability based on the assumption of lack of control over the produced outputs.[139]

The second type refers to large language models (LLMs) which support the functioning of the GenAI. Compared to "deterministic programs", these models can respond according to the varying conditions. To illustrate, ChatGPT, which is also an LLM, is based on "statistical optimisation to infer patterns from data".[140] In practice, this means that the algorithm is responsible for analyzing the input in order to give outputs resulting from such analysis.[141] In addition,

> Machine learning algorithms are often statistical, detecting patterns in data that enable the algorithms to automatically build – without additional manual programing by human engineers – internal computer models of a phenomenon to make further predictions or automated decisions about future data it receives, i.e. new examples of the phenomenon at issue.[142]

136 *Moffatt v Air Canada 2024*..., pp. 6–9.

137 K.P. Soh, V. Ng, *Chatbots and liability*..., p. 4. See more: J. Soh, *Legal Disposition and Artificially-Intelligent Attributions* "Legal Studies" 2023, vol. 43, issue 3, pp. 583-586.

138 J. Soh, *Legal Disposition and Artificially-Intelligent*..., p. 583.

139 K.P. Soh, V. Ng, *Chatbots and liability*..., p. 5.

140 *Ibidem.*

141 *Ibidem.*

142 P. Huberman, *Tort law, corrective Justice and the problem of autonomous-machine-caused harm*, "Canadian Journal of Law & Jurisprudence" 2021, vol. XXXIV, no. 1, p. 110.

Under the second premise, "the established rules of attribution did not, or should not, apply to AI".[143] This standpoint assumes that AI systems are not liable. In this light, it is worthwhile to acknowledge that:

> Accordingly, AAs' [autonomous agents] relative independence extends beyond not being controlled by humans in real time, but to their self-selection of methods to achieve programmed goals. This is not to say that AAs have discretionary powers or wills of their own. They are deterministic systems, their outputs defined by inputs received. Moreover, AAs' ultimate goals are those of their human designers and users, not their own. Nevertheless, due to AAs' emergence, it is difficult – if not impossible – to fully trace or predict connections between environmental inputs and ensuing changes in AAs' algorithms and behaviours.[144]

Overall, the generated AI outputs are considered hybrid evidence in majority of cases. Therefore, they combine both testimonial and real evidence. This is reflected in the profile data or academic summaries provided by Google Scholar. Importantly, these outputs include various types of elements such as the information 'memorized' from the training data in the form of code samples, images, conversations, writings, audio, video, among others. In fact, part of this data may include testimonial input, whereas the others have been extracted from external or even live sources. In this light, it might be difficult to determine whether generative AI evidence amounts to hearsay or not. On the other hand, the opposite might occur and thus it might be relatively easy to distinguish human-made statements from automatically generated data. In order to make such a distinction, it is thus crucial to undergo a careful and item-by-item analysis of the particular evidence.[145]

Despite the above challenges and concerns, it is important to acknowledge that the field of software has been designed to generate reliable software that had to be correct, but not always safe. It is thus crucial to remember that once the trained expertise does not fulfill its goals, there is still human oversight and a "common sense" that could be applied. In contrast, the AI systems are not equipped with "common sense" in case of any failure. In fact, it also results in elaborating the concept of the human-in-the-loop (HITL), which is discussed further.[146]

Overall, the rules of evidence concern primarily the orality of evidence. Therefore, most of this type of evidence is delivered by witnesses and their testimony in court that can be achieved in person or through videoconferencing or audio links. This entails that even though affidavits are produced by GenAI, they would still fall within the scope of human testimony due to the existence of human deponents. As such, humans are still responsible for the content of such generated affidavits. Accordingly, "where AI evidence is tendered in evidence, it

143 K.P. Soh, V. Ng, *Chatbots and liability*..., p. 5.
144 P. Huberman, *Tort Law, corrective justice*..., p. 111.
145 D. Seng Kiat Boon, *'To Admit or Not to Admit*..., p. 22–23.
146 *Ibidem*, p. 6.

is ostensibly admitted as documentary evidence pursuant to a hearsay exception or as real evidence".[147]

Further, even though there is no comprehensive legal framework covering the admissibility or relevance of AI-generated evidence in international arbitration, the Chartered Institute of Arbitrators (CIArb) in its Guideline on the Use of AI in Arbitration (2025) referred to these issues. Under Article 6.6, this Guideline provides that:

> In assessing whether AI-assisted or AI-generated content may be admitted to the record, arbitrators may (where relevant) assess the extent to which source data for the machine-generated content is on the record. Where the link between evidential source material and the model output is not clear, and where that link is a relevant factor in assessing whether the content should be admitted, arbitrators may seek submissions from the parties to explain how inputs from the record are linked to machine-generated outputs.[148]

This provision reflects an evolving approach considering the use of AI in terms of evidentiary standards. It is thus crucial to pay attention to both transparency and traceability of the machine-generated content. Equally important is seeking clarification from the parties when there is a link between the records and AI outputs. In fact, this is crucial in balancing both procedural fairness and party autonomy with the "black-box" dilemma (discussed in the last chapter).

Lastly, it is worth mentioning two different new categories of AI-based evidence, namely those related to AI-generated forgeries and deepfake technology. Under the first, AI-generated forgeries, it becomes relatively difficult to verify whether particular content is handwritten by a human or originates from AI. This might become a practical problem, most notably in the case of unscrupulous parties who are willing to use AI technology for the sake of creating fake documentary, photographic, or video evidence to be presented during arbitral proceedings. Even though forgeries cannot be classified as a new phenomenon, particularly the digital ones, they may be regarded as challenging to identify for the naked eye. Against this background, it is noteworthy that:

> As new forgery methods arise, forgery detection software follows (admittedly at a slightly slower pace). It remains to be determined how forged evidence can be safeguarded against, without leaving the door open for any shrewd defendant to argue that genuine, adverse evidence is in fact fake (the 'deepfake defence'). To account for this uncertainty in the international arbitration context, perhaps all digital evidence will need to be accompanied by

147 *Ibidem*, pp. 7–8.

148 CIArb Guideline on the Use of AI in Arbitration (2025), p. 13, https://www.ciarb.org/media/m5dl-3pha/ciarb-guideline-on-the-use-of-ai-in-arbitration-2025-_final_march-2025.pdf.

a counsel's statement of authenticity or expert opinion confirming that the content has been examined and is authentic and reliable.[149]

The second category related to deepfakes has emerged in the wake of the fast development of new technologies, and it might pose concerns related to privacy and the reliability of AI-based evidence[150]. These concerns can be analyzed from different perspectives. Under the first perspective, the deepfake technology might result in challenges concerning privacy and security, mostly with regard to biases and responsibility. Therefore, "Deepfake technology can introduce or exacerbate biases, both overt and subtle, in various ways. Biases may be present in the training data used to create deepfake algorithms, or they may be introduced intentionally by creators. These biases can manifest in terms of race, gender, age, and other characteristics".[151] Given the ethical perspective, it is thus recommended that technology itself, including solutions developed within deepfake technology, does not spread and amplify any biases. To address these challenges, it is thus crucial to follow ethical principles which stress the significance of transparency, consent, and accountability of developers.[152]

In sum, it is necessary to bear in mind that:

> While digital evidence is ubiquitous in international arbitration, we often assume it is identical to physical (or 'real') evidence [...]. Questions regarding the authenticity, admissibility, reliability, burden of proof, and potential loss of 'veracity' of digital evidence are ever more pressing. Qualitative decision-making requires both a familiarity with the technology involved, and a solid understanding of the challenges associated with digital evidence. Still, there is little to no guidance on how to handle digital evidence, or how to avoid and mitigate the types of technological interference [...].[153]

To address these concerns, it is thus recommended to benefit from expert testimony regarding any suspicions or allegations on AI-generated evidence. Equally important is to require the parties who are willing to submit any AI-based evidence,

149 *The guide to evidence in International Arbitration – Second Edition. Artificial Intelligence in Arbitration: Evidentiary Issues and Prospects*, "Global Arbitration Review" 2024, ed. A. Kläsener, M. Magál, J. Neuhaus, p. 12, https://www.baerkarrer.ch/userdata/files/publications/2023/rvs06r8disjbgis29fya.pdf. Accessed onJune 7,2025.

150 See more: S. Lim, H. Shim, *No secrets between the two of us: privacy concern over using AI agents*, "Cyberpsychology: Journal of Psychosocial Research on Cyberspace" 2022, vol. 16, issue 4, https://doi.org/10.5817/CP2022-4-3.

151 A. Golda et al., *Privacy and security concerns in enerative AI: a comprehensive survey*, "EEE Access" 2024, vol. 12, p. 48135.

152 *Ibidem*.

153 M. Apostol, *Arbitration tech Toolbox: blind spots in arbitration – when technology distorts evidence without direct human intervention*, "Kluwer Arbitration Blog" January 2, 2025, https://arbitrationblog.kluwerarbitration.com/2025/02/01/arbitration-tech-toolbox-blind-spots-in-arbitration-when-technology-distorts-evidence-without-direct-human-intervention/. Accessed on 07.06.2025.

possibly susceptible to manipulation, to attach the evidence of authenticity as well[154].

### *2.3.4.1 Distributed Ledger Technology (DLT)*

To start with, the Distributed Ledger Technology (DLT) was defined by the World Bank as "a novel and fast-evolving approach to recording and sharing data across multiple data stores (or ledgers). This technology allows for transactions and data to be recorded, shared, and synchronized across a distributed network of different network participants".[155] According to the definition of Taxonomy included in the UNCITRAL Report, DLT should be understood:

> in terms of a bundle of technologies and methods that are deployed to implement and maintain a ledger (or database) that is shared, replicated and synchronized on multiple networked computers (or servers). Thus, a distributed ledger technology system ("DLT system") is the system (comprising software and hardware components) that supports the deployment of those technologies and methods. DLT systems differ in their design, governance, purpose and use.[156]

Under another definition, DLT means "a decentralized database shared across a network of peer-to-peer machines, typically linked via the Internet. It can be architected to allow multiple parties to record and update information. DLT typically harnesses multiple elements such as an information technology infrastructure, an Internet connection, and data".[157] Technically, these elements can be divided into four different groups such as a 'cryptographic hash' (i.e. data in a block), a 'consensus mechanism' (i.e. Proof of Stake), a platform (i.e. a layer one protocol), and digital assets (i.e. fungible tokens).[158]

In addition, DLT can be classified according to twofold features. In this view, they can be regarded either as public/private ledger or permissioned/permissionless access to it. Therefore, the first distinction is based on who is allowed to participate in operating the system and thus to run a computer that contributes to the ledger

154 M. Barakat Friedman, M. Ansari, *Artificial wisdom or automated folly? Practical considerations for arbitration practitioners to address the AI conundrum*, "New York Law Journal" January 27, 2025, p. 4, https://www.sullcrom.com/SullivanCromwell/_Assets/PDFs/General/Mehdi-Ansari-NYLJ-Article-AI-Arbitration.pdf. Accessed on June 7, 2025.

155 *Distributed Ledger Technology (DLT) and Blockchain. FinTech Note No.* 1, "World Bank Group" 2017, p. IV, https://documents1.worldbank.org/curated/en/177911513714062215/pdf/122140-WP-PUBLIC-Distributed-Ledger-Technology-and-Blockchain-Fintech-Notes.pdf. Accessed on June 3, 2025.

156 *Legal issues relating to the use of distributed ledger technology in trade*, "United Nations Commission on International Trade Law" 29.05.2024, p. 3, https://uncitral.un.org/sites/uncitral.un.org/files/1175_for_submission1.pdf. Accessed on March 6, 2025.

157 *Ibidem.*

158 *Ibidem.*

(the so-called node). In view of the public ledger, there is a decentralized network that allows to participate without any restrictions, whereas the private ledger allows access merely to a limited number of participants, most notably those who have already been pre-identified.[159]

Under the second classification, namely permissioned or permissionless nature of DLT, a key issue is to determine whether there is a need to have permission before taking part in the ledger. In practice, it refers to determining whether an identification of the user is regarded as a pre-condition that must be fulfilled prior to their participation. The permissionless DLT does not require any identification which theoretically means that any interested user is allowed to participate without the identification process.[160]

Considering features of the DLT, it provides persistence of information, also known as immutability. In practice, the modification of any information that has been stored in the ledger is permitted merely in case of achieving a consensus. In fact, this feature can have further implications. To illustrate, if the enterprise decides to record its assets on DLT, it would be easier to confirm their existence, which might be useful in the case of pre-insolvency restructuring. Therefore, it remains crucial to ensure the correctness of data. To avoid any inconsistencies and incorrect data, it is thus recommended that enterprises build in systems with special prevention mechanism.[161]

Moreover, DLT is generally described as lacking cross-ledger interoperability. This means that, for example, an individual distributed ledger cannot interact with other distributed ledgers or even non-DLT applications. This is mainly rooted in the fact that distributed ledgers (most notably those classified as private and custom-built) have been launched for a specific purpose. Given that, they do not operate beyond this scope. One must note, however, that this limitation related to the lack of interoperability can have further ramifications in terms of limited applications of distributed ledgers. It is equally important to mention that the information would be in a "data silo" which entails that it could not be easily transferred or even used by the other systems.[162]

### *2.3.4.2 Blockchain*

Blockchain technology is widely described in Chapter 1, whereas this section focuses on the application of this tool in view of AI-based evidence. Prior to making such an analysis, it is crucial to assess this technology through the lens of transparency, privacy, and data security.

Even though the blockchain technology is considered an advantageous solution considering both transparency and immutability, there are some concerns related

159 *Ibidem.*
160 *Ibidem.*
161 *Ibidem*, p. 5.
162 *Legal issues relating to the use*..., p. 6.

to privacy. In practice, it becomes challenging to properly identify either individuals or entities that are behind a certain transaction. In fact, blockchain opts and employs a solution based on pseudonymity, which means that users are identified according to public names, instead of using their real names or identities. On the one hand, this should be seen as providing a certain level of anonymity. On the other hand, it also results in some privacy concerns, most notably in the legal context. Equally, the same applies to maintaining an accurate level of data security. Even though blockchain technology benefits from cryptographic mechanisms and decentralization, there are some doubts related to its security. In this light, one must note that seeming security may actually be misleading and result in far-reaching consequences. This is particularly important in terms of decreasing the gap between the potentially beneficial aspects of blockchain technology and strong cybersecurity measures. It thus plays a key role in safeguarding sensitive information within legal documents. Apparently, this type of information constitutes an immanent part of the blockchain infrastructure; therefore, it is necessary to prevent any unauthorized access to the blockchain itself.[163]

In addition, the use of blockchain technology also relates to some concerns about data protection. In this context, both the immutable and decentralized nature of blockchain might have an impact on the process of properly managing and safeguarding personal data. To illustrate, once data has been stored on the blockchain, it becomes immutable. In practice, it poses practical challenges in view of trying either to alter or delete such data. In fact, these actions could even lead to invalidating the entire blockchain. Importantly, the immutability should also be analyzed in terms of complying with data protection laws. The General Data Protection Regulation (GDPR) allows for the deletion of personal data upon request. However, it may be challenging in view of the blockchain technology.[164]

Equally important is to prevent any data breaches, most notably in terms of sensitive data. In this context, "Additionally, the transparent nature of blockchain transactions means that any individual with access to the blockchain can view its contents, thereby endangering the privacy of those involved in legal transactions".[165]

To address these issues, it seems necessary to adopt privacy-enhancing technologies which should become an imminent part of the blockchain systems. Therefore,

> These technologies are engineered to anonymise transactions, shield user identities, and prevent sensitive information from being divulged on the blockchain. Techniques such as zero-knowledge proofs and ring signatures enhance anonymity and confidentiality, allowing users to engage in transactions without revealing their identities. Additionally, cryptographic methods

163 A. Zhuk, *Beyond the blockchain hype: addressing legal and regulatory challenges*, "SN Social Sciences" 2025, vol. 5, issue 11, p. 9.

164 *Ibidem*, p. 10.

165 *Ibidem*.

> like homomorphic encryption safeguard sensitive data within the blockchain, ensuring that only authorized parties can access such information.[166]

This entails that both seamless and secure sharing of information should be regarded as a response to blockchain's drawbacks. Through the proper implementation of cryptographic techniques such as encryption, the blockchain itself could limit unauthorized access to information for third parties in order to decipher the included information. Thanks to such solutions regarding data sharing, it would be easier and more effective to maintain both the integrity and confidentiality of data. Importantly, the application of this solution would not compromise the key benefits of blockchain technology, namely transparency and traceability of transactions.[167]

On the other hand, it is worthwhile to remember that the introduction of encryption improves both privacy and security but simultaneously disrupts the full transparency of blockchain technology. In practice, it becomes impossible to read data without the decryption key which might influence the degree of the openness of some blockchain implementations.[168]

Later, along with the increasing use of blockchain technology, the increasing number of cyberattacks and data breaches may become a reality. Nakamoto explains that there is the risk of 51% of cyberattacks to be handled on blockchain. "In a blockchain network, a 51% attack occurs when a single entity or group controls over 50% of the network's computing power, enabling them to manipulate the network and potentially steal sensitive data. Although rare, such attacks pose a substantial risk to the security of blockchain networks".[169] To mitigate these risks, it is thus recommended to implement multi-factor authentication and encryption.

From the legal perspective, the key issue is to focus on the admissibility of blockchain-based evidence. In this context, it is worth noting that the Hangzhou Internet Court in the People's Republic of China is widely regarded as the first court in the world to accept blockchain evidence.[170] This refers to the case of Hangzhou Huatai Yimei Culture Media Co., Ltd. v. Shenzhen Daotong Technology Development Co., Ltd.[171]

Currently, there is also another successful example of blockchain-based evidence stemming from Everledger. This is a blockchain-based platform that provides a digital certificate confirming the authenticity of diamonds. In fact, this type of evidence was submitted before the UK High Court in 2018. The court not

166 *Ibidem.*

167 A. Zhuk, *Beyond the blockchain hype…*, p. 11.

168 *Ibidem.*

169 *Ibidem.*

170 M. Łągiewska, *Digitalization and the use…*, p. 119-121. See more: R. Walters, *Tokens and blockchain evidence in international commercial arbitration: its current status?*, "Arbitration International" 2025, , https://doi.org/10.1093/arbint/aiae041.

171 *Hangzhou Huatai Yimei Culture Media Co., Ltd. v. Shenzhen Daotong Technology Development Co., Ltd. (2018) Zhe 0192 Civil Case, First Court no. 81*, Hangzhou Internet Court of the People's Republic of China, June 27, 2018, https://journals.sas.ac.uk/deeslr/article/view/5080/4973. Accessed on May 26, .2025.

only recognized the evidence but also ruled that it is admissible. Overall, the court issued a ruling that was favorable for the party who presented the proof of ownership confirmed by the blockchain technology.[172]

### *2.3.5 AI-assisted witness' testimony analysis*

Currently, the AI tools have been developed to provide more sophisticated services, including the assessment and analysis of the witness's testimony. Importantly, some of these tools might even be useful in determining the witness's credibility.[173]

To illustrate, an AI-powered tool could be applied for the sake of assessing the credibility of certain statements. In this context, AI is based on "the application of machine learning such that the behaviour of respondents during their statements is compared to previously stored features of true or false statements collected from respondents under controlled conditions".[174]

Importantly, it is possible to follow three main techniques that are commonly used, including an analysis of non-verbal behavior, analysis of verbal behavior, and those based on the brain imaging method (the so-called functional magnetic resonance imaging – fMRI).[175]

One must note that new technologies have been already widely applied. This is reflected by the Court of Arbitration for Sport (CAS), which even allowed presenting polygraph evidence (aka "lie detector") in a few cases.

> The polygraph is a well-known approach to detecting deception…it relies on the measurement of skin conductance, which can be influenced by arousal during deception – it has been repeatedly evaluated and its validity and reliability have been challenged for decades in systematic reviews and evaluations. In addition to questions about its reliability and validity, the polygraph is particularly vulnerable to countermeasures – covert or overt measures taken by the subject of the polygraph in order to distort or undermine any conclusions.[176]

Under another definition, "the polygraph measures galvanic skin response, blood pressure, heart and breathing rates, and perspiration as a proxy for nervous-system

172 A. Zhuk, *Beyond the blockchain hype…*, p. 14.

173 See also: R. Bradshaw, *Deception and detection: the use of technology in assessing witness credibility*, "Arbitration International" 2021, vol. 37, issue 3, pp. 707–720, https://doi.org/10.1093/arbint/aiab007.

174 J. Golub, *Application of artificial intelligence (AI) in the assessment of the credibility of statements in the cross-border taking of evidence in civil and commercial matters*, "JIPITEC" 2023, vol. 14, issue 376, pp. 381–382.

175 *Ibidem*, p. 382.

176 K.N. Kotsoglou, M. Oswald, *Falling behind the PACE: lie detectors, policing and lack of foreseeability – an FOI-based study*, "Legal Studies" 2025, vol. 45, p. 61; See also: *Neuroscience, society and policy*, "The Royal Society Report 2011, 01/11 DES2015.

activity (primarily anxiety) as an (imperfect) proxy for deception".[177] Therefore, due to "leakages" of different physiological cues, particularly concerning both face and hands, the polygraph can identify various signals, including increased levels of anxiety relating to a particular part of the speech. However, these factors cannot be fully considered foolproof in determining the lie.[178]

The above case refers to a situation of an athlete accused of using doping who decided to take a polygraph test in order to demonstrate his evidence. It is worthwhile to note, however, that even though this evidence has been admissible, in practice, the CAS tribunals did put merely little weight on it.[179] In addition, it is noteworthy that:

> AI enhancements can potentially (1) shift the role of the human agent in relation to the subject of the investigation in favor of autonomous, robotic agents; (2) enable the remote and unannounced collection of subjects' data; (3) personalize lie detection analyses using big data-related profiling and surveillance techniques; (4) construct corpora of exemplars of 'lying' so that machine learning devices can be trained; and (5) foster new varieties of multi-factored constructs and data mining routines related to human leakage and other physiological traces associated with lying.[180]

In fact, AI-driven tools have already been implemented for the sake of assessing evidence in forensics. In this light,

> AI plays a critical role in examining electronic data, audio, and video recordings. This is especially relevant in digital forensics, where AI algorithms help sift through enormous volumes of data to locate critical evidence. Example: The FBI has used AI-driven software to analyze digital media from seized devices, helping law enforcement build cases in criminal investigations by identifying faces, voices, and other key indicators from multimedia sources. The following AI algorithms are key to the applications mentioned in the context of legal evidence analysis: Natural Language Processing (NLP), Machine Learning, Predictive Analytics, and Computer Vision.[181]

177 C. Leonetti, *Abracadabra, Hocus Pocus, same song, different chorus: the newest iteration of the "science" of lie detection*, "Richmond Journal of Law & Technology" 2017, vol. XXIV, issue 1, p. 1, https://jolt.richmond.edu/files/2017/12/Leonetti-Final-Copy-2.pdf.

178 J.A. Oravec, *The emergence of "truth machines"? Artificial intelligence approaches to lie detection*, "Ethics and Information Technology" 2022, vol. 24, issue 6, p. 6.

179 R. Bradshaw, *Arbitration tech toolbox: cross examination? There's an app for that*, "Kluwer Arbitration Blog" 06.02.2023, https://arbitrationblog.kluwerarbitration.com/2023/02/06/arbitration-tech-toolbox-cross-examination-theres-an-app-for-that/. Accessed on June 11, 2025.

180 J.A. Oravec, *The emergence of "truth machines"?...*, p. 6.

181 C. Kerdvibulvech, *Big data and AI-driven evidence analysis: a global perspective on citation trends, accessibility, and future research in legal* applications, "Journal of Big Data" 2024, vol. 11, issue 180, p. 2, https://doi.org/10.1186/s40537-024-01046-w.

The so-called "lie-detecting" programs might also be used to check the facts and their compliance with the witness's testimony in arbitral proceedings. In this light, it is noteworthy to set forth that:

> Similar tools could provide automated cite-checking of briefs as well as real-time fact-checking at the hearing. Witness testimony is already routinely recorded and transcribed. Soon, it may be possible to run AI tools on the real-time transcript; if a witness refers to an email or letter in his or her answer, for example, it can cross-check the record and provide counsel with the relevant exhibit reference. Furthermore, an automated fact-checker could verify whether a witness's answer contradicts other evidence on the record or other parts of his or her testimony and alert counsel to the inconsistency.[182]

### *2.3.6 Drafting arbitral awards*

The international arbitration faces some criticisms related to the lack of consistency in rendering arbitral awards. In this context, the "arbitral tribunals render different decisions in similar matters, and as such parties to existing arbitral proceedings go into the dispute settlement arena blindfolded, hand tied, and very much worrisome as there might be a possibility of them losing not just money but time to their opponent".[183] From this perspective, it is much more likely that parties will be open to using AI-supported tools providing the prediction of the outcome of the arbitral proceedings, even prior to filing a case.

Unfortunately, the current development of AI does not meet these requirements thus far. Nonetheless, it is worthwhile to note the existence of the so-called "decision-tree", which makes use of machine learning software to predict the outcomes. This has been widely applied in the US legal sector. In fact, this solution became popular in 2004 due to Andrew Martin. This political scientist and professor at the University of Michigan, supported by his colleagues, decided to benefit from "decision tree" technology in predicting the possible results of the proceedings in the US Supreme Court.

Later, in 2014, Daniel Katz, who is a scientist and a professor of law, elaborated an algorithm that was able to predict the result of a case based on the same "decision-tree" technology with more than 70% accuracy. In 2017, he further developed this technology by employing the so-called forest algorithm. Accordingly, he decided to use precedents from 1815 to 2015, and the trained algorithm provided even better outcomes compared to a "decision tree". In addition, it is also crucial to remember that the European Court of Human Rights also benefits from this new technology since 2016. It applied the so-called Support Vector Machine (SVM), which was elaborated by University College London in cooperation with the University of Sheffield and Pennsylvania State University. In fact, this tool

182 R. Bradshaw, *Arbitration Tech Toolbox*...

183 A.O. Onyefulu-Kingston, *AI-Based Technologies in International*..., p. 652.

provides a 79% accuracy. Therefore, considering international arbitration, this tool would be of significant interest to the parties in order to foresee what the chances of winning or losing the dispute are. Equally, it would also be possible to predict potential compensation depending on the outcome of the proceedings alongside the duration of the case itself. This means that the proper application of such a tool would be seen "as a check and balance on the possible merits or demerits of embarking into such a proceeding and the possibility of exploring alternative dispute settlement mechanisms such as negotiation, mediation amongst others".[184]

In practice, even though AI-powered tools may increase efficiency in terms of handling arbitral proceedings, there are also concerns resulting in the misunderstanding that such proceedings should be relatively quick and cheap. Indeed, it could be one of the benefits; however, efficiency also means: "coming to a just result. It involves according due process. It involves an award that is enforceable. And this involves a balancing".[185] In fact, such an approach in terms of using new technologies requires finding a "golden mean" in properly balancing benefits[186] and threats. In practice, it may lead either to a reduction or even the end of using some technological tools in the course of arbitral proceedings.[187]

To address this question, it is worth referring to one of the dilemmas, namely the potential use of predictive legal solutions in international arbitration. Once arbitrators rely heavily on AI-predicted outcomes of the case, the key principle of professional practice may challenge both the independence and impartiality of arbitrators. This entails that "AI should be deployed in tandem with human arbitrators".[188] Even though such an approach seems to be interesting, there are practical challenges that need to be faced. Indeed, arbitrators applying such AI-powered tools should have a certain level of proficiency in terms of technological competence, much higher than a basic level. In addition, one of the most important criticisms with regard to AI systems in international arbitration refers to the lack of transparency in their application.[189]

AI may also be helpful in drafting arbitral awards. Depending on the use of AI-powered tools, there is a different level of supervision proposed by the Paulsson-Suresh Progressive AI Supervision Scale (hereafter "Paulsson-Suresh Scale"). Therefore, this concept recognizes two extremes such as minimal supervision (level 1) and full supervision (level 5).

If the AI performs basic tasks, including making corrections on spelling and grammar, it falls within the first level of supervision. In this light, an arbitrator is

184 *Ibidem*, p. 652.

185 K. Fach Gómez, *The Technological Competence…*, p. 37.

186 See more: J. Liu, *The human impact on arbitration in the emerging era of artificial intelligence*, "Contemporary Asia Arbitration Journal" 2024, vol. 93, pp. 91–115.

187 K. Fach Gómez, *The Technological Competence…*, p. 37.

188 *Ibidem*. See more: N. Ahmad, *Smart resolutions: exploring the role of artificial intelligence in alternative dispute resolution*, "Cleveland State Law Review" 2025, vol. 73, issue 2, pp. 273–297.

189 *Ibidem*.

allowed to trust the vendor support.[190] Further, evaluation of a single document along with the production of summaries and translations has been classified as a level 2. Given that, it requires limited supervision and intervention in view of the design, implementation, and monitoring. Under the Paulsson-Suresh Scale, such AI-powered tools can carry out simple tasks instead of an arbitrator.[191]

Drafting a procedural history of the arbitral proceedings alongside uncontested facts given the parties' submissions is deemed to require moderate supervision. The same applies in the case of using AI to analyze large documents to find out the key topics and generate concise summaries that may be used in the arbitral awards. In this regard, AI performs tasks related to informational analysis and thus may complete complex tasks. As such, it needs moderate supervision (level 3) due to its potential influence (either direct or indirect) on the arbitral award. To reduce potential negative consequences of such AI-powered tools, it is advised to use AI tools specifically designated for the legal sector. There is also a need for human oversight and occasional intervention. In addition, arbitrators must carefully assess and validate the generated output in terms of the accuracy of the analysis, results, and summaries.[192]

If an arbitrator would like to use AI for cost calculation in the arbitral award, such analysis will require a high level of supervision (level 4). In this regard, AI systems perform more complex tasks and thus not only the outcomes but also the process should be constantly supervised by the arbitrator. Further, the arbitrator should interpret such AI-generated content in making his own decisions. Such close monitoring by the arbitrator is crucial in ensuring compliance with the principles of international arbitration. Failure to comply with this requirement may result in some negative consequences when AI could potentially affect the substantive part of the arbitral award.

Finally, if an arbitrator uses AI to "support evaluation across multiple documents and checking for consistency with prior stance of the arbitrator in published awards/articles" and "flagging inconsistencies in evidence"[193], the arbitrators' adjudicative mandate is transferred to AI and thus falls within the highest level of supervision (level 5). According to the Paulsson-Suresh Scale, such actions need full monitoring by an arbitrator due to AI-drawn conclusions that may affect substantive parts of the arbitral awards.[194]

Overall, the Paulsson-Suresh Scale marks a useful explanation of how AI tools may be applied in the process of drafting arbitral awards. Given that, AI tools may

190 M. Paulsson, S. Suresh, *AI: The modern tribunal assistant – impact on enforceability of arbitral awards under the New York convention*, "Jus Mundi Arbitration Review" 2024, vol. 1, issue 1, p. 117, https://jusmundi.com/en/document/pdf/publication/en-ai-the-modern-tribunal-assistant-impact-on-enforceability-of-arbitral-awards-under-the-new-york-convention. Accessed on April 27, 2025.

191 *Ibidem*.

192 *Ibidem*.

193 *Ibidem*, p. 118.

194 *Ibidem*.

be allowed to prepare technical drafts where there is merely general information about the background of the dispute and the procedural history.

On the other hand, it is also crucial to remember that overreliance on AI-supported prediction tools may even lead to the violation of due process and fair hearings. Given that, it might be even seen as a destructive tool. From this perspective, "if parties can decipher who will win or lose, the loser may be frightened of going into arbitration and wasting resources if they are eventually going to lose. They may decide to settle out of court, in this case outside of arbitration".[195]

In fact, the case of international arbitration differs from court litigation, most notably due to the lack of publishing arbitral awards. Arbitration, which is considered a private dispute resolution mechanism, benefits from the confidentiality principle. Importantly, this is widely considered one of the most cherished attributes of arbitration itself. In this view, the Secretary General of the ICC mentions in his report that "parties in an arbitral dispute place the highest value on confidentiality as this is one of the most essential attributes in arbitration".[196] In addition, it is worthwhile to note that confidentiality is also rooted in procedural rules. To name a few examples, Article 30 of the London Court of International Arbitration Rules,[197] Article 44 of the Swiss Rules on International Arbitration,[198] Articles 3 and 9 of the SCC Arbitration Rules[199] explicitly stipulate confidentiality during arbitral proceedings. Historically, this doctrine was first outlined in the Dolling-Baker v Merrett case "where Parker LJ delivering the lead judgment in March 1990, stated

195 A.O. Onyefulu-Kingston, *AI-Based Technologies in International...*, p. 653.

196 *Ibidem*, p. 652.

197 "Article 30.1 The parties undertake as a general principle to keep confidential all awards in the arbitration, together with all materials in the arbitration created for the purpose of the arbitration and all other documents produced by another party in the proceedings not otherwise in the public domain, save and to the extent that disclosure may be required of a party by legal duty, to protect or pursue a legal right, or to enforce or challenge an award in legal proceedings before a state court or other legal authority. The parties shall seek the same undertaking of confidentiality from all those that it involves in the arbitration, including but not limited to any authorised representative, witness of fact, expert or service provider". See: *LCIA Arbitration Rules 2020*, https://www.lcia.org/Dispute_Resolution_Services/lcia-arbitration-rules-2020.aspx#Article%2030. Accessed on June 10, 2025.

198 "Article 44.1. Unless the parties expressly agree in writing to the contrary, the parties undertake to keep confidential all awards and orders as well as all materials submitted by another party in the framework of the arbitration proceedings not already in the public domain, except and to the extent that a disclosure may be required of a party by a legal duty, to protect or pursue a legal right, or to enforce or challenge an award in legal proceedings before a judicial authority. This undertaking also applies to the arbitrators, the tribunal-appointed experts, the secretary to the arbitral tribunal, the members of the board of directors of the Swiss Arbitration Centre, the members of the Court and the Secretariat". See: *Swiss Rules of International Arbitration (Swiss Rules) 2021*, https://www.swissarbitration.org/wp-content/uploads/2023/08/Swiss-Rules-2021-EN.pdf. Accessed on 10.06.2025.

199 Article 3. Unless otherwise agreed by the parties, the SCC, the Arbitral Tribunal and any administrative secretary of the Arbitral Tribunal shall maintain the confidentiality of the arbitration and the award. See: *SCC Arbitration Rules 2023*, https://sccarbitrationinstitute.se/wp-content/uploads/2024/12/SCC_Arbitration_Rules_2023_English.pdf. Accessed on 10.06.2025.

that parties are under some form of 'Implied Obligation' to keep arbitral proceedings private and confidential".[200]

On the other hand, it is also worthwhile to remember that the doctrine of confidentiality has not been recognized globally. In practice, some jurisdictions do not recognize this principle in terms of obligation. To illustrate, the case of Esso Australia Resources Ltd v Ministry of Energy and Mineral confirmed that "privacy of arbitral process does not give rise to an obligation of confidentiality, thereby rejecting the decision of the English court. However, even in a situation like this, the awards are not fully published except of consented by parties".[201]

Therefore, to address this challenging problem of insufficient data in arbitration, specific databases have been launched such as the Dispute Resolution Data (DRD). This database includes macro data concerning arbitral proceedings originating from 18 different arbitral institutions (i.e. the ICC, AAA). Importantly, this data has been collected from 5,000 arbitral proceedings and involved 185 countries. Currently, some AI-powered tools have been developed such as ArbiLex, Ravel Law, and Solomonic. The first one, ArbiLex, has been designed as an AI prediction tool based on Bayesian machine learning.[202] In fact, it identifies the "risk factors that may be occasioned if parties resort to arbitration".[203] One must note, however, that the outcomes differ due to the different circumstances of a particular case. The second, Ravel Law, is also an AI-powered prediction tool that can "predict hundreds of cases from several law firms at the same time".[204] The last, Solomonic, has been developed for the sake of predicting and analyzing cases simultaneously.[205]

## 2.4 Two stages of AI implementation in international arbitration

Throughout the constant advancements of AI, the world would face new changes in terms of economic, social, and cultural background. Indeed, such changes would

200 A.O. Onyefulu-Kingston, *AI-Based Technologies in International*..., p. 653.

201 *Ibidem.*

202 "Bayes / Bayesian / Bayes' Theorem: A general term used to describe Algorithms and other methods that estimate the overall Probability of some eventuality (e.g., that a Document is Relevant), based on the combination of evidence gleaned from separate observations. In Electronic Discovery, the most common evidence that is combined is the occurrence of particular words in a Document. For example, a Bayesian Algorithm might combine the evidence gleaned from the fact that a Document contains the words "credit", "default", and "swap" to indicate that there is a 99% Probability that the Document concerns financial derivatives, but only a 40% Probability if the words "credit" and "default", but not "swap", are present. The most elementary Bayesian Algorithm is Naïve Bayes; however, most Algorithms dubbed "Bayesian" are more complex. Bayesian Algorithms are named after Bayes' Theorem, coined by the 18th century mathematician, Thomas Bayes. Bayes' Theorem derives the Probability of an outcome, given the evidence, from: (i) the probability of the outcome, independent of the evidence; (ii) the probability of the evidence, given the outcome; and (iii) the probability of the evidence, independent of the outcome". See: *The Grossman-Cormack Glossary*..., p. 9.

203 A.O. Onyefulu-Kingston, *AI-Based Technologies in International*..., p. 653.

204 *Ibidem.*

205 *Ibidem.*

also be seen in the dispute resolution landscape; thus, they would also impact the arbitration itself. Orlando Federico Cabrera Colorado predicts that there would be two different stages of the AI implementation within the framework of international commercial arbitration. Given that, the first stage refers to the construction of a "complementary relationship between predictive machines and humans".[206] According to this concept, even though AI would serve arbitrators, arbitral institutions, and counsels in their daily work, the final decision would be rendered by humans. This entails that AI-powered technologies will reduce the work overload of arbitrators in their routine activities. Therefore, the entire arbitral proceedings would be more efficient.[207]

In addition, Orlando Federico Cabrera Colorado believes that the AI system may be implemented either through "rule system" or "expert system". Given this concept, "the rules are encoded into the system as 'if x occurs, then y'".[208] In practice, such a system would be able to capture the knowledge of the human arbitrator, which will be transferred to the computer system as the expert knowledge. Such a transfer requires that "the knowledge is encoded as rules".[209] Once the programmer sets the code, he can easily make changes to properly correct the flaws. However, this approach also has some limitations based on the size of its rules.[210]

On the other hand, once the first stage is completed, the new arbitral institutions would emerge. Indeed, their structure will differ significantly from the current ones. They would have AI, which will be a pillar in terms of their decision-making. Once this stage is achieved, lawyers will have to learn more about the proper use of such new technologies and their limitations. In the wake of these technological advancements, there will be a need for lawyers specializing in algorithm development, machine learning (ML), and data interpretation, among others. It seems inevitable that AI will be widely applied in international arbitration and thus create a new standard in dispute resolution. From the perspective of arbitrators, AI will be useful in terms of facilitating the comparison between the submitted evidence and furthering the process of finding conflicting facts within such evidence.[211]

International arbitration seems to be a relatively easily adaptable environment for AI. Indeed, AI could serve in many different aspects of arbitration by accomplishing a variety of tasks such as "appointment of arbitrators, legal research, proof reading briefs, translations, case management and document organization, cost estimation, stenographic services, simultaneous interpretation, and drafting standard selections of an arbitration award such as the procedural history".[212]

206 O.F. Cabrera Colorado, *The future of international arbitration in the age of Artificial Intelligence*, "Journal of International Arbitration" 2023, vol. 40, issue 3, pp. 301–302.

207 *Ibidem*.

208 *Ibidem*, p. 305.

209 *Ibidem*.

210 *Ibidem*.

211 *Ibidem*, p. 302.

212 *Ibidem*, p. 303.

# 3 Legal issues involved in using AI in international arbitration

## 3.1 Legal framework

### *3.1.1 "Hard law" regulations on using AI*

#### *3.1.1.1 Council of Europe Framework Convention on Artificial Intelligence and Human Rights, Democracy and the Rule of Law*

Council of Europe Framework Convention on Artificial Intelligence and Human Rights, Democracy and the Rule of Law ("Framework Convention") opened for signature on 5 September 2024. Currently, there are 16 signatories to this Convention thus far.[1] It provides a legal framework on using AI tools that may potentially lead to discrimination in digital contexts. The chief purpose of this Convention is "to ensure that activities within the lifecycle of artificial intelligence systems are fully consistent with human rights, democracy and the rule of law" (Article 1.1).[2] In addition, this Framework Convention also defines the term "artificial intelligence systems" which should be understood as

> a machine-based system that, for explicit or implicit objectives, infers, from the input it receives, how to generate outputs such as predictions, content, recommendations or decisions that may influence physical or virtual environments. Different artificial intelligence systems vary in their levels of autonomy and adaptiveness after deployment.[3]

According to Article 5.1, it is crucial that each Party adopts or maintains measures for the sake of ensuring that "AI systems are not used to undermine the integrity, independence and effectiveness of democratic institutions and processes, including the principle of the separation of powers, respect for judicial independence and access to justice". It is worthwhile to note that this provision can also have an impact on international arbitration. In this light, AI systems cannot be used in

1 *Signatories, Council of Europe Framework Convention on Artificial Intelligence and Human Rights*, https://www.coe.int/en/web/artificial-intelligence/the-framework-convention-on-artificial-intelligence. Accessed on June 24, 2025.

2 *Council of Europe Framework Convention on Artificial Intelligence and Human Rights, Democracy and the Rule of Law*, https://rm.coe.int/1680afae3c. Accessed on May 23, 2025.

3 *Ibidem*, Article 2.

DOI: 10.4324/9781003667834-4

violation of judicial independence and access to justice. This means that AI systems are permitted as long as they uphold the fundamental principles of arbitration. The most notable of these principles are those related to the integrity of arbitral proceedings, the process of rendering an arbitral award, and due process.

Furthermore, the Framework Convention requires the "adequate transparency and oversight requirements tailored to specific contexts and risks".[4] Equally, this provision also applies to activities undertaken within the lifecycle of AI systems such as the identification of content produced by these systems. Therefore, this provision imposes two different principles, namely transparency and oversight.[5] Indeed, both principles are crucial in ensuring the proper application of AI-powered tools in arbitral proceedings. More in-depth discussions on this topic will be set forth in Chapter 4.

The Framework Convention also refers to both privacy and personal data protection. Under its current status,

> Each Party shall adopt or maintain measures to ensure that, with regard to activities within the lifecycle of artificial intelligence systems: a) privacy rights of individuals and their personal data are protected, including through applicable domestic and international laws, standards and frameworks; and b) effective guarantees and safeguards have been put in place for individuals, in accordance with applicable domestic and international legal obligations.[6]

The above provision is particularly significant within the context of international arbitration, namely the principle of confidentiality. Parties involved in the arbitral proceedings should be ensured that their data are well protected while using AI-powered tools. This becomes crucial in order to maintain the integrity of arbitral proceedings and due process. Any leakage of sensitive data related to the dispute may result in far-reaching consequences for the parties and the arbitral tribunal.

To sum up, the Framework Convention, albeit not directly, has a significant impact on international arbitration. In fact, this Convention introduces some considerations in view of due process and fairness in arbitral proceedings, arbitrator independence, data governance, and explainability, among others. Considering both due process and fairness, it is recommended to use AI-powered tools with respect to the parties' procedural rights. Arbitrators should also cautiously employ AI systems and thus not excessively rely on them. In fact, both opaque and biased content may challenge the arbitrator's independence and impartiality. In addition, it is also advised to meet transparency and accountability thresholds.

4 *Ibidem*, Article 8.

5 *Ibidem*.

6 *Ibidem*, Article 11.

#### *3.1.1.2 EU AI Act*

The Artificial Intelligence Act – Regulation (EU) 2024/1689 ("EU AI Act")[7] is widely considered a first comprehensive AI law globally. It has been adopted as a digital strategy of the EU for the sake of ensuring better conditions in view of developing and using such emerging innovations. The first draft of this law was proposed by the European Commission in April 2021. This regulation provides a risk-based AI classification system that can be employed in different applications.[8]

In view of the above, it is necessary to relate such considerations to arbitration. In fact, the activities conducted by arbitrators may concern different scopes of the EU AI Act. Mari Scherer classifies these scopes as follows: material, personal, territorial, and temporal.[9]

First, the material scope refers to a risk-based approach that has been adopted by the EU AI Act. In this light, it considers economic activities based on the possible harm that may result from using AI systems. It also implies various regulatory duties depending on the level of risk.[10]

Equally, it is also crucial to answer the question of whether arbitrators use high-risk AI systems. Under the EU AI Act, AI systems are deemed high-risk if they are

> intended to be used by a judicial authority or on their behalf to assist a judicial authority in researching and interpreting facts and the law and in applying the law to a concrete set of facts, or to be used in a similar way in alternative dispute resolution.

In addition,

> AI systems intended to be used by alternative dispute resolution bodies for those purposes [i.e. use and assistance in researching and interpreting facts and the law and in applying the law to a concrete set of facts] should also be considered to be high-risk when the outcomes of the alternative dispute resolution proceedings produce legal effects for the parties.[11]

7 *Regulation (EU) 2024/1689 of the European Parliament and of the Council of 13 June 2024 laying down harmonised rules on artificial intelligence and amending Regulations (EC) No 300/2008, (EU) No 167/2013, (EU) No 168/2013, (EU) 2018/858, (EU) 2018/1139 and (EU) 2019/2144 and Directives 2014/90/EU, (EU) 2016/797 and (EU) 2020/1828 (Artificial Intelligence Act) (Text with EEA relevance)*, "EUR-Lex", https://eur-lex.europa.eu/legal-content/EN/TXT/?uri=CELEX%3A32024R1689. Accessed on April 25, 2025.

8 *EU AI Act: first regulation on artificial intelligence*, "Topics: European Parliament" June 8, 2023, https://www.europarl.europa.eu/topics/en/article/20230601STO93804/eu-ai-act-first-regulation-on-artificial-intelligence. Accessed on April 25, 2025.

9 M. Scherer, *We need to talk about...the EU AI Act*, "Kluwer Arbitration Blog" May 27, 2024, https://arbitrationblog.kluwerarbitration.com/2024/05/27/we-need-to-talk-about-the-eu-ai-act/. Accessed on April 26, 2025.

10 *Ibidem.*

11 *Regulation (EU) 2024/1689...*, Recital 61; C. Lüttenberg, I. Beimel, S.J. Heetkamp, *How does the EU AI Act apply to arbitration?*, "Daily Jus" January 14, 2025, https://dailyjus.com/legal-tech/2025/01/how-does-the-eu-ai-act-apply-to-arbitration. Accessed on June 15, 2025.

In practice, this provision has far-reaching ramifications for the arbitral proceedings. First, arbitration is one of the methods of alternative dispute resolution. Second, an arbitral award is binding upon the parties, which means that it has some legal effects on them. Therefore, if the arbitral tribunal uses such AI systems during arbitral proceedings, they may be classified as high-risk systems depending on the purpose of their application. High-risk systems fall within this category as they have, even potentially, some influence on "democracy, the rule of law, individual freedoms, and the right to a fair trial". In contrast, if such AI systems have been used for "purely ancillary administrative activities, [...] such as the anonymization or pseudonymization of court judgments, documents or data, communication between staff or administrative tasks",[12] they would not be deemed high-risk. Given that, the purpose of performing such actions with the support of AI tools will result in their classification as high-risk systems or not. This means that each time it is needed to first analyze the purpose of the AI system and not automatically classify it as high-risk.

The EU AI Act provides exceptions in categorizing AI systems as high-risk. These exceptions result from Article 6(3) which stipulates as follows:

> where it does not pose a significant risk of harm to the health, safety or fundamental rights of natural persons, including by not materially influencing the outcome of decision making. The first subparagraph shall apply where any of the following conditions is fulfilled:
>
> a. the AI system is intended to perform a narrow procedural task;
> b. the AI system is intended to improve the result of a previously completed human activity;
> c. the AI system is intended to detect decision-making patterns or deviations from prior decision-making patterns and is not meant to replace or influence the previously completed human assessment, without proper human review; or
> d. the AI system is intended to perform a preparatory task to an assessment relevant for the purposes of the use cases listed in Annex III. [...].[13]

Importantly, these exceptions already refer to many different AI tools widely applied in arbitration. To name a few examples, AI-powered tools are implemented not only for payments of advances but also take part in the process of calculating and monitoring deadlines that may be specified by the arbitral tribunal. Second, such AI tools are used to enhance the presentation of finalized orders or review the chronologies in the ongoing proceedings. Third, AI plays a significant role in verifying the consistency of rendered arbitral awards with the previously issued decisions. If there are any inaccuracies in this regard, this may require the arbitral tribunal to conduct a further review. Finally, AI systems are helpful in terms of creating chronology along with the summaries of the facts. They may be used in

12 *Ibidem*.
13 *Regulation (EU) 2024/1689...*, Article 6(3).

searching for case law and literature reviews based on the legal issue involved in a particular case.[14]

The interpretation of this provision has already confirmed that there are many different examples of AI application that fall beyond the scope of high-risk systems. On the other hand, it is also worth noting that the EU AI Act provides (extensive) obligations in the case of employing such systems. Therefore, if the above-mentioned exceptions do not apply in specific circumstances, the arbitral tribunal is required to take more straightforward actions to address these challenges. If individuals decide to use high-risk AI systems, the arbitral tribunal must take more decisive actions, including technical and organizational measures. They may also cover specialized training. In addition, "Arbitral tribunals must retain the logs automatically generated by the high-risk system used for at least six months".[15]

Importantly, the EU AI Act implies penalties in the case of violations of these provisions. However, each Member State is obliged to specify its own punishment. Under Article 99(4)(e) of the EU AI Act, the maximum fine for breaches of these obligations shall be up to 15 million EUR.

Overall, in the case of work of arbitral tribunals, the use of AI systems as (preparatory) activities that are far from determining and interpreting both facts and legal provisions alongside applying the law to specific facts do not fall within the scope of high-risk systems. Even if such AI systems are used "to assist in the determination and interpretation of facts and legal provisions and in the application of the law to specific situations" that may not be categorized as high-risk in the case of complying with the conditions specified in Article 6(3) of the EU AI Act. Despite these two specific circumstances, all other AI systems are deemed to be classified as high-risk. In this light, it is worthwhile to note that although there is no explicit reference to AI systems replacing human behavior or the personal mandate of an arbitrator, they are likely forbidden under the EU AI Act. Generally, AI systems are supposed to be exempt from being classified as high-risk under Article 6(3) of the EU AI Act. However, arbitral tribunals are encouraged to assess the potential application of the EU AI Act to their systems. Such measures are necessary to fulfill the obligations arising from the EU AI Act along with some potential legal consequences in this regard.[16]

Second, the personal scope of the EU AI Act refers to the distinction between various entities. Under the EU AI Act, deployers means "a natural or legal person, public authority, agency or other body using an AI system under its authority except where the AI system is used in the course of a personal non-professional activity".[17] In this light, it is worth noting that "Members of an arbitral tribunal are natural persons with a personal mandate and cannot act as legal entities. Arbitral institutions should also be considered in the personal scope of application, although

14 C. Lüttenberg, I. Beimel, S.J. Heetkamp, *How does the EU...*

15 *Ibidem.*

16 *Ibidem.*

17 *Regulation (EU) 2024/1689...*, Article 3(4).

their administrative work is less likely to fall within the category of high-risk AI systems".[18] Further on, deployers of high-risk activities are also required to abide by various regulatory obligations arising from Article 26(1) of the EU AI Act. Given this provision, "Deployers of high-risk AI systems shall take appropriate technical and organisational measures to ensure they use such systems in accordance with the instructions for use accompanying the systems".[19]

Third, the territorial scope of the EU AI Act applies in the case of "deployers of AI systems that have their place of establishment or are located within the Union" and "providers and deployers of AI systems that have their place of establishment or are located in a third country, where the output produced by the AI system is used in the Union" (see: Article 2(1)(b) and (c).[20]

In practice, the provisions of the EU AI Act may have significant implications for arbitral proceedings, albeit not straightforward. From the literal wording of Article 2(1)(b) of the EU AI Act, we may deduce an unworkable scenario. For example, in the case of a three-member arbitral tribunal, the EU AI Act will be applicable merely to those arbitrators who either have their domicile or are based within the EU. Therefore, to avoid this kind of inconsistency with regard to the treatment of the arbitral tribunal's members, it is thus recommended to make use of the collective link to the seat of the arbitral tribunal. Despite the efforts to anchor jurisdiction to the seat of the arbitral tribunal, "if the arbitral tribunal comes from EU Member States but its seat is located outside the EU, the AI Act would not apply".[21] This begs the question of whether the drafters of the EU AI Act intentionally included such provisions and thus associated its application to the seat of the arbitral tribunal. Such a theory seems to be doubtful and questionable on the grounds of Article 2(1)(b) which refers to the deployers that are located within the EU.

Moreover, from scratch, the EU AI Act has the aim "to protect against the harmful effects of AI systems in the Union".[22] Even though Article 2(1)(c) may partially offset the inconsistent treatment mentioned above, there are more ambiguities in view of the following phrase: "the output produced by the AI system is used in the Union".[23] Therefore, these provisions can have a significant impact on the arbitral award. In the case of AI systems used by the arbitral tribunal, the output influences the award, and further it also has some legal consequences for the party based within the EU. In practice, the wording included in the EU AI Act may pose many questions. To name a few, "is the location of one of the parties in the EU thus sufficient to conclude that the 'output produced by the AI system is used in

18 C. Lüttenberg, I. Beimel, S.J. Heetkamp, *How does the EU AI Act apply to arbitration?*, "Daily Jus" January 14, 2025, https://dailyjus.com/legal-tech/2025/01/how-does-the-eu-ai-act-apply-to-arbitration. Accessed on April 25, 2025.

19 *Regulation (EU) 2024/1689...*, Article 26(1).

20 *Ibidem*, Article 2(1)(b) and (c).

21 C. Lüttenberg, I. Beimel, S.J. Heetkamp, *How does the EU...*

22 *Regulation (EU) 2024/1689...*, Recital 1.

23 *Ibidem*, Article 2(1)(c).

the EU"? Or, otherwise, is it sufficient that an award could ultimately be enforced against assets located in the EU"?[24] Any positive answer to these questions could be equal to significant extraterritorial consequences of the EU AI Act. In practice, this means that "it could apply even if the seat of the arbitration is outside the EU, the arbitrators are based outside the EU, and one of the parties is located outside the EU".[25]

Last, four scope refers to the temporal effect of the EU AI Act, most notably with regard to the high-risk systems that will apply 24 months after its coming into force (Article 113).[26]

### *3.1.2 "Soft law" regulations on using AI*[27]

The term "artificial intelligence" (AI) seems ambiguous and difficult to define. Nevertheless, it is worth noting that on November 23, 2023, the United Nations Educational, Scientific and Cultural Organization (UNESCO) issued the Recommendation on the Ethics of Artificial Intelligence. The Recommendation was not adopted to provide a single definition of AI. Rather, it focuses on the features of AI systems that are crucially relevant from an ethical standpoint. This approach considers constant and rapid changes in light of technological development. From this perspective, AI systems have the capacity to process data and information. Because of this capacity, such systems exhibit intelligent behavior. In practice, this means they can engage in reasoning, learning, perception, prediction, planning, and control.[28]

The UNESCO Recommendation outlines three significant elements. The first considers the following:

> AI systems are information-processing technologies that integrate models and algorithms that produce a capacity to learn and to perform cognitive tasks leading to outcomes such as prediction and decision-making in material and virtual environments. AI systems are designed to operate with varying

24 M. Scherer, *We need to talk...*

25 *Ibidem.*

26 *Ibidem.*

27 International Council for Commercial Arbitration (ICCA) also referred to the use of AI within its newly adopted sourcebook. According to Article 10, "To the extent that the use of artificial intelligence in the arbitration by the arbitral tribunal, the parties and other participants is not regulated by the applicable law or institutional, ad hoc or other rules chosen by the parties, the tribunal and the parties shall discuss, as early as possible, whether to have regard to any published or other guidelines on the use of artificial intelligence in arbitration". See more: *ICCA Drafting Sourcebook for Logistical Matters in Procedural Orders with the Assistance of the Permanent Court of Arbitration Peace Palace, The Hague*, "The ICCA Reports No. 2: Kigali Special Edition" 2025, p. 5, https://cdn.arbitration-icca.org/s3fs-public/document/media_document/ICCA%20Drafting%20Sourcebook%20Kigali%20Edition.pdf. Accessed on June 25, 2025.

28 *UNESCO Recommendation on the Ethics of Artificial Intelligence issued on 23 November 2023*, United Nations Educational, Scientific and Cultural Organization (UNESCO), https://www.unesco.org/en/legal-affairs/recommendation-ethics-artificial-intelligence. Accessed on October 13, 2024.

> degrees of autonomy by means of knowledge modelling and representation and by exploiting data and calculating correlations.[29]

Additionally, the Recommendation outlines a few methods that AI systems can use: machine learning (ML) and machine reasoning (MR). The former includes deep learning and reinforcement learning, while the latter refers to "planning, scheduling, knowledge representation and reasoning, search, and optimization".[30]

The second element focuses on the ethical questions regarding the use of AI systems, which are crucial throughout the entire life cycle of AI systems. It is important from the initial research and design stages through deployment and use. It is worth noting that this element also includes maintenance, operation, trade, financing, monitoring and evaluation, validation, end-of-use, disassembly, and termination.[31]

The Recommendation also refers to actors involved in AI, which can be broadly defined as "any actor involved in at least one stage of the AI system life cycle, and can refer both to natural and legal persons, such as researchers, programmers, engineers, data scientists, end-users, business enterprises, universities and public and private entities, among others".[32]

The final third element addresses novel ethical concerns associated with the implementation of AI systems. Consequently, the focus is directed towards the:

> decision-making, employment and labour, social interaction, health care, education, media, access to information, digital divide, personal data and consumer protection, environment, democracy, rule of law, security and policing, dual use, and human rights and fundamental freedoms, including freedom of expression, privacy and non-discrimination.[33]

Such ethical challenges are fueled by the potential threats and risks related to the use of AI algorithms, which may lead to the production or reinforcement of existing biases. This phenomenon may consequently lead to an escalation in discrimination, prejudice, and stereotypes.[34]

Subsequent sections delve into the "soft law" regulations on using AI that have been adopted by various arbitral institutions.

#### *3.1.2.1 AAA-ICDR*

The American Arbitration Association – International Centre for Dispute Resolution (AAA-ICDR) introduced a set of guidelines covering AI use in ADR in November 2023 and thus became the first arbitral institution to pay attention

29 *Ibidem.*
30 *Ibidem.*
31 *Ibidem.*
32 *Ibidem.*
33 *Ibidem.*
34 *Ibidem.*

to these issues. The so-called "Principles Supporting the Use of AI in Alternative Dispute Resolution" have been launched for the sake of "enhancing ADR practices through AI, balancing innovation with [our] enduring commitment to legal integrity and service excellence".[35] These rules aim to properly integrate the use of AI within the framework of alternative dispute resolution mechanisms with respect to both legal integrity and service. Therefore, these principles pay attention to "maintaining competence, confidentiality, advocacy, impartiality, independence, and process improvement when using AI".[36]

According to the first principle, namely competence, all participants of the ADR mechanisms, including legal professionals, arbitrators, and mediators, are obliged to be proficient in using AI technologies and understand not only benefits and risks but also their uses and ethical considerations. Therefore, to achieve this goal, it is recommended that such professionals constantly update their knowledge of new AI-technologies in order to better understand their advancements.[37]

Secondly, AAA-ICDR's Principles also pay attention to confidentiality issues while using AI tools. In practice, it is important to ensure the safety of sensitive data throughout actions aimed at prohibiting "unauthorized access, leakage, or misuse of confidential data". Such an approach is particularly important in the case of "large datasets, opaque machine learning models alongside uncertain data protocols".[38]

Thirdly, under the principle of advocacy, it is advised to promote not only the accuracy but also the expediency and candor of AI tools. This means that the AI tools may be applied and used merely in cases when best complying with the interests of clients and the integrity of the justice system.[39]

Fourthly, all outputs provided by the AI tools should be scrutinized carefully to ensure impartiality. In practice, participants using AI-powered systems should not over-rely on the generated content.[40] Given that, it is important to check the results provided by the AI and not take them fully for granted. Indeed, this principle is also linked to independence while exercising judgments.[41] In case of arbitral awards, there is no doubt that arbitrators have been appointed in a particular case based on their knowledge, experience, and expertise. Indeed, they are merely responsible for their awards and work. This entails that even if they take advantage of using

35 *Principles supporting the sse of AI in alternative dispute resolution*, "The American Arbitration Association®-International Centre for Dispute Resolution (AAA-ICDR)" November 2023, https://go.adr.org/rs/294-SFS-516/images/Principles%20Supporting%20the%20Use%20of%20AI%20in%20Alternative%20Dispute%20Resolution.pdf. Accessed on January 3, 2025.

36 André Guskow Cardoso, Elizabeth Chan, Luísa Quintão, Cesar Pereira, *Generative Artificial Intelligence and Legal Decision-making*, Global Trade and Customs Journal 2024, vol. 19, issue 11&12, p. 719.

37 Principles supporting the use of AI…, p. 1.

38 *Ibidem*.

39 Principles supporting the use of AI…, p. 2.

40 *Ibidem*.

41 *Ibidem*.

AI-powered tools, including GenAI, they must check the outputs to comply with principles and rules applicable in international arbitration.

Lastly, it is recommended to make use of AI tools for the sake of increasing not only accessibility, efficiency, but also fairness in terms of ADR mechanisms. Apparently, many AI-powered tools should already be seen as useful in view of handling administration, services, and related legal frameworks.[42] This approach confirms that it would be rather difficult to avoid AI tools in the daily life of arbitration work. Nevertheless, there is a need to find a balance between the implementation of such (Gen)AI-powered tools with respect to fundamental principles of international commercial arbitration.

Importantly, these Guidelines are rather rigoristic by suggesting that legal professionals should enhance their proficiency in AI technologies to fully understand not only benefits but also challenges and potential risks related to their use. Likewise, some ethical considerations arise because of considering AI integration as not complying with the principle of confidentiality and not compromising the quality of the arbitration process itself.[43]

In the wake of technological advancement, the AAA-ICDR decided to issue new rules governing the use of AI in the form of "Guidance on Arbitrators' Use of AI Tools" which were adopted in March 2025.[44] This Guidance is particularly dedicated to providing recommendations to arbitrators. Indeed, on the one hand, arbitrators are encouraged to embrace AI-driven tools. On the other hand, they are also obliged to abide by the Code of Ethics for Arbitrators in Commercial Dispute and the so-called Code of Professional Responsibility for Arbitration of Labor-Management Disputes. Both Codes have the aim of upholding fairness, integrity, and confidentiality of the arbitral proceedings, which are commonly considered a core value of arbitration.

This Guidance is divided into three parts, namely considerations when using AI tools, confidentiality and data protection, and competence and professionalism. The first part consists of four considerations that should be taken into account by arbitrators during arbitral proceedings. Accordingly,

> AI tools provide valuable assistance but occasionally generate incomplete or inaccurate information. Arbitrators should apply their expertise to critically evaluate and verify outputs and to ensure that information aligns with the standards of accuracy and reliability required in arbitration. When using AI tools, arbitrators should cross-reference outputs against primary sources to ensure accuracy.[45]

42 *Ibidem*.

43 A. Guskow Cardoso, E. Chan, L. Quintão, Cesar Pereira, *Generative Artificial Intelligence and Legal...*, p. 720.

44 *AAA-ICDR Guidance on Arbitrators' Use of AI Tools — March 2025*, https://go.adr.org/rs/294-SFS-516/images/2025_AAA-ICDR%20Guidance%20on%20Arbitrators%20Use%20of%20AI%20Tools%20%282%29.pdf?version=0. Accessed on June 10, 2025.

45 *Ibidem*, p. 1.

This recommendation aims to prevent overreliance on and unconscious replication of AI-generated output, as this can compromise due process, especially when inaccurate or false information is involved. The arbitrator is solely responsible for providing correct information in arbitral awards. This is particularly important given the need to maintain fairness and due process. Reliance on AI-powered tools to enhance the arbitration process must not compromise the principles of fairness and due process, which must always be the arbitrator's top priority. To avoid challenges related to fairness or due process, arbitrators must comprehend how AI-driven tools function, particularly in terms of their utility and limitations. This knowledge is necessary to assess the feasibility of incorporating these tools fairly into arbitral proceedings. Importantly, this approach aligns with Canon I of the Code of Ethics for Arbitrators in Commercial Disputes.[46]

Furthermore, arbitrators must maintain control over the decision-making process. While the use of AI-powered tools to support the arbitrator's work is permitted, it is strictly prohibited for these tools to replace the arbitrator's judgment and expertise. It is equally important to note that, even if arbitrators use AI tools for legal research or evidence analysis, they must ensure that the reasoning and evaluation processes remain independent.[47] This provision confirms that AI is merely a supportive tool and cannot substitute for a human arbitrator.

Arbitrators must also disclose their use of AI tools to the parties, especially if it could materially impact the arbitral proceedings or influence the reasoning behind the final decision.[48] It is crucial to maintain transparency with the parties in order to prevent challenges based on due process violations.

The second part stresses that arbitrators must protect confidential information while using secure tools and platforms complying with data security standards. It is equally important that arbitrators refrain from uploading confidential information, including party names or case-specific details, into AI systems unless they are certain that strict data protection measures are in place. To reduce these risks, the AAA-ICDR Guidance recommends using AI tools that comply with strict data security and confidentiality measures. These precautionary steps are crucial in upholding the principle of confidentiality and preventing the disclosure of sensitive information, whether intentional or not.[49]

Finally, arbitrators are encouraged to follow new technological advancements which might be useful in the course of arbitral proceedings. In addition, the AAA-ICDR emphasizes that "Many AI tools are intuitive and accessible, enabling easy incorporation into a practice. Developing proficiency with AI tools reflects an arbitrator's commitment to professionalism and continuous improvement".[50]

46 *Ibidem.*
47 *Ibidem.*
48 *Ibidem.*
49 *Ibidem*, p. 2.
50 *Ibidem.*

Overall, the newly adopted Guidance should be viewed as a means of helping arbitrators employ AI-powered tools in accordance with the fundamental principles of the arbitration process. Although these recommendations seem general, they address key issues related to the proper application of AI by arbitrators.

In May 2025, the AAA-ICDR issued additional regulations in the form of the "AAAi Standards for AI in ADR" ("Standards"), which provide solutions to be implemented by ADR administrators, neutrals, and advocates. Regarding arbitration, the Standards apply to arbitral institutions, arbitrators, and the parties' legal representatives. They include six different standards that should be implemented in the arbitral proceedings such as ethical and human-centric values, privacy and security, accuracy and reliability, explainability and transparency, accountability and adaptability.[51]

The first standard related to ethical and human-centric values requires cautious application of AI tools within arbitral proceedings. The arbitral institutions are encouraged to design AI systems that comply not only with ethical standards but also safeguard fair and unbiased outcomes alongside equity in dispute resolution. Therefore, the implementation of AI tools should be handled with respect to values and lead to mitigating biases. In turn, arbitrators who are willing to use AI tools are obliged to comply with the existing ethical obligations, most notably in terms of ensuring the human perspective in the process of rendering judgments while using AI. In addition, arbitrators should also carefully scrutinize the use of AI by parties and their legal representatives to mitigate possible risks of overreliance of one of the parties on AI-powered tools. From the perspective of parties' legal perspective, it is crucial to carefully verify the AI-generated outputs in relation to recognized legal principles which imply a duty of human control.[52]

Under the second standard, the key issue is to ensure both privacy and security. Arbitral institutions should thus manage data responsibly to protect not only data confidentiality but also integrity. It is also crucial to provide system reliability based on the undertaken measures for the sake of mitigating possible external threats and increasing operational resilience. In this light, arbitrators should confirm the privacy and security standards of any AI-powered tools which are used for document translation, analytics, scheduling, or any other purpose. Likewise, the same applies to legal representatives.[53] In fact, this standard plays a significant role in educating the different stakeholders of arbitral proceedings about both privacy and security. It is thus recommended to first verify these parameters of AI-supported tools prior to their use to comply with the best standards in arbitration.

Third standard concerns accuracy and reliability and thus seeks to mitigate challenges to hallucinated or biased outcomes generated by AI tools. This requirement applies equally to all actors of arbitral proceedings who should every time

51 *AAAi Standards for AI in ADR*, "AAA-ICDR" May 2025, https://go.adr.org/rs/294-SFS-516/images/AAAi_Standards_for_AI_in_ADR.pdf?version=0. Accessed on June 10, 2025.

52 *Ibidem*, Standard 1: Ethical and Human-Centric Values.

53 *Ibidem*, Standard 2: Privacy and Security.

verify the accuracy of such outcomes and their compliance with industry standards. Therefore, human oversight cannot be underestimated in this respect.[54]

The fourth standard refers to the principles of explainability and transparency. Under this concept, each participant of arbitral proceedings is required to understand the outputs generated by AI. This is particularly important in the case of arbitrators who should weigh the probative value of AI-produced outputs within the parties' submissions. In addition, they should carefully verify them in order to eliminate possible misstatements, bias, or dubious references. Accordingly, in case of any doubts, they should also seek clarification from AI and inform the parties about this process.[55] This standard reflects the need to provide a transparent process of rendering an arbitral award where all parties concerned can understand how such an award was reached. Currently, the AI systems often represent a "black-box" dilemma which is regarded as a challenge. More in-depth analysis concerning these challenges is provided in Chapter 4.

The fifth standard relates to accountability in using AI systems. From the perspective of arbitral institution, it is necessary to carefully choose the AI system as a provider of services that not only ensures reliable performance but also complies with the values rooted in international arbitration. Arbitrators, in turn, are required to enhance their working knowledge of AI capabilities and thus properly assess risks, benefits, along with ethical considerations. In this light, the AAAi Standards recommend remembering to "ensure [that] automated document summaries or data analysis [should] never overshadow firsthand examination of evidence and arguments".[56] Legal representatives should always apply human scrutiny of AI-generated outputs and confirm their compliance with international standards.[57]

The last, sixth standard, pays attention to adaptability. Such a flexible attitude towards using AI tools is necessary for the sake of enhancing a culture of innovation with respect to professional expertise. Therefore, arbitrators are encouraged to constantly update their knowledge on new technologies, including AI tools. Under these standards, they can "incorporate AI-assisted scheduling, translation, evidence organization, and other tools if they enhance clarity and minimize delays, but [they should] evaluate every dispute according to its unique context".[58]

In sum, one must note that AAA-ICDR encourages arbitrators to implement AI-powered tools within arbitral proceedings. On the other hand, it also seeks to implement a certain standard in using these tools to comply with the specificity and uniqueness of a particular dispute. Considering legal representatives, they are also encouraged to benefit from these AI-supported tools in order to better support the goals of international arbitration. Indeed, it can be achieved through streamlining

54 *Ibidem*, Standard 3: Accuracy and Reliability.

55 *Ibidem*, Standard 4: Explainability and Transparency.

56 *Ibidem*, Standard 5: Accountability.

57 *Ibidem*, Standard 5: Accountability.

58 *Ibidem*, Standard 6: Adaptability.

discovery, expediting legal research, and delegation of some administrative tasks to AI tools, among others.[59]

#### *3.1.2.2 SVAMC Guidelines of the use of artificial intelligence in international arbitration*

The Silicon Valley Arbitration and Mediation Center's (SVAMC) Guidelines on the Use of Artificial Intelligence in Arbitration ("Guidelines") are widely considered to be the first comprehensive regulations on AI acknowledged by the international arbitration community. These Guidelines were issued on April 30, 2024 for the sake of addressing the most recent issues related to the use of AI in arbitral proceedings. Importantly, the Guidelines include a definition of AI which "refers to computer systems that perform tasks commonly associated with human cognition, such as understanding natural language, recognising complex semantic patterns and generating human-like outputs".[60] One must note that there is no uniform and only one definition of AI widely accepted. In addition, the current definitions may also change and evolve based on the advancement of new technologies. Therefore, the Guidelines provide a relatively broad definition of AI to cover not only the already existing types of AI but also future ones which would be probably more "autonomous, complex, multifunctional, and probabilistic than traditional automation tools based on rule-based deterministic logic".[61]

In addition, the Guidelines have been adopted for the sake of establishing general principles on how to use AI in arbitration rather than strict rules to be followed. Therefore, these Guidelines aim to serve as advisory measures that could be easily adopted to both specific case circumstances and new technological contexts. Given that, the SVAMC Guidelines aim to enhance fairness, efficiency, and transparency of the arbitral proceedings while using AI tools. In practice, these rules may be incorporated fully or in parts depending on the parties' arbitration agreements and/or decisions made by the arbitral tribunal alongside in the course of arbitral proceedings, including Procedural Orders.[62]

These Guidelines recognize multi-faceted and multi-jurisdictional characters of arbitral proceedings globally. In the context of international arbitration which involves complex, cross-border disputes, the SVAMC principles are in line with new trends. Therefore, they could be applied in the case of "an arbitration seated in Paris, governed by Mexican law, with hearings in Hong Kong" which is not an exceptional case in this type of dispute resolution. Against this background, there is a need to compromise different domestic and international standards in view of using AI in arbitration. Furthermore, these Guidelines explain that they are not

59 *Ibidem*, Standard 6: Adaptability.

60 *Silicon Valley Arbitration and Mediation Center's Guidelines on the Use of Artificial Intelligence in Arbitration*, https://svamc.org/wp-content/uploads/SVAMC-AI-Guidelines-First-Edition.pdf, p. 8. Accessed on January 5, 2025.

61 *Ibidem*, p. 13.

62 *Ibidem*.

intended to replace the already existing and binding AI laws or regulations. By contrast, they should be seen as an additional international benchmark which lays down a foundation for further discussions over both the ethical and effective use of AI tools within the framework of international arbitration. As such, they intend to help all participants of the arbitral proceedings, including parties, tribunal, institutions and other actors to manage the proper integration and application of AI tools.[63]

It is also worthwhile to remember that modern AI systems benefit from machine learning, namely different types of computer science techniques that are useful in terms of not only learning patterns but also providing intelligent predictions. It is possible based on data that have been uploaded for the sake of their training. Indeed, machine learning algorithms were invented some time ago and they have been commonly applied by dispute resolution professions. To name a few examples, they were widely used for checking the spelling and grammar, email spam filters, optical character recognition ("OCR") or even machine translation.[64]

Importantly, the SVAMC Guidelines include seven different rules that should apply in international arbitration to provide a uniform standard on the use of AI within such proceedings.

###### 3.1.2.2.1 ALL PARTICIPANTS IN ARBITRATIONS

The SVAMC Guidelines identify three different rules that apply to all participants in arbitrations who are dealing with AI-powered tools.

According to the first Guideline, participants of arbitral process should be aware of the functionality, limitations, and risks of using AI. By limitations of such risks, the SVAMC means "their tendency to perpetuate biases contained in the training data, their propensity to mix up or invent information to fill gaps in knowledge, and their inability to identify the true logic or sources of information used to produce a given output".[65] Such an awareness is needed to properly mitigate not only limitations but also risks associated with the use of AI tools. This is particularly important in view of Generative AI. Currently, such tools are prone to perpetuating biases in training data, fabricating or distorting information as a response to filling gaps in their knowledge alongside lacking transparency in terms of reasoning processes or sources of information behind their generated outputs. To mitigate such pitfalls, it is thus recommended to review the terms of service along with data management practices prior to using such AI tools. This might be crucial in assessing whether a particular tool is in line with requirements on confidentiality, privacy, and data security, among others. Equally, being mindful of such limitations and risks, participants of arbitral proceedings should seek professional assistance from technical

63 *Ibidem*.
64 *Ibidem*, pp. 13–14.
65 *Ibidem*, p. 15.

experts. Moreover, the GenAI may also produce some erroneous, hallucinated, or biased content (discussed further).[66]

Second guideline refers to confidentiality which is commonly recognized as one of the fundamental principles of international commercial arbitration. Given this rule, all participants should carefully make use of their AI tools with respect to the existing obligations on safeguarding confidential information. Importantly, such information is defined broadly to encompass "privileged, private, secret, or otherwise protected data".[67] This means that all participants of arbitral proceedings should refrain from submitting any confidential information to AI-powered tools without proper review and authorization.[68]

In addition, while safeguarding confidentiality, all participants are also required to abide by policies regarding "recording, storage, and use of prompt or output histories and of any other confidential data submitted to the AI tool".[69] This guideline pays attention to precautionary measures to safeguard the essence of arbitration itself. It also has the aim to ensure the reliability of the proceedings and confidence that all the information provided within its framework would not go beyond the process of dispute resolution. This is particularly important in view of certain AI tools that may store information provided by users for various reasons and even claim their rights to all input information. In this regard, the use of publicly available AI tools during arbitral proceedings represents a risk in disclosing confidential information. On the other hand, both business-oriented or privacy-oriented AI tools and providers developed comparable functionality with stronger protection mechanisms to safeguard confidentiality. In this context, it is also advised to engage technical experts.[70]

Overall, this guideline does not recommend to fully reject AI tools but stresses their proper application in terms of safeguarding confidentiality in the case of submitting confidential information. Therefore, participants should first verify different AI-powered tools in view of their data use and retention policies to choose the one that offers the most secure solutions. It is also advised to redact or even anonymize data submitted to AI to minimize the potential negative consequences to the best extent.

The final, third guideline considers the need for disclosure. In general, the SVAMC Guidelines do not necessarily advocate disclosure of AI tools during arbitral proceedings. Instead, they recommend that such decisions be made on a case-by-case basis in light of the specific circumstances of a dispute. There is no doubt that due process and any applicable privilege would have a significant impact on that final decision.[71] On the other hand, the Guidelines admit that, in certain situations, a need for disclosure may result from professional conduct rules or as a tool

66 *Ibidem*, pp. 15–16.
67 *Ibidem*, p. 9.
68 *Ibidem*.
69 *Ibidem*.
70 *Ibidem*, p. 17.
71 *Ibidem*, p. 10.

preventing the other participants from being misled. Currently, due to the lack of more specific provisions, the disputes associated with the questions of AI-related disclosure should be dealt with using the existing procedures like the other types of disclosure. This means that the arbitral tribunal would normally resolve this issue under the procedural rules governing the arbitration.[72]

However, if any participant is willing to use AI tools, the SVAMC Guidelines recommend assessing such tools in view of the following factors: 1. "the name, version, and relevant settings of the tool used; 2. a short description of how the tool was used; and 3. the complete prompt (including any template, additional context, and conversation thread) and associated output".[73] In this regard, it is worth noting that the AI-generated content depends highly on both the inputs provided by the user and the characteristics of such AI system. For that reason, once a disclosure is necessary, it should provide enough information to reproduce and assess the results generated by AI. In practice, it thus means the disclosure of the entire conversation history along with additional materials that have been uploaded to the AI tool upon a prompt. Equally, this guideline also would apply in the case of other non-generative AI tools equipped with evaluative features, including recommender or classification systems.[74]

##### 3.1.2.2.2 PARTIES AND PARTY REPRESENTATIVES

The SVAMC Guidelines provide two specific principles dedicated particularly to the parties and their representatives. The first one refers to the duty of competence or diligence in using AI tools during arbitral proceedings. Under this rule, "party representatives shall observe any applicable ethical rules or professional standards of competent or diligent representation when using AI tools in the context of an arbitration".[75] In addition, it also provides a need to review the AI-generated content, if used, to prepare submissions. Therefore, the aim of such review is to check whether the output is accurate in view of a factual and legal standpoint. Both parties and their legal counsels shall bear a legal responsibility for any uncorrected mistakes or even inaccuracies resulting from the use of AI-powered tools in arbitration.[76]

This guideline outlines potential risks that may result from assigning some legal tasks to AI tools. For example, if a party representative asks AI to summarize cases, write parts of briefs or oral submissions, or conduct legal research, a lack of review of the AI-generated output may lead to information far from the factual and legal perspective. Depending on the Generative AI tool, it may produce errors or even hallucinations alongside incorrect legal citations or mistakes regarding both

72 *Ibidem*, p. 17.
73 *Ibidem*, p. 10.
74 *Ibidem*, p. 17.
75 *Ibidem*, p. 11.
76 *Ibidem*.

the presentation and interpretation of facts, evidence, and legal authorities. In this regard, it is possible that the arbitral tribunal and opposing party may ask a party, witness, or expert more detailed questions regarding the extent of AI-generated content. Even though there is no independent standard for conducting such a review, party representatives on record will bear legal responsibility in the case of non-compliance with this rule.[77]

Moreover, it is also crucial to remember that AI-induced errors are not equally severe. In practice, some mistakes may be either inadvertent, inconsequential, or have no effect on the arbitral proceedings. By contrast, sometimes AI-generated errors and hallucinations may significantly impact the integrity of the arbitration process or lead to a manipulated presentation of facts, law, or evidence. In practice, depending on the AI-induced errors, the arbitral tribunal may take different actions. In the case of an inaccurate submission because of AI use, the tribunal may decide to dismiss the submission, require the party to make necessary corrections, and lower credibility of such documents, among others.[78] Therefore, this guideline provides step-by-step advice on how to deal with possible errors in AI-generated content and how to overcome possible challenges in this regard.

Under the second guideline, parties, their representatives and experts should restrain from using AI-powered tools that might, even potentially, impact the integrity of the arbitration process or interfere with the conduct of arbitral proceedings.[79] Even though there are many benefits and advantages of employing AI tools, their potential misuse may compromise due process and lead to manipulation in view of the tribunals' findings.[80]

Likewise, it is also forbidden to use AI tools that may falsify evidence, undermine its authenticity, or mislead either the arbitral tribunal or the opposing party.[81] In this regard, it is also worth noting that GenAI, along with deepfake technologies, poses more risks in manipulating or falsifying evidence than before. In addition, developments in AI may even lead to producing fakes that are difficult to distinguish from authentic materials. However, it is also crucial to remember that fraudulent behaviors or misconduct, including the submission of false documents or engaging in the so-called "guerilla tactics"[82] may happen both with and without the use of AI.

In sum, the SVAMC Guidelines should be seen as a response to this challenging problem. They identify elevated risks and remind the parties that fairness and integrity are key issues in the arbitral proceedings. Given that, parties, their

77 *Silicon Valley Arbitration and Mediation*..., p. 18.

78 *Ibidem*.

79 *Ibidem*, p. 11.

80 *Ibidem*, p. 19.

81 *Ibidem*, p. 11.

82 See more: *Guerilla Tactics in International Arbitration*, ed. G.J. Horvath, S. Wilske, Wolters Kluwer 2013.

representatives and experts should restrain from using AI tools to undermine the fairness of the arbitration process in any case.[83]

#### 3.1.2.2.3 ARBITRATORS

The SVAMC Guidelines include two different recommendations for arbitrators willing to use AI in the proceedings. The first one refers to the non-delegation of decision-making responsibilities to any AI tool. This principle aims to present arbitrator's independence in terms of analyzing the facts, the law, and the evidence.[84] An arbitrator is equipped with the personal and non-delegable function of rendering an arbitral award. Therefore, he cannot simply transfer such power to an AI-powered tool. On the other hand, this guideline should not be seen as a prohibition or ban on using AI tools in order to support their independent analysis. This means that AI tools might be used for the sake of assisting arbitrators in their work, including both analyses of the facts, arguments, evidence, and the law as well as the process of rendering an arbitral award.[85] Even though AI tools have been designed to perform all these tasks, they should not replace human arbitrators in any case. As such, while acting as an arbitrator, he must fulfill his duties in terms of discretion, responsibility, and accountability. This guideline aims to avoid, even unintentional, transfer of the personal mandate of arbitrators to AI tools. To achieve this goal, an arbitrator must carefully assess any AI-generated output to verify its accuracy. In addition, he should also be fully responsible for any errors or inaccuracies resulting from using AI tools. Equally, once an arbitrator relies on AI to analyze arguments or draft partially a decision or arbitral award, he cannot merely adopt the AI-generated output without making sure that this content reflects his own personal and independent analysis of both issues and evidence in the ongoing arbitral proceedings. Indeed, this guideline should be considered a landmark in terms of reminding arbitrators that, despite the technological advancements, he is still personally responsible for rendering decisions and awards. Even though AI-powered tools may significantly improve efficiency and provide valuable insights, the arbitrator himself remains solely responsible for making final decisions. In this regard, the human element plays a critical role in view of preserving both the fairness and integrity of the arbitration itself.[86]

Under the second guideline, namely respect for due process, "an arbitrator shall not rely on AI-generated information outside the record without making appropriate disclosures to the parties beforehand and, as far as practical, allowing the parties to comment on it".[87] This provision safeguards not only transparency in the arbitral proceedings but also the parties' right to be heard. Equally, the obligations

83 *Ibidem*, p. 19.
84 *Ibidem*, p. 12.
85 *Ibidem*, p. 19.
86 *Ibidem*, p. 20.
87 *Ibidem*, p. 12.

to disclose the use of AI tools may differ depending on the particular AI tool that has been employed.[88]

It is also worth noting that certain jurisdictions employ the principle of *iura novit arbiter*[89] which means that "arbitrator knows the law." According to this principle, the arbitrator is allowed to apply laws, case law alongside precedents even if they have not been cited by the parties of the arbitral proceedings. In addition, it has been recognized by investment treaty arbitrations and the International Court of Justice (ICJ). The scope of such authority may be different across jurisdictions. This guideline, however, cannot be seen as an interference with the application of *iura novit arbiter*, if appropriate in a case.[90]

In addition, if the AI tool does not provide any sources related to its output that may be easily verified, an arbitrator must not assume that they exist or have been properly characterized by the AI tool.[91] This guideline requires that an arbitrator carefully evaluate any AI-generated output to ensure its reliability.

To sum up, one must note that these Guidelines are widely considered a landmark in establishing a principle-based legal framework for the use of AI within arbitral proceedings. Indeed, AI-powered tools have become much more popular and commonly applied in international arbitration. Therefore, the SVAMC Guidelines were introduced to provide all participants in arbitral proceedings with a framework in terms of the potential application of AI. In addition, it is worth noting that these Guidelines offer solutions that may be applied in both domestic and international arbitration. Nonetheless, the SVAMC Guidelines apply only once agreed upon by the parties or followed by the decision of the arbitral tribunal.

#### *3.1.2.3 Guide to the use of artificial intelligence in cases administered under the SCC rules*

In the wake of SVAMC Guidelines and the adoption of EU AI Act, the Stockholm Chamber of Commerce (SCC) also issued its own Guide to the use of artificial intelligence in cases administered under the SCC rules ("SCC Guide") which was adopted on October 16, 2024. This Guide refers to multifarious programs that represent capabilities linked to human intelligence. The SCC also repeated the definition of the artificial intelligence system that has been introduced in the EU AI Act under Article 3(1). In this light, AI systems are deemed to adopt their behavior

88 *Ibidem*, p. 20.

89 For a more thorough examination of the discussion regarding its application across civil and common law jurisdictions, refer to the following sources: C. Bao, *Iura Novit Arbiter: truth or fiction?*, "American Review of International Arbitration" 2022, vol. 32, issue 4; J. Jemielniak, S. Pfisterer, *Iura Novit Arbiter revisited: towards a harmonized approach?*, "Uniform Law Review" 2015, vol. 20, issue 1, pp. 56–80, https://doi.org/10.1093/ulr/unv009.

90 *Silicon Valley Arbitration and Mediation…*, p. 12.

91 *Ibidem*.

through the analysis of effects related to the previous actions. Based on such analysis, the AI systems can take their own autonomous decisions.[92]

On the one hand, the SCC Guide makes reference to various ways of using AI-powered tools within the context of arbitration, including legal research; concept searching; editing and proof-reading; translations and interpretations; transcriptions; generating briefing notes, diagrams, and summaries of texts; drafting communications and submissions; document production; document management; reviewing, analyzing, and presenting of evidence; drafting cross-examination questions; and arbitrator appointments and case-value analysis. This list is not exhaustive and expands constantly because of fast advancement in new technologies.[93]

On the other hand, the SCC Guide also highlights the potential of using AI tools in dispute resolution for the sake of reducing costs alongside increasing efficiency. However, the EU AI Act also classified certain AI systems used by arbitral tribunal "in researching and interpreting facts and the law and in applying the law to a concrete set of facts"[94] as high-risk systems. In this light, it is worthwhile to note that the SCC Guide does not prohibit the use of AI systems for these purposes. Instead, it requires us to consider four factors such as confidentiality issues, quality, integrity, and non-delegation of decision-making power.

Under the first factor, there is a need to pay attention to confidentiality while using AI-powered tools. It might result, even unintentionally, in the AI systems impacting confidentiality issues either by the arbitral tribunal or the parties of the dispute. Therefore, the SCC Guide encourages disclosing any use of these tools, including "how any data input is employed and deployed when using AI".[95]

Second factor refers to the quality of outputs generated by the AI systems. In this view, it is crucial to remember that both biases and incorrect or false information may result from using AI-powered tools. Equally, these systems may also generate false or manipulated evidence. To address this challenging problem, it is thus advised that "AI systems should be equipped with technical solutions to mark and detect AI-generated or manipulated content, using reliable and interoperable methods".[96] Following this recommendation may be crucial in determining any inconsistencies or hallucinations (discussed further) due to imperfect solutions employed by AI-powered tools. Given that, arbitral tribunals, being aware of such possible negative ramifications of AI systems, should ensure the adequate quality of their decisions. In this light, effective human oversight is needed to avoid possible reduction of quality in decisions made by arbitral tribunals. Practically, the SCC

92 *SCC Guide to the use of artificial intelligence in cases administered under the SCC rules*, "SCC Arbitration Institute" October 16, 2024, https://sccarbitrationinstitute.se/wp-content/uploads/2024/12/scc_guide_to_the_use_of_artificial_intelligence_in_cases_administered_under_the_scc_rules-1.pdf. Accessed on May 21, 2025.

93 *SCC Guide to the use of artificial intelligence*..., pp. 2–3.

94 EU AI Act, Recital 61, Annex III, 8(a).

95 *SCC Guide to the use of artificial intelligence*..., p. 3.

96 *Ibidem*.

Guide recommends the proper level of review and verification of AI-generated outputs prior to their use in arbitral proceedings.[97]

In view of the third factor, the integrity of arbitral proceedings is crucial in the successful operation of the arbitral tribunal. Therefore, to achieve this goal, both transparency and accountability are of key importance. They can be achieved through the disclosure of any AI use considering both research and interpretation of facts and the law or the application of the law to facts. Importantly, such a disclosure may also play a significant role in ensuring the parties' right to be heard alongside the arbitral tribunal's mandate.[98]

The last four factor relates to the non-delegation of decision-making mandate. In this context, the AI-powered systems can be used for the sake of supporting the decision-making process of arbitral tribunals. However, these systems cannot replace them. Importantly, arbitral tribunals should fully execute their mandate and thus it is forbidden to delegate both the decision and the reasoning to anyone or anything.[99]

Compared to the SVAMC recommendations, the SCC Guide is rather general in scope, albeit addressing the chief principles in using AI systems during arbitral proceedings. As such, it represents a framework of conduct without detailed advice in response to the fast-developing landscape of new technologies. One must admit, however, that these four factors are at the heart of arbitral proceedings, and they play a significant role in preserving the fundamental principles of international arbitration, namely due process and confidentiality. In this context, the SCC positions itself as a modern institution that seeks to keep pace with technological advancements. In addition, the SCC does not remain neutral in addressing challenges resulting from the digital era and thus would be seen as a reliable institution in view of using AI systems in arbitral proceedings.

#### *3.1.2.4 CIArb Guidelines on the use of AI in international arbitration*

The Chartered Institute of Arbitrators (CIArb), which is one of the leading and most renowned arbitral institutions globally, issued its "Guidelines on the Use of AI in Arbitration (2025)" on March 19, 2025. These Guidelines have been introduced to assist not only arbitrators but also parties, their representatives, and other actors of the arbitral proceedings in taking advantage of using AI while mitigating risks associated with the integrity of the arbitration, parties' procedural rights, and enforceability of arbitral awards or settlement agreements. The Guidelines have been divided into four parts, namely 1. Benefits and Risks of the Use of AI in Arbitration, 2. General Recommendations About Use of AI in Arbitration, 3.

97 *Ibidem.*
98 *Ibidem.*
99 *Ibidem.*

Parties' Use of AI in an Arbitration, and 4. Use of AI by Arbitrators.[100] At first glance, the structure follows the SVAMC Guidelines discussed above.

However, CIArb Guideline provides a legal definition of terms, such as AI, AI Tool, GenAI Tool, hallucination, Machine Learning (ML), Natural Language Processing (NLP), among others. Importantly, CIArb adheres to the definition of AI established by the OECD, namely:

> AI is a machine-based system that, for explicit or implicit objectives, infers from the input it receives, how to generate outputs such as predictions, content, recommendations, or decisions that can influence physical or virtual environments. Different AI systems vary in their levels of autonomy and adaptiveness after deployment.[101]

In addition, the definition of GenAI is based on the IBM website and refers to "an AI Tool consisting of deep-learning models capable of generating narrative text, computer code, financial analysis, mathematical calculations, graphics or other output which either serves as a substitute for human-generated output or materially modifies human-generated output".[102]

#### 3.1.2.4.1 GENERAL RECOMMENDATIONS

The general recommendations provide some guidance for both the parties and arbitrators. Prior to using the AI tool in arbitral proceedings, it is recommended to first understand its technology, function, and underlying data, most notably in terms of possible risks. This is essential in the context of minimizing possible negative ramifications of AI that may have an impact on "due process rights, the rule of law, the administration of justice, the credibility and legitimacy of arbitration, and the environment".[103] To achieve this goal, parties and arbitrators should investigate AI-related laws, regulations, and court rules in the relevant jurisdictions.[104]

Such recommendations are interesting, but they may result in many challenges in practice. First, neither party nor arbitrators are qualified as IT experts to assess the possible risks resulting from employing a specific AI tool. Nowadays, in the wake of launch of ChatGPT on November 30, 2022, many OpenAI sources have been developed globally, including a significant number of Chinese AI tools that are popping up like mushrooms after the rain. To name a few examples, fully up-to-date, there exist such tools as Ernie, DeepSeek, Qwen 2.5-Max, and Kimi, among others. Second, it might be difficult to predict possible ramifications on due process

100 *CIArb Guideline on the Use of AI in Arbitration (2025)*, p. 1, https://www.ciarb.org/media/m5dl-3pha/ciarb-guideline-on-the-use-of-ai-in-arbitration-2025-_final_march-2025.pdf. Accessed on April 25, 2025.

101 *Ibidem*, p. 2.

102 *Ibidem*.

103 *Ibidem*, p. 9.

104 *Ibidem*.

without further understanding of the functions and functionality of a particular AI tool. Likewise, it would be difficult, if not impossible, to prevent challenges to the arbitral award that has been produced with the support of an AI tool. The parties rarely share their further steps on where they will be seeking recognition and enforcement of an arbitral award.

In addition, the CIArb Guideline goes further and provides that "Unless the Tribunal and the parties expressly agree to the contrary in writing (subject to any applicable Mandatory Rule), the use of an AI Tool by any participant in the arbitration shall not diminish their responsibility and accountability that would otherwise apply to them without the use of an AI Tool".[105]

#### 3.1.2.4.2 PARTIES

CIArb Guideline gives arbitrators power to decide whether parties can use AI tools within arbitral proceedings. Given that, arbitrators may give directions for such use and take decisions in the form of procedural rulings, unless expressly prohibited by the parties or any mandatory laws, regulations, policies, and institutional rules. In addition, the arbitral tribunal may even appoint a special AI expert to understand the functioning of a certain AI tool or aspects, including some potential ramifications they may have on the ongoing arbitral proceedings. Importantly, under CIArb Guidelines, "arbitrators may regulate the use of AI by parties with a view to preserve the integrity of arbitral proceedings which they oversee and ensure the validity and enforceability of any ensuing awards".[106] This is essential in terms of the arbitrator's role, namely he is responsible for safeguarding the integrity of the arbitration process and the rendering of a valid and enforceable arbitral award. Given that, the arbitrator may take decisions that compromise the use of AI tools if he sees potential risks to the arbitration.

According to the CIArb Guidelines, an arbitrator is advised to record decisions concerning the use of AI tools in the form of procedural order. Such decisions can be changed during arbitral proceedings. However, "If the use of AI was contentious, the arbitrators may consider addressing the use of AI in its award".[107] Likewise,

> If parties fail to comply with directions or procedural orders on the use of AI, arbitrators should assess any impact of that failure on the proceedings. Arbitrators may thereafter take any measure to remedy that failure, make any further rulings on the use of AI, draw any appropriate conclusion (including drawing adverse inferences, if appropriate), or take such failure into account when awarding costs.[108]

105 *Ibidem*.
106 *Ibidem*, p. 11.
107 *Ibidem*.
108 *Ibidem*.

In practice, failure to comply with the AI procedural orders made by the arbitrator may imply some further implications, including additional costs of the arbitral proceedings. This begs the question, however, how such costs should be calculated.

On the other hand, it is recommended by the CIArb Guideline to fully respect the party's autonomy in making decisions on the arbitral proceedings. This means that the use of AI tools may be considered the same way as the other factors of the arbitration process, including seat, language, number of arbitrators, governing rules, etc. However, the fast development of new technologies changes the landscape of dispute resolution and implies new duties for arbitrators. Given that, "when the arbitrator receives a request for arbitration, it should ascertain whether and how the parties provided for the use of AI in their arbitration agreement".[109] Further on, if such agreement is silent or ambiguous in this regard, and thus parties have not discussed this issue in their early communications neither with the arbitral institution nor arbitrators, the arbitrators are deemed to take a proactive role in encouraging parties to express their will on that matter during the first case management conference or at a later point. Finally,

> The parties may discuss the subject of the use of AI. Although, the arbitrators may intervene in the discussion to clarify what AI Tools or classes of tools may be available to the parties, how they could be used in the course of the arbitral proceedings, any risks thereof (e.g., as to accuracy, privacy etc.), and any other issues of that the arbitrators or the institution consider the parties should be aware.[110]

In view of the above, the arbitrator should be familiar with different types of AI tools, their functions and possible ramifications they may have on the arbitral proceedings. This is crucial in view of ensuring the integrity and due process of the arbitration. In practice, it may require arbitrators to undergo special training on AI to better fulfill their role in the digital environment.[111]

In contrast, if the parties fail to reach a consensus over the use of AI in arbitral proceedings, arbitrators would be competent to make such a decision given the circumstances of the disputed case. When deciding whether to use AI or not, arbitrators should consider both potential advantages (for example, cost reduction or time efficiency) and possible risks. The latter refers to foreseeable impacts on the evidence, fairness, due process, and confidentiality issues, among others. It is thus necessary to assess not only nature but also the features of the AI tool. Given

109 *Ibidem*, p. 12.

110 *Ibidem*.

111 For instance, the Hong Kong International Arbitration Center (HKIAC) set up "the Hub" in response to fast technological advancement on May 9, 2025. Against this background, "The Hub aims to identify and respond to the evolving needs of arbitrators in a technology-driven world by (i) addressing practical challenges in the use of legal technology; (ii) fostering knowledge exchange through curated content; and (iii) providing structured, institutional support to accelerate technology adoption in arbitration". See more: *HKIAC Launches the Hub*, "HKIAC" May 9, 2025, https://www.hkiac.org/news/hkiac-launches-hub. Accessed on June 25, 2025.

that, arbitrators must analyze "data underpinning the output produced, the presence of any bias, as well as the quality, accuracy, and security of the AI Tool".[112] Consequently, many different factors must be considered prior to making a decision on the possible use of a particular AI tool during arbitral proceedings. To illustrate, in the case of any challenges regarding the biases of an AI tool, arbitrators should examine, if possible, data provided for model training. In addition, they may even require the party to disclose "any debiasing tools used within the model and any audits conducted for bias".[113]

In practice, this guideline reflects the need to verify logical reasoning in AI-generated outputs. In the case of any doubts, arbitrators should ask the parties about the links between their inputs and the content provided by GenAI.

In a nutshell, all participants of the arbitral proceedings should also abide by AI laws and regulations even if they do not explicitly focus on the arbitral proceedings. Importantly, such provisions may have a significant impact on both arbitrators' and parties' decisions regarding the use of a specific AI tool. In this regard, it may result in allowing, prohibiting, or limiting the use of AI tools in the course of the arbitration process. This is crucial, most notably in terms of some laws and regulations, which while being mandatory, may influence not only the validity but also enforceability of arbitral awards. Given that, compliance with general regulations on AI policy is needed to avoid any challenges and annulment of arbitral awards.

Further on, the CIArb Guidelines refer to disclosure of use of AI tools. It says that such disclosure may be mandatory in the case of AI tools that have an impact on the evidence, results of the arbitral proceedings, or "otherwise involve a delegation of an express duty toward the arbitrators or any other party".[114] In addition, disclosure may be needed to enhance transparency of the arbitration, preserve the integrity of the entire process, and/or ensure the validity and enforceability of arbitral awards. This means that the arbitrators may even require parties to make such AI disclosure, including party-appointed experts along with factual witnesses. In this view, "arbitrators may make directions as to the type of AI covered by the obligation to disclose, circumstances in which disclosure is required, to whom disclosure is to be made and within which timeframe".[115] An arbitrator may issue such a procedural order within the entire arbitral proceedings. Once a party is obliged to make an AI disclosure, an arbitrator further evaluates a party's compliance. Importantly, the arbitrator should also consider any inconsistency with regard to disclosure and the duty of confidentiality or any legal impediment that may explain its position in withholding specific case-related information. If a party fails to disclose the use of AI, the arbitrator may inquire of the party and ask for the party's comments on that issue.[116]

112 *CIArb Guideline on the Use of AI in Arbitration (2025)*, p. 12.
113 *Ibidem*, p. 13.
114 *Ibidem*.
115 *Ibidem*.
116 *Ibidem*.

In sum, in the wake of AI development, arbitrators are deemed to possess more technological knowledge and skills to provide parties with guidance and assistance on how to use such tools safely in arbitral proceedings. The CIArb Guideline provides detailed provisions reflecting this new trend in arbitration resulting from the increasing use of AI tools in the legal industry.

#### 3.1.2.4.3 ARBITRATORS

The CIArb Guidelines do not remain silent in discussing the use of AI tools by arbitrators for the sake of improving the arbitral process along with the quality of its decision-making. In general, arbitrators may use AI tools if they keep full control over the decision-making process and do not transfer it to AI. Given that, arbitrators must remain independent in their judgments. In addition, they should avoid using AI that could potentially compromise the integrity of the arbitral proceedings or the validity or enforceability of rendered arbitral awards. Arbitrators are also required to oversee independently the outcomes of AI-generated content, most notably in terms of its accuracy and correctness. Such precautionary actions are needed to avoid any biases and distortions in the arbitral awards. Furthermore, the CIArb Guidelines specify that "the Tribunal should avoid delegating any tasks to AI Tools, such as legal analysis, research and interpretation of facts and law, or application of the law to the facts, if such use could influence procedural or substantive decisions".[117] This provision should be regarded as a confirmation that AI is merely an additional tool aiming to enhance the efficiency of the arbitral proceedings. Importantly, AI has not been allowed in arbitration to replace arbitrators who are responsible for handling the processing based on their specific knowledge, experience, and skills. In practice, it may become difficult, however, to assess whether arbitrators abided by this rule. Despite this fact, arbitrators would still bear a legal responsibility with regard to all aspects of the arbitral award.

Interestingly, the CIArb Guidelines also recommend prior consultations with the parties over the arbitrator's use of AI. This solution aims to allow parties to make comments and express their willingness or objections to using such tools during their arbitral proceedings. As a result, "If the parties disagree on the use of AI by the arbitrators, the arbitrators should refrain from using the specified AI Tool".[118] Moreover, in the three-panel arbitrations, arbitrators should also discuss among themselves the use of AI in a particular proceeding.

In sum, the CIArb Guidelines provide relatively limited regulations on the use of AI by arbitrators. In brief, these recommendations are rather general and do not specify different types of AI tools. In practice, even AI-supported tools aimed at checking grammar and punctuation may be forbidden if the parties strongly reject AI in their proceedings. Therefore, too many simplifications in recognizing AI tools may lead to some challenges. These Guidelines are focused on the use of

117 *Ibidem*, p. 16.
118 *Ibidem*.

GenAI that could potentially compromise due process of the arbitral proceedings and result in challenging the arbitral award. This standpoint is commonly acknowledged by the international arbitration community. There is no doubt that AI is allowed only to support arbitrators in their daily work and not replace them. This begs the question of how to properly balance these approaches in taking advantage of new technologies, including AI solutions, with respect to the fundamental principles of the arbitration process. A set of recommendations addressing these questions will be provided in the book's conclusion.

Overall, the CIArb Guidelines are widely regarded as a milestone in the responsible adoption of AI tools in international arbitration. Importantly, they should therefore be seen as promoting innovation in the field of dispute resolution with respect to ethical standards. In this respect, they are also seen as an answer to some questions on how to properly address legal and procedural challenges arising from the use of AI-driven technologies in arbitration. In this context, it is worth recalling the EU AI Act which will enter into force in August 2026 and thus will have an impact on the AI systems used in the "administration of justice and democratic processes".[119] Arbitration itself also falls within the scope of this administration. This means that as of August 2026, arbitrators who use high-risk AI systems for the purpose of "researching and interpreting facts and the law and in applying the law to a concrete set of facts, or to be used in a similar way"[120] will have to comply with the EU AI Act. This is already evident in the CIArb Guidelines, most notably in the non-delegation of any tasks to AI concerning legal reasoning, fact-finding, and application of the law to the facts.

#### *3.1.2.5 VIAC note on the use of artificial intelligence in arbitral proceedings*

First and foremost, the Vienna International Arbitration Center ("VIAC") Note was adopted in April 2025 in response to the fast development of AI-powered tools. Apparently, it does not assume a specific definition of AI but instead seeks to cover a broad range of new AI-powered tools in response to the fast advancements in this field. This Note provides six rules to be followed by stakeholders participating in arbitral proceedings governed under the VIAC.

The majority of these provisions repeat the already existing recommendations such as ethical rules and professional standards, non-delegation of decision-making process, confidentiality standards. However, this Note includes more detailed information on the use of AI and its proper management by both parties and arbitrators. In this context,

119 C. Morgan, *AI-volution in arbitration: the new Chartered Institute of Arbitrators (CIArb) Guidelines*, "Herbert Smith Freehills" March 26, 2025, https://www.herbertsmithfreehills.com/notes/arbitration/2025-03/ai-volution-in-arbitration-the-new-chartered-institute-of-arbitrators-guidelines. Accessed on April 30, 2025.

120 *Ibidem*.

> Arbitrators shall, within their discretion and where they consider necessary, facilitate the parties' and any third parties' (e.g. experts, court reporters) understanding and use of AI tools. They may wish to discuss in the case management conference, the potential use of AI in them proceedings, the requirement of disclosure as well as the potential impact of AI on the arbitration timeline and costs.[121]

This recommendation requires that the arbitrator himself first understand the functioning of the AI tool and, based on his knowledge, guide the other stakeholders of arbitral proceedings about its possible use. In practice, it imposes a new requirement for arbitrators to enhance their technological competence[122] which becomes a new standard in the digital environment.

Equally important is the prior notification that the arbitrator himself is willing to use a certain AI tool, including the name and scope of tasks to be completed with this technological support. In response, the parties should be given the opportunity to comment on these AI-powered tools. Indeed, this requirement aims to protect the arbitrator from challenges to the arbitral award based on the violation of due process resulting from the lack of disclosure of AI in arbitral proceedings.[123] To mitigate these risks, the VIAC Note suggests reaching an agreement on the use of AI concerning both confidentiality and transparency in the form of Procedural Order No. 1, for example.[124] This rule is in accordance with the CIArb Guideline.

Interestingly, the VIAC Note explicitly refers to the use of AI regarding evidence. In this context, VIAC represents a rather flexible approach by stating that "In relation to the submission of factual and expert evidence, it is within the arbitrators' discretion to decide whether to request disclosure of evidence produced by AI or with the support of AI". It is also supplemented by the following provision: "It is within the arbitrators' discretion to determine the admissibility, relevance, materiality, and weight of any evidence produced by the parties with the support of AI".[125] Therefore, the arbitrator is fully responsible for making rules on the possible disclosure of AI-generated evidence.

Finally, the VIAC Note assumes no liability or responsibility in the case of any AI-related violations or breaches regardless of being an arbitrator or party within the arbitral proceedings held by the VIAC.[126]

121 *VIAC Note on the Use of Artificial Intelligence in arbitration proceedings*, "Vienna International Arbitration Center" April 2025, Art. 5.1, p. 3. https://www.viac.eu/wp-content/uploads/2025/04/VIAC-Note-on-AI-1.pdf

122 See more: S. Migliorini, *Automation & augmentation: Artificial Intelligence in international arbitration*, "Jus Mundi Arbitration Review" 2024, vol. 1, issue 1, pp. 119–130.

123 *Ibidem*, Art. 5.2, p. 3.

124 *Ibidem*, Art. 5.3, p. 3.

125 *Ibidem*, Art. 6, p. 3.

126 *Ibidem*, p. 4.

## 3.2 Human rights concerns on using AI in international arbitration

### *3.2.1 Right to a fair trial*

Richard Susskind analyzed the potential relation between AI and dispute resolution in his book entitled "Online Courts and the Future of Justice".[127] In this context, he sought to answer the question of whether "litigants always want judicial decisions, or do they simply want their problems resolved swiftly, efficiently, and fairly"?[128] Further, Susskind even stressed that "automated systems could, in the future, in many cases, provide quicker and more consistent outcomes than traditional courts, even if they are not perfect".[129]

Ensuring fairness in using AI systems is one of the key challenges. Even if the AI systems are seen as a response to the workload of humans while increasing accuracy, they also pose many new challenges related to human safety and autonomy. In this context, one of the most important concerns refers to the risk of bias (discussed further) that may even result in unjust decisions. It is crucial to address this challenge in view of ensuring the right to a fair trial. In addition, it is worthwhile to remember that AI systems are not equipped with common sense like humans. Under this concept, these systems lack causality which is understood as the ability to match cause and effect. In practice, it leads to far-reaching consequences. Therefore, "AI systems are not properly able to grieve a concept and apply a solution to a new, unknown problem".[130] In this light, it is important to remember that AI systems do not "reason" like humans do.[131]

The term "fairness" refers to a complex concept that requires an interdisciplinary approach. In fact, it lies at the intersection of legal and technical sciences, and thus both perspectives relate to each other. Importantly, despite the introduction of various methods for the sake of mitigating bias in AI systems, only a few of them fulfill legal requirements.[132] Fairness is commonly repeated in the legal sciences, albeit it still remains rather a theoretical concept that lacks a proper implementation in practice. It also introduces different dimensions. To illustrate, the first dimension refers to the understanding of fairness within the context of equality and equity. The former requires equal treatment for all individuals, whereas the latter considers justice in terms of distributing resources or opportunities depending on individual needs. In addition, "overall fairness refers to the principle that legal procedures and

127 R. Susskind, *Online Courts and the Future of Justice*, Oxford University Press 2019.

128 S. Embry, *AI-Powered arbitration: Is Arbitrus.ai the future of dispute resolution?*, "TechLaw Crossroads" February 20, 2025, https://www.techlawcrossroads.com/2025/02/ai-powered-arbitration-is-arbitrus-ai-the-future-of-dispute-resolution/. Accessed on April 23, 2025.

129 *Ibidem.*

130 M. Kattnig et al., *Assessing trustworthy AI: Technical and legal perspectives of fairness in AI*, "Computer Law & Security Review: The International Journal of Technology Law and Practice" 2024, vol. 55, p. 1.

131 See more: M.M. Louwerse, *Understanding Artificial Minds through Human Minds: The Psychology of Artificial Intelligence*, Routledge 2025.

132 M. Kattnig et al., *Assessing trustworthy AI...*, p. 2.

processes should be fair and impartial. This is commonly interpreted that all persons are equal in relation to the legal system and treated with dignity, respect, and equality".[133] This is particularly significant in terms of possible restrictions of rights or opportunities for individuals as a result of using AI systems. In this context, not only automated decision-making systems but also decision support systems may lead to problematic situations resulting from their data usage and potential impact on individuals.[134]

In practice, fairness also implies that both processes and procedures should be free from discrimination, bias, or prejudice towards individuals. In consequence, the proper processes maintained in the court system also affect people's image of procedural fairness. Equally, the existence of such fairness also impacts people's behaviors and thus their compliance with the law. According to Lind and Tyler, there are threefold elements of procedural justice, including the possibility to express an opinion, the recognition of the decision-making process in terms of a fair and unbiased process along with the adequate level of both respect and dignity as a reflection of positive behavior towards the parties.[135]

Furthermore, an examination of Tyler's concept reveals the presence of four elements associated with procedural fairness. In summary, these principles can be outlined as follows: voice, signifying the opportunity for expression (the right to be heard); neutrality, which is equivalent to the impartiality of the decision-maker; respect, exemplified by the proper treatment of the parties involved with dignity and courtesy; and trust, understood in terms of the perceived legitimacy of the process.[136]

Aside from the procedural fairness, there is also a substantive fairness which is reflected in the content and outcome associated with the decisions or processes. Thanks to substantive fairness, they reflect just and equitable decisions which are rendered as a result of assessing the merits and facts of a particular case. Compared to procedural fairness dedicated to the "fairness of the process that leads to a decision", substantive fairness pays attention to the decision itself.[137]

There is no doubt that AI is constantly changing the dispute resolution landscape by providing new solutions. To illustrate, Arbitrus.AI offers a service including the drafting of an arbitration clause that would allow Fortuna Arbitration's AI-driven system to settle disputes. This AI-powered tribunal ensures "fast, fair, and efficient dispute resolution".[138] Once purchased, Arbitrus.AI generates a Policy Number which allows initiating a case in its platform. In fact, this solution provides the same consequences as typical arbitration and thus decisions rendered by Arbitrus .ai are both final and binding upon the parties. As a fully AI-powered platform, it

133 *Ibidem.*
134 *Ibidem.*
135 *Ibidem.*
136 *Ibidem.*
137 *Ibidem.*
138 *Atribitrus.ai contract coverage*, "Arbitrus.ai", https://www.arbitrus.ai/contract. Accessed on April 27, 2025.

allows the handling of many different types of evidence, namely large documents, written testimony, video testimony, and photographs, among others.[139]

The Arbitrus.AI is thus a response to current challenges of arbitration itself, which is very often slow, expensive, and cumbersome. Brian Potts, who is the co-founder of this platform, designed this AI-powered tool for the sake of deciding matters within the framework of the contract. In the case of litigation, disputes are often not only unpredictable but also wide-ranging. In contrast, contractual arbitration concerns predefined issues and provides a testing ground for the AI-powered decision-making process. Even if there are many concerns over the idea of using machines to decide legal disputes, Arbitrus.AI addresses these challenges by providing services able to handle complex legal and equitable concepts. In this view,

> As Richard Susskind predicted back in 2019, the future of dispute resolution may increasingly reduce the level of human involvement but AI systems that provide fast, consistent, and fair decisions. By reducing the transactional costs of dispute resolution, AI could level the inherent unfairness where one side has ample resources and the other does not.[140]

In this sense, Arbitrus.AI seeks to complete this vision by providing AI services in the context of arbitration.

### *3.2.2 Due process*

#### *3.2.2.1 Hallucinations as a result of AI-generated false information*

Hallucinations[141] refer to AI-generated content that falls within two categories of being either fabricated or impossible to be properly verified. This poses serious risks to arbitral proceedings, most notably in the case of using such content without the careful scrutiny. It might have far-reaching consequences for all stakeholders in arbitration, including legal professionals who heavily rely on the content generated by AI tools. This is particularly challenging in the context of using these tools for the sake of collecting evidence or formulating legal arguments. In the wake of hallucinations produced by AI, various inaccuracies may interfere with the legal reasoning process through distortions that lack a factual basis. This may lead to compromising both the credibility and integrity of the legal argumentation.[142]

139 *Resolve your disputes in a fraction of the time*, "Arbitrus.ai", https://www.arbitrus.ai. Accessed on April 27, 2025.

140 S. Embry, *AI-Powered arbitration…*

141 Damien Charlotin follows the AI hallucinations cases on his website. Up to June 30, 2025, he identified 161 cases concerning the hallucinated content produced by the GenAI. The entire list of cases is available on the website: https://www.damiencharlotin.com/hallucinations/. Accessed on June 17, 2025.

142 Y. Abdel Latif, *Hallucinations in large language models and their influence on legal reasoning: Examining the risks of AI-generated factual inaccuracies in judicial processes*, "Journal of Contemporary Interdisciplinary Methodological Research & Development (JCIMRD)" 2025, p. 10.

LLMs, which produce such hallucinations, are widely considered a transformation of the Natural Language Processing (NLP) and thus they are equipped with strong performance in completing multiple tasks. Nonetheless, one must note that they usually generate inaccurate or even hallucinated outputs, most notably in the case of domain-specific or knowledge-intensive queries.[143]

In addition, it is worthwhile to mention that the so-called Masked Language Modeling (MLM) also contributes to generating hallucinated content. MLM is defined as:

> a training technique used in Natural Language Processing (NLP); a branch of AI focused on enabling machines to understand human language. In MLM, random words in a sentence are hidden or 'masked', and the model's task is to predict these missing words based solely on the context provided by the other words in the sentence. This process helps the AI to grasp language nuances, improve its comprehension, and become better at generating coherent, contextually appropriate text.[144]

Matthew Dahl et al. introduce the distinction between three different types of legal hallucinations. According to the first one, a model produces hallucinations that are inconsistent with or misrepresent the original query. This type of hallucination is commonly acknowledged as closed-domain or intrinsic hallucination. Importantly, these issues may play a significant role in completing tasks that need a high level of accuracy between the input and output. To illustrate, this is the case of machine translation or text summarization. Within the legal context, such inaccuracies may have detrimental consequences, most notably in the case of court decisions' summaries, drafts of legal texts and documents alongside the identification of crucial arguments set forth by the opposing party.[145] Equally, this type of hallucination may result in various negative ramifications in international arbitration. This applies particularly in the case of too much reliance on the AI-generated outputs, most notably in terms of summaries of the arbitral hearings, preparing requests for arbitration or statements of claim along with drafting of arbitral awards.

Second type of legal hallucination concerns the situation when the generated content "either contradicts or does not directly derive from its training corpus".[146] This type is, after Agrawal et al., widely known as open-domain or extrinsic hallucination. Ideally, the produced output should comply with the training data regardless of whether the information pertaining to this particular corpus is factually or objectively accurate. Within the legal context, this hallucination may result in

143 G. Agrawal et al., *Mindful-RAG: A study of points of failure in Retrieval Augmented Generation*, "2nd International Conference on Foundation and Large Language Models (FLLM)" 2024, p. 607, doi: 10.1109/FLLM63129.2024.10852457.

144 R.R. Khan, *The AI Glossary: Demystifying 101 Essential Artificial Intelligence Terms for Everyone*, CRC Press (Taylor&Francis Group) 2025, p. 76.

145 M. Dahl et al., *Large legal fictions: Profiling legal hallucinations in large language models,* "Journal of Legal Analysis" 2024, vol. 16, p. 67, https://doi.org/10.1093/jla/laae003.

146 *Ibidem.*

"challenges to those aiming to fine-tune the kind of general-purpose foundation models".[147] This concerns not only research memos but also templates or stylistic guidelines, among others. In this light, the content generated by the model complies with institutional knowledge alongside guidelines. Nonetheless, one must note that

> insofar as creativity is values, certain legal tasks – such as persuasive argumentation – might actually benefit from some lack of strict fidelity to the training corpus; after all, a model that simply parrots exactly the text that it has been trained on could itself be undesirable.[148]

In practice, the adjustment of the LLM model's temperature can result in enhanced creativity. On the other hand, it may also lead to more likely hallucinated outputs. Importantly, to define the contours of the "unwanted hallucinations" in a specific context, there is a need for value judgments which represent the balance between both fidelity and spontaneity.[149]

The last, third type of hallucination occurs in the situation when an LLM produces outputs that are far from fidelity to the real-world facts. This occurs regardless of how these LLMs have been trained or prompted. In fact, this is another type of open-domain hallucination that differs from the others by focusing on factual accuracy. In this view, the key issue is to verify whether the generated response really reflects the objective reality. Considering the legal field, "this is perhaps the most alarming type of hallucination, as it can undermine the accuracy required in any legal context where a correct statement of the law is necessary".[150]

In sum, the LLMs can generate hallucinated legal responses that are either factually incorrect or completely fabricated. Even though currently there is no universal definition of legal hallucinations, they refer to erroneous or illogical content produced by AI in the legal context. Nowadays, scholarly consensus upholds that hallucinations represent an inherent part of the LLMs. This means that irrespective of "the model's architecture, learning algorithms, prompting strategies, or training data, hallucination appears to be an unavoidable part of any calculable LLM".[151]

To address the shortcomings of LLMs resulting in hallucinations, the Retrieval Augmented Generation (RAG) techniques have been developed. Accordingly, the RAG allowed LLMs to draw upon and further incorporate external knowledge sources in the form of structured knowledge graphs (KGs). Even the integration of KGs does not solve all the problems related to producing inaccurate outputs for complex queries. There are twofold challenges in this regard such as reasoning failures and structural limitations. The former refers to the LLMs' difficulties in properly interpreting the user's queries and applying context-based cues. The

147 *Ibidem*.

148 *Ibidem*, p. 68.

149 *Ibidem*.

150 *Ibidem*.

151 B.A. Herrera-Tapias, D. Hernández Guzmán, *Legal hallucinations and the adoption of Artificial Intelligence in the judiciary*, "Procedia Computer Science" 2025, vol. 257, p. 1187.

latter, in turn, concerns failures arising from inadequate attention to the organization of knowledge sources (i.e. knowledge graphs) alongside the reliance on irrelevant evaluation metrics.[152]

Garima Agrawal et al. believe that the so-called Mindful-RAG might be a solution to these challenges. Under this concept, the Mindful-RAG is considered:

> an approach that re-engineers the retrieval process to be more intent-driven and contextually aware. Mindful-RAG is not merely an alternative method; it represents a comprehensive approach aimed at the development of more effective KG-RAG systems. Unlike traditional methods that primarily rely on semantic similarity or structural cues, Mindful-RAG suggests to leverage the intrinsic parametric knowledge of LLMs to accurately discern the intent behind queries. This approach not only guides the retrieval process to ensure that the extracted context from the KG is relevant but also aligns it with the original intent of the query. Additionally, Mindful-RAG introduces advanced contextual alignment techniques for efficient knowledge graph navigation and incorporates a validation step to ensure the generated response meets the intended requirements.[153]

Overall, to ensure that generated content is not only legal but also contextually appropriate, it is necessary to address the randomness of the LLMs' processes. To achieve this goal, prioritizing the so-called deterministic decoding techniques, in the form of beam search, is highly recommended. Indeed, they provide more reliable and consistent outputs compared to sampling-based approaches. Furthermore, the incorporation of an error-checking layer is needed to identify any differences concerning legal reasoning, citation accuracy, or even procedural steps. In this light, the creation and further development of hybrid systems that combine parametric (stored) knowledge with external resources, namely databases, case law repositories alongside live updates, are widely seen as a solution to the current situation. Therefore, the case-specific evidence precedence would prevail over general knowledge.[154]

Lastly, in order to accurately interpret laws and evidence, LLMs should be equipped with more structured legal frameworks. They should also rely heavily on enhanced legal reasoning and logic systems. It is equally crucial to provide transparency and explainability in generating outputs (discussed further). These features would play a significant role in outlining the model's reasoning process alongside references to applicable legal sources and facts. This is essential for allowing users to understand and verify the AI-produced content.[155]

152 G. Agrawal et al., *Mindful-RAG: A Study...*, 607.

153 *Ibidem.*

154 B.A. Herrera-Tapias, D. Hernández Guzmán, *Legal hallucinations and the adoption...*, p. 1187.

155 *Ibidem*, p. 1187.

#### *3.2.2.2 Biases in AI decision-making*

The predictive model is based on the data which are widely considered the core component therein. The data used for the model's training may lead to undesirable properties, most notably within the context of the decision-making process. Accordingly, these properties are commonly recognized as biased,[156] even if they can be classified either as statistical or societal biases. The former refers to non-representative sampling and a measurement error. The latter, in turn, includes social structures and the so-called past injustices that have already existed within particular data. Therefore, once biased data is used for the sake of training a predictive model, it can result in undesirable properties. To address this challenging problem, it is thus crucial to properly identify any biases and to mitigate even potential influence on the trained model.[157]

In fact, there are various types of biases that can result from "the origin of data, the chosen processing steps and methods, or even the selection of training and evaluation metrics".[158] In order to mitigate this risk, the feature hunting opts for a greedy approach which tests different features to classify tasks prior to identifying the highest improvement. This approach is recommended instead of testing features following a hypothesis. On the other hand, Hellström et al. advocate for a different approach, namely the taxonomy of various types of bias. Under this concept, aside from the bias existing within the data, there are also many different biases such as those resulting from "historical or social norms, learning bias of the model and evaluation bias".[159]

To name a few examples of bias after Kattnig et al., it is worth recalling algorithmic, historical, representation, sampling, measurement, omitted variable, aggregation, evaluation, and popularity biases. Even if this list is not exhaustive, it already represents a set of problems existing in predictive models. Under the concept of algorithmic bias, the bias itself is not reflected in the present data. In contrast, it results from the algorithm's structure alongside design decisions. In practice, this model can lead to different outcomes in unfairly treating groups depending on specific conditions. Unlike humans, AI systems are not equipped with intuitive judgment or common sense and thus they cannot make nuanced decisions. In practice, their limitations in properly interpreting the context of the situation can further influence the results. In addition, these systems cannot distinguish correlation from causation. In this light, AI systems need further training data. Even though computational tools are designed to identify and reduce biases in certain data sets, they

156 See more: M.F. Labanieh et al., *Navigating legal and ethical conundrums of using AI-generated content (AI-GC) systems in arbitration*, "Proceedings of the 12th UUM International Legal Conference 2023 (UUMILC 2023)", pp. 271–281, doi: 10.2991/978-94-6463-352-8_21.

157 M. Kattnig et al., *Assessing trustworthy AI...*, p. 8.

158 *Ibidem.*

159 *Ibidem.*

fail to address deeper social, cultural, and ethical dimensions associated with both biases and discrimination.[160]

The second type refers to historical bias, which is based upon the pre-existing inequalities and socio-technical issues embedded in the real world. In this context, it is worthwhile to note that such biases exist despite the data that are perfectly measured and sampled. In addition, these AI models can generate harmful or discriminatory outputs. In fact, this type of bias is associated with gender, ethnicity, cultural norms, alongside social structures.[161]

Third, the so-called representation bias occurs if the collected data do not properly reflect the existing diversity within the population. Following this bias, the datasets may also be non-representative or unbalanced. Given that, certain subgroups may be excluded, or other anomalies may exist. Due to these shortcomings, the AI models can generate unfair results, most notably for minority groups.[162]

Fourth, sampling bias resembles the previous one and arises in the situation when the training data does not represent the target population. In practice, some groups are disproportionately represented, or they can be omitted in the dataset in view of the actual distribution in society. This may lead to overrepresentation of groups or discrimination against those who are underrepresented.[163]

Fifth, measurement bias results from the fact "how features are chosen, utilized, and measured".[164] In this regard, there are features or labels serving as proxies for broader concepts. In addition, "If those proxies are poor reflections or the target constructs are computed differently across groups, these proxies become problematic. Hence, this bias results from using mismeasured proxy features".[165]

Sixth, omitted variable bias reflects the situation when important features have not been taken into account by the model in generating output.[166] To properly assess the situation, the model needs to analyze the overall situation to produce a trustworthy result.

Seventh, the aggregation bias refers to generalizations about individuals that are based on the data concerning the entire population. Under this bias, the relationship between inputs and outputs is the same in all subgroups. This arises due to wrongly applied patterns that have been observed in one group and thus there is an assumption about their significance to others, even if meaningful discrepancies between them exist. Accordingly, this generalization can lead to inadequate performance of the model on all subgroups and thus there is no group properly represented in any case.[167]

160 *Ibidem.*
161 *Ibidem.*
162 *Ibidem.*
163 *Ibidem.*
164 *Ibidem.*
165 *Ibidem.*
166 *Ibidem.*
167 *Ibidem.*

Eight, evaluation bias arises in the case of a model that goes through assessment based on a benchmark dataset. In fact, this dataset does not fully refer to the intended target population. Even if the models themselves are trained according to the specific datasets, their performance is assessed through the benchmark datasets. This means that such datasets are considered standard tools in terms of comparing different machine learning models. Nonetheless, it might also occur that these benchmarks are neither diverse nor representative. Given that, they perform well merely on the benchmark subset, which can be even preferred by mistake.[168]

The last, ninth example of bias is commonly known as popularity bias. In this case, the recommender systems favor items with a higher number of ratings or interactions compared to less frequently rated ones. Accordingly, these items become more popular and much more recommended than the less rated, despite the actual user performances. Even if the bias might appear harmless, it might also result in mismatched recommendations that are contrary to individual interests. To illustrate, "this bias might seem unproblematic, however, e-Recruiting recommender system might be used to recommend applicants to a recruiter, based on their profiles. Whereby the profile or specific attributes of applicants might amplify this bias and lead to an unfair distribution of exposure".[169]

#### *3.2.2.3 Discrimination*

To start with, it is worthwhile to note that some observers focus on discriminatory AI, which is regarded as a danger, whereas others see AI as a solution to end discrimination. Before making a more in-depth analysis of the discrimination issues while using AI tools, it is advised to remember that human decision-making also includes prejudices and stereotypes. Indeed, properly designed algorithms may even avoid this type of situation and identify hidden forms of discriminations.[170]

AI might have a discriminatory effect in different situations. To illustrate, algorithms can even reinforce entrenched social inequalities and stereotypes in the case of being trained on datasets reflecting these features. In addition, the predictions made by AI can be difficult, if not impossible, to verify.[171]

First, the discriminatory effect of AI may be seen in the case of profiling and using this tool in decision-making. The term 'profiling' is defined in the General Data Protection Regulation (GDPR) and "means any form of automated processing of personal data consisting of the use of personal data to evaluate certain personal aspects relating to a natural person, in particular to analyse or predict aspects concerning that natural person's performance at work, economic situation, health,

168 *Ibidem.*

169 *Ibidem.*

170 A. von Ungern-Sernberg, *Discriminatory AI and the Law: Legal Standards for Algorithmic Profiling* [in:] *The Cambridge Handbook of Responsible Artificial Intelligence: Interdisciplinary Perspectives*, ed. S. Voeneky, P. Kellmeyer, O. Mueller, W. Burgard, Cambridge University Press 2022, p. 252.

171 *Ibidem*, pp. 252–253.

personal preferences, interests, reliability, behaviour, location or movements".[172] In this light, profiling relates to the automated process which can have an impact on humans, most notably those who rely heavily on the outcomes generated by AI such as patterns, correlations, and prediction of human characteristics. Therefore, the term "profiling algorithm" can be described as "intelligent". This means that such an algorithm has been designed to solve a particular problem. This is mainly possible due to the predictions concerning unknown facts which derive from pattern-based analysis.[173]

The process of profiling requires several steps to be achieved, including (1) collecting data for the sake of training; (2) building a model in order to predict outcomes grounded on specific predictors (the so-called training algorithms); and (3) the application of this model to a certain person (based on the screening algorithm). Importantly, both the first and the last steps are related to the processing of personal data, whereas the second step relies on anonymized data.[174] In addition, one must note that

> Data protection law only applies to personal data, i.e. information relating to an identified or identifiable natural person. Since it is not necessary to train a profiling algorithm on personalised data, datasets are regularly anonymised before the second step. Some authors suggest that data subjects whose personal data have been collected during the first step should have the right to object to anonymisation, as this also constitutes a form of data processing.[175]

In fact, these findings are crucial in three ways. First, discriminatory AI algorithms might have an impact on selecting the arbitrator for a particular case. If the algorithm acts in such a discriminatory way, it might reject a person, even with better qualifications and experience, based on these unfair factors. Second, this type of AI could also harmfully evaluate one of the parties and thus produce outcomes against this party. Apparently, these generated contents could compromise the principle of equality and thus the due process as well. Finally, the use of discriminatory AI could also have far-reaching negative consequences in the case of assessing the witness's credibility and his testimony. In fact, this tool could make decisions based on high-context culture, for instance. Overall, these examples already confirm that AI-driven profiling might include discriminatory features that would enhance the imbalances in the arbitral proceedings. It is thus advised that both arbitral institutions and tribunal scrutinize the outcomes provided by AI to overcome this kind of obstacles and challenges.

172 Regulation (EU) 2016/679 of the European Parliament and of the Council of April 27, 2016 on the Protection of natural persons with regard to the processing of personal data and on the free movement of such data, and repealing Directive 95/46/EC (General Data Protection Regulation), Article 4(4), https://eur-lex.europa.eu/legal-content/EN/TXT/HTML/?uri=CELEX:32016R0679. Accessed on June 5, 2025.

173 A. von Ungern-Sernberg, *Discriminatory AI and the Law*..., p. 254.

174 *Ibidem*, pp. 254–255.

175 *Ibidem*, p. 255.

In the case of decision-making, it is thus recommended to follow anti-discrimination law[176]. In this context, it is worthwhile to note that the anti-discrimination laws are applicable not only to human decisions but also to those generated by machines. This means that this law does not presuppose the existence of humans as an indispensable factor to render a decision. In this view, "it is not relevant for anti-discrimination law whether a decision has been made solely by an algorithm, solely by a human being (based on the profile), or by both (i.e. by a human being accepting or not objecting to the decisions suggested by an algorithm)".[177]

### *3.2.3* ***Privacy***

The term privacy[178] is included in institutional rules. In this light, it is crucial to note that national laws are silent in this respect. This is mainly since national laws do not provide any specific provisions regarding third parties' involvement in arbitral proceedings. It results from the lack of a parallel framework within the UNCITRAL Model Law concerning the privacy of international commercial arbitration. This loophole is filled by the rules of arbitral institutions which opt for presumptive privacy in the case of arbitral hearings.[179] To illustrate, Article 26(3) of the ICC Rules stipulates that

> The arbitral tribunal shall be in full charge of the hearings, at which all the parties shall be entitled to be present. Save with the approval of the arbitral tribunal and the parties, persons not involved in the proceedings shall not be admitted.[180]

176 See more: J. Gerards, F. Zuiderveen Borgesius, *Protected grounds and the system of non-discrimination law in the context of algorithmic decision-making and artificial intelligence*, "Colorado Technology Law Journal" 2022, vol. 20, pp. 1–55.

177 A. von Ungern-Sernberg, *Discriminatory AI and the Law...*, p. 257.

178 See more: C. Bartneck, C. Lütge, A. Wagner, S. Welsh, *An Introduction to Ethics in Robotics and AI*, Springer, 2121, pp. 61-70.

179 N. Teramura, L. Trakman, *Confidentiality and privacy of arbitration in the digital era: pies in the sky?*, "Arbitration International" 2024, vol. 40, p. 285, https://doi.org/10.1093/arbint/aiae017.

180 International Chamber of Commerce (ICC) Arbitration Rules, in force as of January 1, 2021, Article 26(3), https://iccwbo.org/wp-content/uploads/sites/3/2020/12/icc-2021-arbitration-rules-2014-mediation-rules-english-version.pdf. Accessed on June 6, 2025.

Likewise, many other arbitral institutions, including for instance SIAC,[181] HKIAC,[182] and DIAC[183] followed the same rules admitting the default privacy nature in the case of arbitral hearings.

Nonetheless, one must note that privacy has not been fully covered by arbitral rules and thus omit more detailed provisions regarding concerns in using AI tools in international arbitration that would compromise the privacy issues. Apparently, there are various practical challenges to the use of generative AI, most notably related to privacy during arbitral proceedings. In this context, it raises many questions on how to treat AI-generated data[184] according to the existing and binding data privacy laws and who is responsible for ensuring their relevant protection. This is particularly important in view of cross-border data flows, and international arbitration cannot be seen as an exception in this regard. Since the outset, generative AI models benefit from data derived from multiple jurisdictions. Apparently, each jurisdiction also includes its own specific data protection laws. This entails that "ensuring compliance with varying regulations while maintaining seamless data access for AI development becomes a challenge".[185]

From the perspective of arbitral institutions, it is recommended to establish protocols concerning data collection, storage, sharing, and disposal. Considering data storage, in order to prevent unauthorized access and data breaches, it is necessary to use encryption and access controls. In contrast, data sharing requires more specific agreements with third parties, namely AI providers, to ensure the accurate level of privacy and security of data used within the AI models. [186]

181 "Article 39.3. Unless otherwise agreed by the parties, all hearings shall be conducted in private, and any recordings, transcripts, or documents used in relation to the arbitration shall be subject to the confidentiality provisions in Rule 59". See: *2025 Arbitration Rules of the Singapore International Arbitration Centre*, https://siac.org.sg/wp-content/uploads/2024/07/SIAC-Rules-7th-Edition_100325-full.pdf. Accessed on June 25, 2025.

182 "Article 22.7 Hearings shall be held in private unless the parties agree otherwise. The arbitral tribunal may require any witness or expert to leave the hearing room at any time during the hearing". See: *2024 HKIAC Administered Arbitration Rules*, https://www.hkiac.org/arbitration/rules-practice-notes/administered-arbitration-rules/hkiac-administered-2024-1#27. Accessed on June 25, 2025.

183 "Article 26.5. Unless the Tribunal directs or the parties agree otherwise, all meetings and hearings shall be held in private. Persons not involved in the arbitration shall not be admitted to the hearings without the approval of the Tribunal and the parties." See: *2022 DIAC Arbitration Rules*, https://www.diac.com/wp-content/uploads/2024/04/DIAC-Arbitration-Rules-2022_EN.pdf. Accessed on June 25, 2025.

184 See more: A. Alamäki, M. Mäki, R. Ratnayake, *Privacy Concern, Data Quality and Trustworthiness of AI Analytics* [in:] *Proceedings of Fake Intelligence Online*, ed. H. Teoksessa Ketamo, P. O'Rourke, Pori 2019, pp. 37–42.

185 A. Golda et al., *Privacy and Security Concerns...*, p. 48137.

186 *Ibidem*, p. 48138.

### 3.3 Copyright issues of AI-generated content in international arbitration

To start with, it is worthwhile to note that in the wake of fast advancement of AI, the existing and binding IP legislation remains silent on the protection of AI-generated works. Therefore, they do not refer to both creative works resulting from the use of AI technology and the so-called computer-generated works. The latter means "creative content generated exclusively by computer algorithms or programs and fails to address the complex issues surrounding AI-generated works".[187]

From scratch, the law has the aim to protect human authors in recognizing the originality and creativity of their works. In this context, the prior identification of an author plays a crucial role in granting such protection and thus is commonly considered a prerequisite of "copyrightability". Further, in the wake of confirming copyright and intellectual property (IP) law, the notion of "authorship" appears. In fact, the existing IP legal framework was shaped far before the emergence of new technologies, including AI. In consequence, this begs the question of who should be regarded as an author of AI-generated works. In fact, this issue has become highly contentious. Accordingly,

> Given the significant impact of AI-generated works and their substantial role in the creative process, it is now essential and unavoidable for legislative policymakers to establish a clear legal framework that defines the precise legal relationship between computers and their operators or programmers. By doing so, courts will be empowered to address the authorship of computer-generated works and allocate ownership rights accordingly.[188]

The World Intellectual Property Organization (WIPO) has indicated that the legal status of AI-produced content including text, images, and other creative works remains unclear. This indicates the absence of a uniform consensus regarding the inclusion of such content within the framework of IP protection.[189] Similarly, the question of ownership of these rights is still unresolved. It is imperative to acknowledge that, in instances where a GenAI output is not subject to intellectual

187 H. Gaffar, S. Albarashdi, *Copyright protection for AI-generated works: Exploring originality and ownership in a digital landscape*, "Asian Journal of International Law" 2025, vol. 15, p. 24, doi: 10.1017/S2044251323000735.

188 *Ibidem*. See more: P. Samuelson, *Allocating ownership rights in computer-generated works*, "University of Pittsburgh Law Review" 1986, vol. 47, issue 1, pp. 1185–1228.

189 See more: S.S. Chen, *The dawn of AI-generated content: Revisiting compulsory mediation and IP dispute resolution*, "Contemporary Asia Arbitration Journal" 2023, vol. 16, issue 2, pp. 91–115.

property (IP) law protection,[190] contractual provisions may be present to elucidate the ownership status of the content in question.[191]

First, it is important to note that IP laws were written and adopted long before GenAI emerged. This results in uncertainty over whether IP can exist in AI outputs and who would own any such rights. While this may not be an issue for certain IP rights, such as trademarks, there is widespread concern regarding copyright.[192]

On the other hand, some recent patent applications have named an AI system, DABUS, as an inventor. Despite these efforts to provide IP protection, the applications were rejected on the grounds that no human inventor was involved. This suggests that "it is unclear whether generative AI can create inventions without human inventors or if such inventions are patentable".[193]

### *3.3.1 United States*

To start with, it is noteworthy that within the framework of the legislative history of the 1976 Copyright Act, "the history of copyright law has been one of gradual expansion in the types of works accorded protection".[194] Indeed, the development of new technologies and particularly AI created many practical challenges regarding intellectual property (IP) issues. Additionally, different countries have different approaches. For example, in March 2023, the US Copyright Office issued guidance on registering works that include content generated by AI. According to this guidance, a human's creative contribution must be indicated. According to the US Copyright Office's[195] decisions, "a user's text prompt alone may not establish copyright, as the prompt merely influences the output".[196] Historically, the US District Court of Columbia held a case on the copyrightability of AI-generated content in 2023. Accordingly, the plaintiff was against the Office's decision refusing the registration of the image which was described in his application as "autonomously

190 H. Estramant, *AI and the protection of copyright and intellectual property: Policy considerations – Complex technology – simple solutions*, "Diplomatic Magazine" February 4, 2024, https://diplomatmagazine.eu/2024/02/04/ai-and-the-protection-of-copyright-and-intellectual-property/. Accessed on November 26, 2024.

191 *Generative AI: Navigating Intellectual Property*, "IP and Frontier Technologies", WIPO 2024, https://www.wipo.int/export/sites/www/about-ip/en/frontier_technologies/pdf/generative-ai-factsheet.pdf, p. 10. Accessed on November 26, 2024.

192 *Ibidem*, p. 10.

193 *Ibidem*.

194 *Copyright and Artificial Intelligence: Part 2: Copyrightability*, "A Report of the Register of Copyrights" January 2025, p. 1, https://www.copyright.gov/ai/Copyright-and-Artificial-Intelligence-Part-2-Copyrightability-Report.pdf. Accessed on June 25, 2025.

195 See H. Gaffar, S. Albarashdi, *Copyright protection for AI-generated works: Exploring originality and ownership in a digital landscape*, "Asian Journal of International Law" 2024, https://www.cambridge.org/core/journals/asian-journal-of-international-law/article/copyright-protection-for-aigenerated-works-exploring-originality-and-ownership-in-a-digital-landscape/12B8B8D836AC9DDFFF4082F7859603E3. Accessed on November 26, 2024.

196 *Generative AI: Navigating Intellectual...*, pp. 10–11.

created by a computer algorithm running on a machine".[197] In this case, the Court rules that:

> Copyright has never stretched so far, however, as to protect works generated by new forms of technology operating absent any guiding human hand, as plaintiff urges here. Human authorship is a bedrock requirement of copyright. That principle follows from the plain text of the Copyright Act. The current incarnation of the copyright law, the Copyright Act of 1976, provides copyright protection to 'original works of authorship fixed in any tangible medium of expression, now known or later developed, from which they can be perceived, reproduced, or otherwise communicated, either directly or with the aid of a machine or device'. The 'fixing' of the work in the tangible medium must be done 'by or under the authority of the author'. In order to be eligible for copyright, then, a work must have an 'author'.[198]

In January 2025, the Copyright Office produced another report which refers to the concept of "authorship by adoption". Accordingly, the user can achieve the so-called creative judgment through accepting the AI-generated outputs. Given this approach, if a user "repeatedly enters prompts until the output matches their desired expression" it is no different than an "artist who continues to dab paint on the canvas until the image matches the painter's vision".[199] Nonetheless, the US Copyright Office stated that the sole use of prompts cannot be deemed sufficient in terms of providing human control over the generated outputs and thus does not grant the user of such an AI-powered system the authorship. Instead, prompts, even highly detailed, aim to forward instructions for the AI system in order to prevent unprotectable ideas. Therefore, if the detailed prompts could potentially embrace the user's desired outcomes, they cannot be currently deemed to control the process of producing AI-supported content.[200]

On the other hand, it is also noteworthy that:

> if a user edits, adapts, enhances, or modifies AI-generated output in a way that contributes new authorship, the output would be entitled to protection. They argued that these modifications 'should be assessed in the same way as…editorial or other changes to a pre-existing work'. Although such works would not technically qualify as 'derivative works', derivative authorship provides a helpful analogy in identifying originality. Again, the copyright

197 *Copyright Registration Guidance: Works Containing Material Generated by Artificial Intelligence*, "United States Copyright Office" March 2023, p. 2, https://www.copyright.gov/ai/ai_policy_guidance.pdf. Accessed on June 23, 2025.

198 *Stephen Thaler v Shira Perlmutter, Register of the Copyrights and Director of the United States Copyright Office, et al.*, Civil Action No. 22-1564 (BAH), pp. 8–9, https://ecf.dcd.uscourts.gov/cgi-bin/show_public_doc?2022cv1564-24. Accessed on June 25, 2025.

199 *Copyright and Artificial Intelligence…*, p. 17.

200 *Ibidem*, p. 18.

would extend to the material the human author contributed but would not extend to the underlying AI-generated content itself.[201]

### *3.3.2 China*

A case concerning infringement between Li and Liu was handled by the Beijing Internet Court (BIC).[202] The court issued a ruling that is widely considered a turning point in Chinese copyright law. First, the BIC confirmed that AI-generated images are copyrightable. Second, the court approved the idea that a user benefits from copyright on an AI-generated image. According to Chinese Copyright Law, such a person has the right to authorship. In this case, the plaintiff used open-source GenAI (Stable Diffusion) to generate an image of a woman, which was then published on the Chinese social media platform Little Red Book. The plaintiff then realized that the defendant had also published the same image without permission. Consequently, the plaintiff filed a lawsuit against the defendant.[203]

Additionally, the plaintiff believed that AI tools used to create pictures were similar to traditional cameras used to take photos. Photographers had to use their skills to take perfect pictures by adjusting different parameters, and thus they also benefited from copyrights. Currently, despite technological advancements in camera shutters, photographers still have copyrights to the photos they take. In the disputed case, the plaintiff followed the same logic. Therefore, he provided many descriptions to adjust the outcome to best fit his requirements and expectations.[204]

First, the BIC confirmed that the AI-generated image is classified as work under the Chinese Copyright Law as follows:

> According to Article 3 of the Copyright Law of the People's Republic of China (hereinafter referred to as the Copyright Law), 'The works mentioned in this Law refer to intellectual achievements that are original and can be expressed in a certain form in the fields of literature, art, and science', when examining whether the object for which the plaintiff claims copyright constitutes a work, the following elements should be considered: 1. Whether it falls under the realm of literature, art, or science; 2. Whether it is original; 3. Whether it is expressed in a certain form; 4. Whether it is an intellectual achievement. In this case, the pictures involved is no different from the

201 *Copyright and Artificial Intelligence…*, p. 25. See more: M.A. Lemley, *How Generative AI turns copyright upside down*, "Science & Technology Law Review" 2024, vol. XXV, pp. 21–44, https://law.stanford.edu/wp-content/uploads/2024/09/2024-09-30_How-Gerative-AI-Turns-Copyright-Upside-Down.pdf.

202 *Li v Liu*, Beijing Internet Court, (2023) Jing 0491 Min Chu No. 11279, https://english.bjinternetcourt.gov.cn/pdf/BeijingInternetCourtCivilJudgment112792023.pdf. Accessed on June 25, 2025.

203 *Li v Liu*, Beijing Internet Court…, p. 1; Wang Yuqian, J. Zhang, *Beijing Internet Court Grants Copyright to AI-Generated Image for the First Time*, "Kluwer Copyright Blog" February 2, 2024, https://copyrightblog.kluweriplaw.com/2024/02/02/beijing-internet-court-grants-copyright-to-ai-generated-image-for-the-first-time/. Accessed on November 25, 2024.

204 *Li v Liu*, Beijing Internet Court…, p. 12.

> photos and paintings that people usually see; obviously it falls under the category of art and is expressed in a certain form, so elements 1 and 3 are met.[205]

Second, the BIC defined "intellectual achievements" as intellectual activities performed by humans. In the disputed case, the plaintiff had to perform such activities to create an image of a woman. This meant adjusting queries, prompts, and parameters to create an image that reflected the desired aesthetic value. Additionally, the plaintiff selected the image after receiving 150 prompts and making changes to it.[206] The BIC acknowledged that the disputed image was created based on the plaintiff's intellectual input.[207]

In contrast, the term "originality" was understood through the plaintiff's personalized choices and the aesthetic value of the disputed image. In practice, this meant that the plaintiff had to provide many prompts and adjust the parameters to achieve the final output.[208]

The BIC confirmed that the plaintiff has the right to authorship under Article 11 of the PRC Copyright Law. This provision limits the definition of an "author" to natural persons or legal entities. Additionally, the designers of the AI model cannot be classified as authors. They are involved in the creation of AI tools, not a specific image. Therefore, the BIC granted the plaintiff the right of authorship by recognizing his direct intellectual contribution. Importantly, the court also stressed that any use of AI must be disclosed to ensure good faith and public notice.[209]

In sum, the BIC not only granted plaintiff copyright and stressed that:

> the generative AI model has no free will and is not a legal subject. Therefore, when people use an AI model to generate pictures, there is no question about who is the creator. In essence, it is a process of man using tools to create, that is, it is man who does intellectual investment throughout the creation process, the not AI model. The core purpose of the copyright system is to encourage creation. And creation and AI technology can only prosper by properly applying the copyright system and using the legal means to encourage more people to use the latest tools to create. Under such context, as long as the AI-generated images can reflect people's original intellectual investment, they should be recognized as works and protected by the Copyright Law.[210]

This ruling paved the way for granting copyrightability to AI-generated content in China. In the wake of this pro-technology judgment, more cases were handled by the Chinese courts over different types of works.

205 *Ibidem*, p. 10.
206 Wang Yuqian, J. Zhang, *Beijing Internet Court*..., p. 1.
207 *Li v Liu*, Beijing Internet Court..., p. 11.
208 *Ibidem*, pp. 11–12.
209 *Ibidem*, p. 14.
210 *Ibidem*, p. 13.

### 3.3.3 Europe

Within the European Union (EU), there are currently two main legal instruments dedicated to copyright of AI-generated content, including the Copyright in the Single Market Directive (CDSM)[211] and the EU Artificial Intelligence Act (EU AI Act).

Recently, the case concerning the copyrightability of AI-generated content will be analyzed based on a request for a preliminary ruling pursuant to Article 98(1) of the Rules of Procedure, addressed to the Court of Justice of the European Union (CJEU). The case, Like Company v. Google (Google Search and Google Gemini), concerns a copyright infringement claim.[212] Accordingly,

> The applicant argues that there was continual infringing behaviour on the part of the defendant during the specified period, in view of the fact that the defendant made continual use (by means of reproduction and by making available to the public) of the applicant's protected press publications, in different ways and without its consent. According to the applicant, the extent of the use exceeded the 'use of individual words or very short extracts of a press publication'. The applicant submits that, without the publisher's consent, the title of a press publication, at most, may be used free of charge and that what constitutes a 'very short extract' cannot be determined on the basis of the length of the publications, since to do so could cause significant economic harm in the case of longer text.[213]

The CJEU will address this issue by ruling on a precedent-setting case that establishes the European perspective on copyrights for AI-generated content. Overall, European case law lags behind that of the US and China. Therefore, this ruling would be a significant milestone.

It is doubtful that courts would grant copyrights to AI-generated arbitral awards. Consequently, arbitrators are encouraged to use GenAI to assist them in their work rather than replace them.

211 *Directive (EU) 2019/790 of the European Parliament and of the Council of 17 April 2019 on copyright and related rights in the Digital Single Market and amending Directives 96/9/EC and 2001/29/EC (Text with EEA relevance)*, https://eur-lex.europa.eu/eli/dir/2019/790/oj/eng. Accessed on June 23, 2025.

212 *Summary of the request for a preliminary ruling pursuant to Article 98(1) of the Rules of Procedure of the Court of Justice*, Case C-250/25, https://curia.europa.eu/juris/showPdf.jsf?text=&docid=300681&pageIndex=0&doclang=EN&mode=req&dir=&occ=first&part=1&cid=5661670. Accessed on June 29, 2025.

213 *Ibidem*, p. 5.

## 3.4 Recognition and enforcement of AI-generated arbitral awards

### *3.4.1 1958 New York Convention*

#### *3.4.1.1 Existing legal framework*

Fast developing new technologies with a special focus on AI tools will significantly change the landscape of rendering arbitral awards. It might even occur that such awards will be a result of AI-powered technologies. This begs the question, however, whether it is allowed to recognize and enforce such AI-generated arbitral awards under the 1958 New York Convention. At the outset, it is worthwhile to note that compliance with the requirements specified by the SVAMC and CIArb Guidelines, namely the disclosure of AI use, transparency, party consent, human supervision over the AI-generated outputs along with non-delegation of decision-making processes to any AI tools would likely result in having an enforceable arbitral award under the 1958 New York Convention.[214]

Party autonomy is widely seen as a core of the arbitration. Given that, "party autonomy is best served if the outcome of the arbitration is legitimate and one aligned with the parties' arbitration agreement".[215] In this light, such care is needed for the sake of ensuring both the recognition and enforcement of arbitral awards. In practice, the parties' contractual consent to apply AI-powered tools, that is in line with public policy and mandatory laws, would be enough to achieve this goal. This means that the parties' agreement, regardless of whether it is concluded either in the form of an arbitration agreement or during the arbitral proceedings, would allow for the use AI in order not only to enhance transparency but also to reduce costs of the entire arbitration process.[216]

#### *3.4.1.2 Challenges in recognizing and enforcing AI-generated arbitral awards*

In 1921, Christian Lange, a Nobel Prize laureate, pointed out in his Nobel lecture that "Technology is a useful servant but a dangerous master".[217] This sentence seems to be actual even nowadays and perfectly describes the times we are living in now. There is no doubt that GenAI tools can generate arbitral awards in a short time. Despite these practical advantages of using AI-powered tools in busy times, it is crucial to analyze different challenges in recognizing AI-generated arbitral awards. In fact, these challenges arise from the foundational legal principles of international commercial arbitration, namely the assumption that human arbitrators render decisions and the need to respect due process.

214 M. Paulsson, S. Suresh, *AI: The Modern Tribunal...*, p. 113.

215 *Ibidem*, 114; see more: M.R.P. Paulsson, *The 1958 New York Convention in Action*, Kluwer Law International 2016, pp. 112–114.

216 M. Paulsson, S. Suresh, *AI: The Modern Tribunal...*, p. 114.

217 C. Lange, *Nobel Lecture*, "Nobel Prize Outreach", https://www.nobelprize.org/prizes/peace/1921/lange/lecture/. Accessed on April 27, 2025.

The fast development of new technologies also raises questions on the recognition of AI awards under the New York Convention. According to Article I (2) of this treaty, an arbitral award is considered a decision which can be rendered by arbitrators or a permanent arbitral tribunal. Both terms, namely "arbitration proceedings" and "arbitral procedure", require human interaction. In practice, this entails written or oral presentations alongside debates held between human beings. Equally important is to mention that an algorithm would face challenges in producing a "duly authenticated award" under Article IV (I)(a) of the New York Convention, most notably in the case of understanding the term "authentic" as pertaining to a particular person. In addition, some scholars even point out that AI does not possess human intelligence like judges or arbitrators and thus cannot ensure rendering a fair decision. In contrast, AI operates according to statistical probabilities through the implementation of LLMs. The latter are dedicated to predicting the following word or sentence based on the prompts.[218]

In this light, arbitrators are deemed to be natural persons having legal personality. In contrast, "today's robots are unable to replicate the behavioural functions of a human, and therefore have the potential to significantly dilute the procedural fairness of arbitration".[219] In addition, AI systems are not perfect and thus operate based on the "black boxes" (discussed further). This means that these AI-powered tools are not capable of giving reasons behind making a certain decision. Their application in the arbitral proceedings may thus result in violations of due process principles. David Horton even elaborates such findings as follows:

> opacity is already the norm in arbitration, which is private, confidential, and often features awards that are unwritten. Second, although AI legal prediction tools are still embryonic, they work well in the simple debt collection and employment misclassification disputes that businesses routinely funnel into arbitration. Third, AI programs require little overhead and operate at lightning speed. The ability to streamline the process has become especially important in the last few years, as plaintiffs' lawyers have begun filing mass arbitrations overloading the system with scores of individual claims in an effort to saddle defendants with millions of dollars in fees. For these reasons, companies and arbitration providers have powerful financial incentives to experiment with automating decision-making in certain cases.[220]

Considering the AI-generated arbitral awards, it might occur that arbitration practitioners could challenge such award based on the lack of human qualities, namely

218 M. Lehmann, *The New York Convention's Borderline. Blockchain Arbitration and Artificial Intelligence* [in:] *Transforming Arbitration: Exploring the Impact of AI, Blockchain, Metaverse and Web 3*, ed. M. Piers, S. McCarthy, Radboud University Press 2025, pp. 81–82.

219 R. Walters, *Robots replacing human arbitrators: the legal dilemma*, "Information & Communications Technology Law" 2024, p. 8, https://doi.org/10.1080/13600834.2024.2408155.

220 D. Horton, *Forced robot arbitration*, Cornell Law Review 2023, vol. 109, p. 1, https://papers.ssrn.com/sol3/papers.cfm?abstract_id=4363124.

emotions. In this context, empathy, truth or even anger could be significant from the perspective of the decision-making process. This results from an intrinsic value that a human being should hear a case as a person obliged to comply with the duties of justice and respect.[221] In other words, the so-called emotional intelligence is of key importance in the process of rendering an award. Therefore, the AI cannot fulfill the requirement of being emotionally intelligent in view of the following aspects such as the inability to ensure fairness, identify gray areas and pinpoint contradictions, among others. These features are beyond the legal factors and thus they are linked to human thinking, not machine processes.[222]

Further, the use of AI tools may violate due process and result in rendering unreasoned decisions. In this light, one must note that the existence of algorithmic error might have an impact on the decision-making process. It might occur, however, that one algorithmic error pertains to merely one independent error in a particular case. In contrast, it is also possible that one error exists in a line of code that may influence hundreds of thousands of erroneous decisions. Within the legal context, it is thus difficult, if not impossible, to classify such error either as systematic or individualized without deconstructing the processes. Calo and Citron stress that automated systems may "create instability and uncertainty that upends people's lives''.[223] Chris Chambers Goodman also points out that "While some might refer to these outcomes as 'errors', in some cases the so-called mistaken outcomes are exactly what the algorithm was designed to achieve – or trained to achieve – or both".[224]

Finally, an AI-generated arbitral award may be refused recognition and enforcement based on public policy grounds. Importantly, Article V(2)(b) of the New York Convention provides the mechanism for such refusal by the competent authority in the country where the recognition and enforcement of arbitral award is sought. To answer the question of whether this scenario is possible, it is first crucial to refer to the concept of public policy. Indeed, this concept is not only vague but also relatively difficult to define.

221 G. Argerich, M.B. Noodt Taquela, J. Jorge, *Could an arbitral award rendered by AI systems be recognized or enforced? Analysis from the perspective of public policy*, "Kluwer Arbitration Blog" February 6, 2020, https://arbitrationblog.kluwerarbitration.com/2020/02/06/could-an-arbitral-award-rendered-by-ai-systems-be-recognized-or-enforced-analysis-from-the-perspective-of-public-policy/. Accessed on June 5, 2025.

222 B. Berardicurti, *Artificial Intelligence in International Arbitration: The World is All That is The Case* [in:] *40 under 40 International Arbitration*, ed. C. González-Bueno, Dykinson 2021, pp. 377–392.

223 R. Calo, D.K. Citron, *The automated administrative state: A crisis of legitimacy*, "Emory Law Journal" 2021, vol. 70, issue 4, pp. 819.

224 C. Chambers Goodman, *AI, can you hear me? Promoting procedural due process in government use of artificial intelligence technologies*, "Richmond Journal of Law & Technology" 2022, vol. 28, issue 4, pp. 706–707.

### *3.4.2 Possible solutions*

The recent case LaPaglia v. Valve Corp.[225] raises the question of vacatur of arbitral award because "the arbitrator allegedly relied on AI to such an extent that he 'outsourced his adjudicative role'".[226] Given the background of the case, LaPaglia (the "Claimant") is a consumer of PC games who filed a claim against Valve Corp. (the "Respondent"), which is the owner of the Steam online game store. The dispute was handled by the American Arbitration Association (AAA) with a sole arbitrator, Michael Saydah, and concerned compensation for the higher prices due to alleged antitrust violations committed by Valve Corp. In addition, "the hearing took place over 10 days, generating a 2,000-page transcribed record. The final post-hearing brief was submitted on December 23, 2024, and the Award, at 29 pages long, was issued 15 days later (with Christmas and New Year's in the middle) on January 7, 2025, when Arbitrator Saydah was scheduled to leave for the Galapagos".[227]

In response, the Claimant decided to file a petition for the sake of vacating an arbitral award that had been sent by the AAA on April 8, 2025. This petition was filed before the United States District Court for the Southern District of California ("District Court") according to 9 US Code §§ 10(a)(3), (a)(4) on the grounds that the arbitrator "outsourced his adjudicative role to Artificial Intelligence ('AI')". The Claimant stressed that under Section 10(a)(4) of the Federal Arbitration Act (FAA), namely "where the arbitrators exceeded their powers, or so imperfectly executed them that a mutual, final, and definite award upon the subject matter submitted was not made", it is possible to vacate an arbitral award. To support this petition, the Claimant set forth such facts:

1. "Artificial intelligence was used to draft the award, supplanting Arbitrator Saydah's fact finding and adjudicative role with facts found by a machine. Arbitrator Saydah admitted to the parties that he uses ChatGPT to write articles. Specifically, during a break, Arbitrator Saydah told a story about how he had been assigned to write a short article on an aviation club he was part of, and that he had used ChatGPT to write it to save time (Declaration of William Bucher)".[228]
2. The arbitrator informed the parties that he is going on a trip to Galapagos Islands and thus wants to close the case before he leaves.[229]

225 *Petition to Vacate Arbitration Award; Memorandum of Points and Authorities in Support Thereof, LaPaglia v. Valve Corp.*, No. 3:25-cv-00833, https://www.law360.com/articles/2323342/attachments/0. Accessed on May 1, 2025.

226 *When Arbitrators Use AI: LaPaglia v. Valve and the Boundaries of Adjudication*, "Aceris Law LLC" April 19, 2025, https://www.acerislaw.com/when-arbitrators-use-ai-lapaglia-v-valve-and-the-boundaries-of-adjudication/. Accessed on May 1, 2025.

227 *Petition to Vacate Arbitration...*, p. 3.

228 *Ibidem*, p. 8.

229 *Ibidem*.

3. "Arbitrator Saydah's opinion for Mr. LaPaglia's case has telltale signs of AI generation. The facts section cites facts that are both untrue and not presented at trial or present in the record. For example, Arbitrator Saydah's decision states, without source attribution, that 'Other platforms such as Roblox innovate in other ways with more mature content like horror elements paying off' [...]. But Roblox is a children's game with no horror elements. No testimony or document in the record, or anything, suggested otherwise. This sort of hallucinating or mixing up of facts is frequent when using AI tools to write content. Arbitrator Saydah's seemingly random, uncited reference to Roblox's marketing strategy that is only tangentially related to the parties' dispute betrays the use of artificial intelligence to find 'facts'".[230]
4. In addition, the arbitral award includes the following statements: "Just last year Sony and Microsoft partnered together to explore cloud gaming and streaming solutions using Microsoft Cloud Azure" and that "There is also major competition from China with their own developers and platforms, and also competition from companies in the United States, in the race to capture the Chinese market for PC Games". Neither of these statements were in the record or otherwise evidenced or even argued, and neither fact findings bear any citations, again demonstrating Arbitrator Saydah relied on generative AI to determine the facts of the case and make decisions on market power and competition for him".[231]
5. The LaPaglia's counsel's law clerk decided to use queries to determine whether the arbitrator used ChatGPT by asking it "whether it believed the Roblox paragraph was written by a human or AI. ChatGPT stated that the paragraph's awkward phrasing, redundancy, incoherence, and overgeneralizations "suggest that the passage was generated by AI rather than written by a human"[232] (Affidavit of David Jaffe).

Therefore, the Claimant admits that the arbitral award should be vacated on the grounds that the arbitrator used AI to reach his decision. Such behavior falls beyond the scope of the arbitration agreement which sought to empower "a neutral arbitrator" to settle disputes between the parties. In addition, the Claimant believes that the fact of relying on generative AI in the decision-making process not only interferes with human oversight but also betrays the expectations of the parties to get the award written by a human arbitrator.[233]

In addition, the Claimant cited other US cases, including Move, Inc. v. Citigroup Global Mkts. where the court decided to vacate an arbitral award in the case "where

230 *Ibidem.*

231 *Ibidem.*

232 *Ibidem*, p. 9.

233 *When Arbitrators Use AI...*; J. Yav, *Beyond human judgment: A critical examination of Artificial Intelligence in Arbitration via the LaPaglia v. Valve Corp. Case*, "Yav&Associates" April 21, 2025, https://www.legavox.fr/blog/yav-associates/beyond-human-judgment-critical-examination-37196.htm. Accessed on April 26, 2025.

arbitrators falsified their credentials or made other false representations".[234] That court even stressed that an award should be vacated "where 'there is simply no way to determine whether' an unqualified 'imposter' on the arbitration panel 'influenced other members of the panel or that the outcome of the arbitration was affected by his participation'".[235] Following the analogy, the Claimant believed that if a court decided to vacate a decision in the case of outsourcing the decision-making process to a person other than the appointed arbitrator, the same rule should apply in the case of outsourcing to the AI.[236] Even though the District Court has not rendered its own decision so far, it is worth analyzing possible scenarios in this case in view of the Guidelines on the use of AI in arbitration, namely the SVAMC and CIArb (discussed in detail in 3.1.2.1 and 3.1.2.3).

Under SVAMC Guideline 6 (non-delegation of decision-making responsibilities) and CIArb Article 8 (discretion over use of AI by arbitrators), the use of AI, including generative AI such as ChatGPT, in the process of drafting an arbitral award, is not *per se* forbidden unless the arbitrator does not transfer his decision-making power to AI and is not influenced by the generated outcome in the case of procedural, factual, or legal decisions. In the case LaPaglia v. Valve Corp., the Claimant alleged that the arbitrator violated these guidelines by citing both facts and evidence being outside the record "or otherwise evidenced or even argued". Moreover, the lack of adequate disclosure during the arbitral proceedings, resulting in the inability of the parties to comment, may also be recognized as a violation of due process. Further, both the SVAMC and CIArb Guidelines require the arbitrator to independently verify the accuracy of his statement in the arbitral award. Failure to comply with this guideline may be considered an inappropriate use of AI by the arbitrator. However, the Claimant did not specify in his petition the context of such AI-fabricated facts, their inconsistencies alongside over-generalizations. Even though there is no analysis of their potential influence on the arbitrator's decision-making process, their presence in the final arbitral award has already raised many doubts with this regard. In this light, it is also not specified whether the arbitrator disclosed the use of AI during arbitral proceedings. In light of this, both the SVAMC and the CIArb guidelines recommend disclosing such use and even requesting consent before applying it.[237]

In sum, although the case of LaPaglia v. Valve Corp. is still pending, the Claimant's petition raised significant questions regarding the role of AI in the decision-making process of rendering an arbitral award. As such, it represents the tensions resulting from the intersection of technology and human judgment.[238] The principle of non-delegation forms the basis of the analysis. There is no doubt that arbitrators are considered to be exercising their power and cannot simply delegate

234 *When Arbitrators Use AI...*
235 *Petition to Vacate Arbitration...*, p. 9.
236 *When Arbitrators Use AI...*
237 *Ibidem.*
238 J. Yav, *Beyond human judgment...*

their decision-making responsibilities to a third party regardless of being a human or machine. Even if AI tools may be helpful in completing administrative or drafting tasks, they cannot replace the human arbitrator in his assessment of the case's facts, evidence along with legal issues.[239]

Likewise, transparency also plays a crucial role. Therefore, arbitrators should disclose to the parties the fact that they are using the AI tool, if not seek their consent before using it. Failure to comply with this requirement may result in violation of "the parties' right to a reasoned and accountable decision". Given that, the judicial intervention may be needed to uphold the integrity of the arbitral proceedings.[240] In addition, arbitrators, even if they use AI tools in their work, are still responsible not only for accuracy but also for the integrity and human authorship of the arbitral award.[241]

Finally, this case also stresses the new trend in evidentiary issues regarding the following questions: "How can parties prove that an award – or part of it – was drafted by AI? Are AI detection tools reliable, and how should courts treat such evidence? What if an arbitrator uses AI simply to enhance clarity rather than to substitute reasoning"?[242] In practice, many practical challenges may arise because of using AI tools and there is no uniform standard on these issues thus far.

239 *When Arbitrators Use AI...*
240 J. Yav, *Beyond human judgment...*
241 *When Arbitrators Use AI...*
242 *Ibidem.*

# 4 Response of international arbitration to AI

## Revolution or evolution?

## 4.1 Principles of using AI in international arbitration

### *4.1.1 Human oversight*

At the outset, it is worthwhile to refer to the concept of "human-in-the-loop" (HITL). HITL means "an individual who is involved in a single, particular decision made in conjunction with an algorithm".[1] In fact, the HITLs can take various forms. On the one hand, they may concern a human decision-maker who has the power to decide whether to use an algorithm system for the sake of rendering a decision in a specific case. On the other hand, the HITL systems may also be used "where an individual and algorithm pass off tasks or perform tasks in concert".[2]

In the context of legal practice, these systems are reflected in actions taken by an individual to adjust an algorithm mid-determination. It can be achieved through reconfiguration of search parameters in the case of an e-discovery tool. To illustrate, "they include when an individual determines whether or how to implement an algorithmically informed conclusion, such as the commander who decides against engaging an algorithm's recommended target".[3] Importantly, one could also recognize the existence of individualized contestation as a HITL system in the case of a system enabling or requiring immediate human review of an automated decision prior to its implementation.[4]

In addition, in a narrow view of taking a single decision, there is an assumption that humans are "everywhere" at every level of the automated decision-making process. In this light, the concept of a fully autonomous machine, which is capable of taking an independent decision by itself, is rather a myth. Equally, in view of the system's perspective, it is impossible that such a machine exists or functions without human presence. In fact, this involvement may include various forms such as designing the systems, choosing the relevant data for training, formulating questions to be answered by the system alongside implementing its outputs. In addition, humans are also involved in the process of assessing and refining the

1 R. Crootof, M.E. Kaminski, W. Nicholson Price II, *Humans in the Loop*, "Vanderbilt Law Review" 2023, vol. 76, issue 2, p. 440.

2 *Ibidem*.

3 *Ibidem*.

4 *Ibidem*, pp. 440–441.

DOI: 10.4324/9781003667834-5

decision-making processes implemented by the AI systems. In this context, the human presence and thus involvement impact every stage of the AI systems' operation. Therefore, once we pay too much attention to the individual outcomes or even very specific types of applications of AI systems, various forms of human involvement may change into unregulated backdrop.[5]

Moreover, Meg Jones highlights that a purely algorithmic decision does not exist. In contrast, each system needs human interaction at a particular stage, even if it concerns merely inevitable failures. The similar standpoint is also upheld by Andrew Selbst et al. who believe that all "technical systems are subsystems" which operate within specific social and human environments. In this view, "human-in or human-off-the-loop systems are part of expansive sociotechnical systems which always include humans".[6]

HITL, aka "AI by the people" is crucial due to twofold factors, including "ensuring the proper functioning of the AI application and averting malfunctions".[7] In this context, humans are still responsible for ensuring that the AI system is functioning properly. This is particularly significant given the quality of the explanations. Humans also play a key role in preventing malfunctions. This involves overseeing AI applications to minimize risks, such as data poisoning, that could result in system malfunctions.[8]

In sum, "human-in-the-loop" "refers to a process wherein an AI system is closely monitored by a human, who is responsible for making all final decisions".[9] In other words, it represents the so-called "Augmented Intelligence" where AI systems have been designed in order to enhance human decision-making processes and learn following their interactions with human beings.[10]

In contrast, the term "human-on-the-loop" (HOTL) necessitates human involvement in the form of supervision. In this context, human intervention becomes crucial in addressing the potential challenges posed by AI systems in unexpected or undesirable scenarios.[11] Finally, the concept of "human-out-of-the-loop" refers to the absence of human supervision in the decision-making processes of AI systems. In this situation, the AI system possesses full control over the process, and human intervention is impossible. These AI systems represent so-called "Autonomous Intelligence", meaning they can adapt to various stimuli without human interaction or assistance.[12]

5 *Ibidem*, pp. 439–440.

6 *Ibidem*, p. 443.

7 A. Kouroutakis, *Rule of law in the AI era: addressing accountability and the digital divide*, "Discover Artificial Intelligence" 2024, vol. 4, no. 115, https://doi.org/10.1007/s44163-024-00191-8, p. 5.

8 *Ibidem*.

9 *UNESCO Global toolkit on AI and the role of law for the judiciary*, "UNESCO" 2024, p. 44, https://unesdoc.unesco.org/ark:/48223/pf0000387331. Accessed on June 7, 2025.

10 *Artificial Intelligence & responsible business conduct*, "OECD", p. 3, https://mneguidelines.oecd.org/RBC-and-artificial-intelligence.pdf. Accessed on June 6, 2025.

11 *UNESCO Global Toolkit*..., p. 45.

12 *Artificial Intelligence & Responsible*..., p. 3.

#### *4.1.2 Transparency*

The transparency[13] plays a crucial role in the proper decision-making process. In fact, the internal functioning of the decision-making process is usually hidden, which entails that both methods and key factors behind reaching their conclusions remain unknown to humans. Importantly, this lack of transparency in terms of understanding the working process of AI systems undermines trust and accountability, which have some further ramifications in terms of rule of law. Given that, it refers to both legal and political dimensions of the decision-making process. Against this background, if individuals disagree with the outputs generated by the AI systems, they are frequently unable to understand or challenge the process of reaching a decision (outcome).[14]

In addition, even if a minimum level of transparency is provided, the problem of so-called "black boxes" (discussed further) remains crucial in understanding the reasoning process and further in properly interpreting the outcomes. In other words, even if the algorithm's elements can be accessible, there is still a lack of understanding of how the decisions have been made and thus both the internal workings and logic of rendering a decision are far beyond human control. In this light, this opacity in the algorithm's working process raises serious concerns with regard to the rule of law, most notably in terms of biased or unjust outcomes generated by such AI systems. To confront these challenging issues, the process of maintaining the rule of law requires a certain level of human involvement in the decision-making process alongside a duty to give clear reasons and explanations. In addition, it is also crucial to remember that the appropriate level of human supervision depends on both the nature and specific functions of the AI systems' applications.[15]

Antonios Kouroutakis distinguishes threefold dimensions of the transparency in the decision-making process of AI systems. First, transparency means that humans recognize the use of automated systems. Second, there is also a need to clearly comprehend the internal functioning of the AI systems. This recommendation also encompasses the nature of the training data used for proper programming of these systems. Third, transparency also requires humans to challenge decisions produced by the AI systems. In this view, transparency is not only limited to the use of AI systems but also to the proper understanding of how these systems actually work and how to challenge the decisions produced by them.[16]

There are two approaches to the lack of transparency. Under the first one, "a lack of transparency may arise from the complexity of the algorithm's structure,

13 See also: M. McIlwrath, R. Schroeder, *Transparency in International Arbitration: What are Arbitrators and Institutions afraid of?*, [in:] *Contemporary Issues in International Arbitration and Mediation: The Fordham Papers (2010)*, ed. A.W. Rovine, Brill 2011, pp. 333–356, https://doi.org/10.1163/ej.9789004206007.i-516.96.

14 A. Kouroutakis, *Rule of law...*, p. 2.

15 *Ibidem*.

16 A. Kouroutakis, *Rule of law...*, p. 5.

such as with a deep neural network, which consists of thousands of artificial neurons working together in a diffuse way to solve a problem. This reason for AI being a black box is referred to as 'complexity'".[17] The deep neural network was developed on a mathematical model which is commonly known as "the artificial neuron". It has been designed to represent the same ability to learn like the biological neuron. Although the concept of interconnected artificial neurons was developed in the mid-1980s, nowadays it has evolved into "Deep Neural Networks". This term refers to "several layers of interconnected neurons that are used to progressively find patterns in data or to make logical or relational connections between data points".[18]

According to the second approach, "the lack of transparency may arise because the AI is using a machine-learning algorithm that relies on geometric relationships that humans cannot visualize, such as with support vector machines. This reason for AI being a black box is referred to as 'dimensionality'".[19]

### *4.1.3 Confidentiality*

Confidentiality is commonly considered of crucial importance in international arbitration, which provides not only a discreet but also a private setting for handling disputes. Importantly, confidentiality is regarded as a crucial component of the arbitral proceedings that is appreciated by authorities and users as well. One must note, however, that confidentiality has been addressed differently depending on the jurisdiction. This kind of ambiguity is shaping both the functions and applications of confidentiality, resulting in a lack of a unilateral approach in international arbitration. Recently, there has been a new trend that suggests applying stronger confidentiality requirements. Despite this fact, there are various approaches to this issue. To illustrate, the London Court of International Arbitration (LCIA) Rules explicitly specify that "parties should keep all awards and materials created for the arbitration confidential".[20] In contrast, the ICC Rules of Arbitration[21] does not

17 Y. Bathaee, *The Artificial Intelligence Black Box and the Failure of Intent and Causation*, "Harvard Journal of Law & Technology" 2018, vol. 31, no. 2, p. 901.

18 *Ibidem*, pp. 901–902.

19 *Ibidem*, p. 901.

20 Art. 30.1 of the 2020 LCIA Rules, https://www.lcia.org/Dispute_Resolution_Services/lcia-arbitration-rules-2020.aspx#Article%2030. Accessed on June 26, 2025.

21 This concept is elaborated in the Appendix I – Statutes of the International Court of Arbitration. Article 8 stipulates that "The work of the Court is of a confidential nature which must be respected by everyone who participates in that work in whatever capacity. The Court lays down the rules regarding the persons who can attend the meetings of the Court and its Committees and who are entitled to have access to materials related to the work of the Court and its Secretariat". See: *Appendix I – Statutes of the International Court of Arbitration*, https://iccwbo.org/dispute-resolution/dispute-resolution-services/arbitration/rules-procedure/2021-arbitration-rules/#block-accordion-22. Accesssed on June 26, 2025.

explicitly refer to confidentiality. This means that the arbitral tribunal may take measures to protect confidentiality if the parties express such a will.[22]

Overall, confidentiality exists in international arbitration upon the parties' mutual agreement. In addition, it is also subject to the applicable legal framework resulting from the jurisdiction involved. It is commonly acknowledged that the parties have the power to decide on the confidentiality within the arbitral proceedings.

The development and further integration of AI tools in international arbitration introduced a new paradigm of handling disputes[23]. Importantly, AI-powered innovations are widely considered to establish a new framework in the digital era. In fact, these tools are playing a crucial role in enhancing both efficiency and precision. Therefore, they can be used to complete tasks, including predictive analytics and document review in arbitration. Nonetheless, the use of these tools should also be analyzed in terms of significant challenges related to the confidentiality issues. In this light, the implementation of AI within the framework of international arbitration is based on the exchange of substantial data where both parties and arbitrators are involved. In addition, AI-powered systems might disclose, even unintentionally, either sensitive or private information in the course of the analytical process. This may lead to compromising confidentiality itself. To address these challenges, it is thus crucial to elaborate clearer and more precise regulations and guidelines to properly balance AI's advantages without compromising the key principle, namely confidentiality.[24] In this context, it is also worthwhile to note that the key issue lies in reconciling private activities and confidentiality while using more advanced technologies, most notably in terms of international arbitration. In fact, according to the European Parliament and Council, "there is a need for a new breed of legal professionals who can adapt to this new paradigm and understand the application of technology and the impact it has in the legal sphere".[25]

There is no doubt that confidentiality reflects a key standard in international arbitration. Accordingly, the parties involved should avoid any sharing of confidential information with third parties and the general public. This is mainly a difference between typical court litigation and international arbitration. In fact, the requirement of confidentiality plays a crucial role in safeguarding trade secrets, sensitive information, and privileged materials. In this regard, confidentiality introduces strict limitations concerning external disclosure. One must note, however,

22 "Article 22.3. Upon the request of any party, the arbitral tribunal may make orders concerning the confidentiality of the arbitration proceedings or of any other matters in connection with the arbitration and may take measures for protecting trade secrets and confidential information" 2021 ICC Arbitration Rules, https://iccwbo.org/dispute-resolution/dispute-resolution-services/arbitration/rules-procedure/2021-arbitration-rules/#block-accordion-22. Accesssed on June 26, 2025.

23 See more: P. Shetty, A. Singh Chauhan, *Navigating the Frontier: Assessing the Benefits and Limitations of AI Integration in International Arbitration*, "BCDR International Arbitration Review" 2023, vol. 10, issue 1, pp. 23–58.

24 M-S.A. Malekela, *AI and confidentiality protection in International Commercial Arbitration: Analysis of the existing legal framework*, "Discover Artificial Intelligence" 2025, vol. 5, issue 83, p. 2, https://doi.org/10.1007/s44163-025-00316-7.

25 *Ibidem*.

that in the wake of the increasing use of AI tools, most notably in decision-making processes and evidence evaluation, the substantial volumes of data may be easily uploaded to various AI systems. Indeed, this is one of the key prerequisites of using these tools to best benefit from their functionalities. Given that, "Utilization of AI in international arbitration would necessarily call for documents disclosed in, relevant to, and on the record in the arbitration proceeding to be uploaded into the AI tool or technology.[26]

In fact, the so-called data-driven nature of AI alongside the confidentiality in international arbitration should be seen in terms of obstacles and challenges that need to be addressed by international arbitration. Importantly, the AI systems use large datasets to function properly, and the private information pertaining to the arbitral proceedings may be revealed through unintentional exposure or even unauthorized access to these tools. It may be better illustrated based on the following three hypothetical examples concerning unintentional disclosure of confidential information.

The first one relates to the situation where a lawyer, who represents a party, relied upon generative AI while preparing a legal submission for arbitration, most notably by taking advantage of AI to summarize both key evidence and arguments. Even though the entire process of submission of documents can be sped up due to the use of GenAI, it might occur that confidential information pertaining to another client's case has been contained because of training an AI model. In this scenario, the opposing party discovers the breach of confidentiality, which has an impact on the integrity of the arbitral proceedings. In addition, it also affects the ethical obligations of the lawyer. Consequently, the arbitral tribunal must decide this issue, and thus it may result in delays along with additional costs for the parties as well.[27] This example illustrates that AI models may, even unintentionally, share confidential information. The lack of human oversight and verification of the information provided by the GenAI may compromise the integrity of the proceedings and thus be challenged. It is crucial to remember that there are no perfect AI tools so far, and thus each piece of information should be properly verified by lawyers prior to submission to the arbitral tribunal.

The second scenario refers to the situation when the arbitrator makes use of GenAI in terms of drafting an arbitral award. In this case,

> The AI tool, without the arbitrator's knowledge, incorporates language and analysis from previous awards in other cases, some of which contained sensitive commercial information about the parties involved. When the parties receive the draft final award, and identify any unauthorized use of confidential information, they may challenge the arbitrator's impartiality, potentially leading to the annulment of the award.[28]

26 *Ibidem*.

27 *Ibidem*, p. 2.

28 *Ibidem*, p. 2. See also: LaPaglia case discussed in Chapter 3.

In practice, it may result in many negative consequences for the arbitrator who trusted the outcome of GenAI in terms of his reputation. This is particularly significant in view of being appointed as an arbitrator in future cases.

The last, third example illustrates the case of the party who uses the GenAI for the sake of preparing the chronology of events alongside documents concerning the dispute. Even though the AI system seems to be very helpful in completing these tasks efficiently, some challenges related to the disclosure of confidential information may occur. This includes, for instance, private emails and internal communication that were beyond the parties' disclosure. Nonetheless, once the opposing party discovers such a breach of confidentiality in the ongoing arbitral proceedings, it may challenge its fairness. In addition, it may even result in the exclusion of evidence submitted by the party using GenAI and challenges to the jurisdiction of the arbitral tribunal as well.[29]

The above hypothetical scenarios confirm that the use of GenAI, without human oversight, may be detrimental to the integrity of the arbitral proceedings. Apparently, it may also affect the fairness and due process. Therefore, it is crucial to first understand the functioning of AI tools prior to their implementation and use by any stakeholders of the international arbitration.

Aside from unintentional exposure, the unauthorized access to confidential information by third parties may occur while using AI tools. In this light, the AI systems should be analyzed from the perspective of respecting data privacy. It is important, however, to remember that "Uploading of confidential data in Generative AI tools may still be problematic even with the elevated levels of data security set in those tools. Confidentiality in international arbitration therefore requires efficient cyber protection especially with the integration of AI tools that may be a target of cyber intrusions".[30] The international arbitration practice has already confirmed significant concerns related to security issues in using AI tools. It is thus worthwhile to note that AI systems are not fully protected from hacking, which results in unauthorized access to data and breaches of confidentiality itself. In fact, it occurs due to the large volumes of information that are stored by these AI systems. In addition, in the case of AI tools that are provided by third parties like ChatGPT, the situation becomes much more complicated.

There are more chances that unauthorized individuals access sensitive data. It is thus crucial to remember that it is not merely a hypothetical scenario. This situation has already taken place in real legal proceedings. To illustrate, the case of Gela Mikadze et al. v. Ras Al Khamah Investment Authority et al. confirms it. This case was handled by the Stockholm Chamber of Commerce (SCC) where one of the parties filed a petition to annul the award based on the allegation of violating due process. Accordingly, this party was "alleging that due process has been breached

29 *Ibidem*, p. 2.
30 *Ibidem*.

when a third party, acting on the party's order, stole confidential information from them, their attorney, and the tribunal".[31]

Another example refers to "a coder at Samsung, in search for a fix bug, uploaded lines of confidential code to ChatGPT on two separate occasions. Since ChatGPT, like any other third-party owned Generative AI tool, takes user inputs to train its model, this code was subsequently reproduced in response to users from other organisations".[32] In addition,

> In an arbitration context, similar cases may occur when a lawyer, arbitrator or a party to a commercial arbitration uploads confidential information to any of the used third-party owned Generative AI tool and result to unauthorised access by third parties. This is because, for instance, even though lawyers and arbitration practitioners are generally unfamiliar with AI tools, they use AI tools on tasks like e-discovery, document drafting and reviewing which could sometimes involve uploading confidential information in these tools for the said purposes.[33]

This challenging problem has already been addressed by the ICCA-NYC Bar-CPR Protocol on Cybersecurity in International Arbitration.[34] This provides an overview of the guidelines that are crucial in assessing the personal data protection risks and thus recommends the adoption of information-security measures. Even though this Protocol does not comprise any specific regulations concerning the cybersecurity issues while using AI systems, it has already introduced a legal framework on general cybersecurity measures that should be implemented. Therefore, it focuses on the flow of digital data without paying attention to the data breach risks related to the application of AI tools in international arbitration. In this context, it is important to note that "As AI tools continuously learn, retain and reuse data – not only personal data from the data shared and uploaded to them in form of prompts, the gap on the Cybersecurity Protocol also necessitates carefulness and sufficient oversight by lawyers, arbitrators and parties while sharing unredacted legal documents, or data in AI tools in respect of arbitral proceedings".[35]

Even though the concept of confidentiality has not been recognized globally and thus differs depending on the jurisdiction, the arbitral tribunal might use its power to issue a confidentiality order. Given that, it indicates which of the parameters of the arbitral proceedings are of a confidential nature. To illustrate, the case Resolute

31 *Ibidem.*

32 *Ibidem.*

33 *Ibidem.*

34 *ICCA-NYC Bar-CPR Protocol on Cybersecurity in International Arbitration (2022 Edition) with the assistance of the Permanent Court of Arbitration Peace Palace, The Hague*, https://cdn.arbitration-icca.org/s3fs-public/document/media_document/ICCA-reports-no-6-icca-nyc-bar-cpr-protocol-cybersecurity-international-arbitration-2022-edition.pdf. Accessed on June 25, 2025.

35 M-S.A. Malekela, *AI and Confidentiality...*, p. 2.

Forest Products Inc. v. The Government of Canada[36] confirms this standpoint by referring to types of evidence and materials presented in the arbitral proceedings that are covered by the confidentiality orders. Importantly, many arbitral institutions globally have already provided the possibility to issue a confidentiality order. Nevertheless, even in the case of lack of institutional rules providing such a possibility, the arbitral tribunals have the power to make such orders, which pertain subject to mandatory national laws. In this light, it is worthwhile to remember that "confidentiality orders might explain the parties' implicit or other responsibilities while addressing confidentiality of the arbitral processes. The arbitral tribunal's authority to impose (or remove) confidentiality restrictions on the parties that differ from those imposed by relevant laws or the parties' contract is not totally obvious".[37]

In this context, Gary Born upholds that:

> the arbitral tribunal has both wide procedural control over how the arbitral procedures are conducted and the power to interpret and apply relevant national legislation to the specific facts of each arbitral proceeding. While setting aside the arbitral tribunal's confidentiality order the Court in Commonwealth of Australia v. Cockatoo Dockyard Pty Ltd,[38] stated that, the arbitrator's order 'puts a lid on the direct or indirect use of material prepared for the arbitration, no matter how significant that material may be to the public at large...They purport to remove from public debate matters of legitimate public concern'.[39]

Considering the protection of the integrity of arbitral proceedings while using AI, it is thus advised to preserve the parties from unfavorable results in the arbitration. This is particularly important in the case of collateral uses of disclosures of materials that either have been prepared for or submitted in the course of arbitration because of data breaches. In view of this situation, it is thus crucial that the arbitral authority is empowered to issue confidentiality orders.[40]

In sum, the current status and treatment of confidentiality have not been properly covered and thus remain unsatisfactory. In addition, the application of AI tools poses new risks related to the confidentiality. To address these challenges, it is important to remember that

> arbitral tribunals have procedural authority over the conduct of the arbitral proceedings and authority to interpret and apply applicable national law to the circumstances of arbitral proceedings, that authority should include

36 *Resolute Forest Products Inc. v. The Government of Canada*, https://pca-cpa.org/cn/cases/142/. Accessed on June 25, 2025.

37 M-S.A. Malekela, *AI and Confidentiality...*, p. 2.

38 *Commonwealth of Australia v. Cockatoo Dockyard Pty Ltd.*, https://nswlr.com.au/view/35-NSWLR-689. Accessed on June 25, 2025.

39 M-S.A. Malekela, *AI and Confidentiality...*, p. 2.

40 *Ibidem.*

making mandatory confidentiality orders in line with the applicable principles on the use of AI in arbitration so as to protect the integrity of the arbitral proceedings.[41]

The increasing application of AI-powered tools within international arbitration will also require more attention to safeguard the integrity of the arbitral proceedings alongside the confidentiality issues. The concept of "confidentiality by design" proposed by Mark-Silas A. Malekela seeks to fill the existing gap. In fact, this concept reflects the principle, widely known as "privacy by design" that has been elaborated within the European Union's General Data Protection Regulation (GDPR).[42] Importantly, one must note this approach has been perceived and applied by Jus Mundi in terms of privacy and confidentiality issues related to the application of AI tools. Accordingly, since "privacy by design" requires that data protection is considered in the developing and operating of the systems from scratch, thus the same would apply in the case of "confidentiality by design". In other words, this concept would focus much more on the encryption of data that is used by GenAI within arbitration.[43] Given that, AI systems could develop the so-called built-in mechanisms for the sake of protecting confidential information from being accessed by unauthorized parties or preventing breaches. In this light, confidentiality is not reduced merely to an afterthought, but, instead it represents a core feature that is employed within the AI systems' architecture since their design and inception. Accordingly, these mechanisms should be based on more "advanced encryption, restricted access protocols, secure data storage, and robust anonymization techniques to prevent data leaks or misuse during or after the arbitration process".[44] The example of Jus Mundi has already shown the practical application of "confidentiality by design". Therefore, even if this concept has not been yet defined, it is already pertinent in international arbitration. Jus Mundi helps to address the challenges related to lengthy and complex arbitral awards and national judgments. Bearing in mind that the arbitration process is abundant in highly sensitive commercial, financial, and intellectual property information, Jus Mundi's designers employed AI for the sake of completing document review, supporting decisions, or conducting the case management with respect to confidentiality and privacy risks.[45]

41 T. Hwang, *A proposed model procedural order on confidentiality in International Arbitration: A comprehensive and self-governing code*, "Journal of International Arbitration" 2012 vol. 29, issue 2, pp. 137–169.

42 See more: *Regulation (EU) 2016/679 of the European Parliament and of the Council of 27 April 2016 on the protection of natural persons with regard to the processing of personal data and on the free movement of such data, and repealing Directive 95/46/EC (General Data Protection Regulation)*, https://eur-lex.europa.eu/legal-content/EN/TXT/PDF/?uri=CELEX:32016R0679. Accessed on June 25, 2025.

43 M-S.A.Malekela, *AI and Confidentiality…*, p. 2.

44 *Ibidem.*

45 *Ibidem.*

### *4.1.4 Ethical issues*

Currently, there are no legal frameworks in the form of regulations or even guidelines covering AI ethics in international arbitration. To address this challenging situation, it is thus worth referring to the UNESCO Recommendation on the Ethics of Artificial Intelligence, which was adopted on November 23, 2021, discussed briefly in Chapter 3. Apparently, this Recommendation provides a number of principles that might be applied in international arbitration for the sake of enhancing procedural fairness (due process), legitimacy of the decision-making process, transparency alongside accountability in the case of AI-based or AI-integrated arbitral proceedings.

In this context, it is crucial to recall these values and principles that might be applied to international arbitration. Given this objective, considering values, the respect, protection, and promotion of human rights[46] while using AI systems could be reflected during arbitral proceedings in respect of due process principle. In addition, the value related to ensuring diversity and inclusiveness could play a significant role in the proper training of AI systems in order to appoint arbitrators.[47]

One must note, however, that ethical principles are commonly considered a core of this Recommendation. These principles will be analyzed from the perspective of relevance and significance in international arbitration.

Given these criteria, the most important principle refers to "human oversight and determination". Accordingly, the Recommendation stipulates that

> It may be the case that sometimes humans would choose to rely on AI systems for reasons of efficacy, but the decision to cede control in limited contexts remains that of humans, as humans can resort to AI systems in decision-making and acting, but an AI system can never replace ultimate human responsibility and accountability.[48]

Apparently, in the context of international arbitration, this principle emphasizes that AI tools should never replace human arbitrators' decision-making processes, which are based on their skills, experience, and knowledge. This principle aligns with the "human-in-the-loop" concept, which is highly recommended in arbitration. These measures are necessary to ensure due process, and even if an arbitrator uses AI to draft an arbitral award, a human arbitrator must review and approve the ultimate decision. This standpoint has already been confirmed in the EU AI Act and the CIArb Guidelines.

Second, the principle of "transparency and explainability" is significant in preventing violations of the right to a fair trial. This principle also applies to AI systems with an extraterritorial impact. Additionally, this principle allows those who

46 *UNESCO Recommendation on the Ethics of Artificial Intelligence*, "UNESCO" 2023, p. 18, https://unesdoc.unesco.org/ark:/48223/pf0000381137. Accessed on June 2, 2025.

47 *Ibidem*, p. 19.

48 *Ibidem*, p. 22.

could be affected by a decision based on an AI algorithm to receive explanatory information. Explainability is also necessary to make the outputs generated by AI systems intelligible and provide insights into them. Against this background, the Recommendation defines explainability as:

> the understandability of the input, output and the functioning of each algorithmic building block and how it contributes to the outcome of the systems. Thus, explainability is closely related to transparency, as outcomes and sub-processes leading to outcomes should aim to be understandable and traceable, appropriate to the context. AI actors should commit to ensuring that the algorithms developed are explainable. In the case of AI applications that impact the end user in a way that is not temporary, easily reversible or otherwise low risk, it should be ensured that the meaningful explanation is provided with any decision that resulted in the action taken in order for the outcome to be considered transparent.[49]

Indeed, the recently adopted CIArb Guideline widely recommends this principle, most notably that all stakeholders of arbitral proceedings disclose their use of AI tools. This requirement is particularly significant for arbitrators, as it could protect them from challenges to arbitral awards based on the nondisclosure of AI use in arbitration. It is equally important to ensure that outputs generated by AI tools are explainable, so that the "black box" dilemma is avoided (this will be discussed in more detail further).

Third, the principle of "fairness and non-discrimination" must be properly employed in order to ensure procedural fairness. The Recommendation points out that "AI actors should make all reasonable efforts to minimize and avoid reinforcing or perpetuating discriminatory or biased applications and outcomes throughout the life cycle of the AI system to ensure fairness of such systems. Effective remedy should be available against discrimination and biased algorithmic determination".[50] Therefore, it is crucial to avoid biases in the data used for AI training. This is particularly important for AI tools that are used to make predictions about outcomes or select arbitrators for a particular case. From this perspective, biases could influence the selection of a particular person as an arbitrator. Additionally, this principle supports equality of arms, especially when one party has access to more advanced technology, such as AI tools, than the other.

Fourth, the principle of "responsibility and accountability" should not be underestimated. In this view,

> Appropriate oversight, impact assessment, audit and due diligence mechanisms, including whistle-blowers' protection, should be developed to ensure accountability for AI systems and their impact throughout their life cycle. Both technical and institutional designs should ensure auditability and

49 *Ibidem*, p. 22.
50 *Ibidem*, p. 20.

> traceability of (the working of) AI systems in particular to address any conflicts with human rights norms and standards and threats to environmental and ecosystem well-being.[51]

This principle requires the responsible selection of AI tools that best fit the needs of ongoing arbitral proceedings. This principle may also apply to AI-based evidence, which would require the submitting party to attach a document confirming its reliability. In this context, the party using such AI-generated analysis would be accountable for the reliability and probative value of the evidence. Practically speaking, it is also recommended that an arbitrator guide the parties involved and inform them of the potential far-reaching consequences of using AI-based evidence in arbitral proceedings.

Fifth, the Recommendation emphasizes the importance of ensuring the "right to privacy and data protection". Accordingly, under the UNESCO Recommendation:

> Adequate data protection frameworks and governance mechanisms should be established in a multi-stakeholder approach at the national or international level, protected by judicial systems, and ensured throughout the life cycle of AI systems. Data protection frameworks and any related mechanisms should take reference from international data protection principles and standards concerning the collection, use and disclosure of personal data and exercise of their rights by data subjects while ensuring a legitimate aim and a valid legal basis for the processing of personal data, including informed consent.[52]

This principle seems to be especially important in the case of processing personal and sensitive data. Nonetheless, it is important to acknowledge the practical challenges it presents, primarily due to the absence of a uniform legal framework for data protection. Cross-border disputes, which are often resolved through arbitration, relate to the flow of data across multiple legal systems. In addition, parties stemming from different jurisdictions may use various AI tools that comply with different data protection standards. To address this issue, the arbitration agreement or a procedural order should specify which AI tools may be used and to what extent. This approach would help prevent potential violations of data privacy duties.

Under the last principle, known as "proportionality and do not harm", the key issue is to ensure that "none of the processes related to the AI system life cycle shall exceed what is necessary to achieve legitimate aims or objectives and should be appropriate to the context".[53] Further, the Recommendation even elaborates this concept by providing more detailed information about the process of choosing the accurate AI system. Therefore, under the UNESCO Recommendation,

51 *Ibidem*, p. 23.
52 *Ibidem*, p. 21.
53 *Ibidem*, p. 20.

> The choice to use AI systems and which AI method to use should be justified in the following ways: (a) the AI method chosen should be appropriate and proportional to achieve a given legitimate aim; (b) the AI method chosen should not infringe upon the foundational values […], in particular, its use must not violate or abuse human rights; and (c) the AI method should be appropriate to the context and should be based on rigorous scientific foundations.[54]

In fact, this principle requires the proportionate use of AI tools. The arbitral tribunal should determine how to enhance the effectiveness and efficiency of arbitral proceedings with respect to procedural fairness.

In short, at first glance, the UNESCO Recommendation provides a general overview of AI ethics. However, taking a closer look helps identify principles that could be applied in international arbitration cases. Currently, the key issue is to raise awareness of these principles and provide more training to arbitrators, legal representatives, and arbitral institutions so they can use AI tools in compliance with the well-established standards in this regard.

## 4.2 In search of the "golden mean"

### *4.2.1 AI disclosure and lack of "black box" dilemma*

Disclosing[55] the use of AI in the arbitral proceedings seems to be the new standard in arbitral proceedings, and, thus all stakeholders should comply with this rule.

The "black box" dilemma is linked to the problem of using AI in the decision-making process without proper explanation on how a decision has been reached. Importantly, different types of AI-powered tools, mainly "those based on the machine learning mechanisms, are designed to analyze huge sets of data, find patterns 'hidden' therein, and offer a solution (e.g. a decision to a legal case […])".[56] In other words, such dilemma refers to the "path the AI model takes to reach a result which is not identifiable".[57] In practice, this entails that AI can deliver different outcomes and it is thus difficult, if not impossible, to explain the exact mechanisms and specific reasoning lagging behind such outputs. Therefore, it is not clear "how" and "why" the algorithm itself proposed a particular solution and thus reached a

54 *Ibidem.*

55 See also: E. Chan, K. Limond, *Striking the right balance: approaching disclosure of generative AI-assisted work product in international arbitration*, "b-Arbitra: Belgian Review of Arbitration" 2024, vol. 2024, issue 1, pp. 69–96.

56 B. Brożek, M. Furman, M. Jakubiec, B. Kucharczyk, *The black box revisited. Real and imaginary challenges for automated legal decision making*, "Artificial Intelligence and Law" 2024, vol. 32, p. 427.

57 B. Praštalo, *Arbitration Tech Toolbox: AI as an Arbitrator: Overcoming the "Black Box" Challenge?*, "Kluwer Arbitration Blog" August 23, 2024, https://arbitrationblog.kluwerarbitration.com/2024/08/23/arbitration-tech-toolbox-ai-as-an-arbitrator-overcoming-the-black-box-challenge/. Accessed on April 28, 2025.

certain decision.[58] This is mainly related to the lack of transparency which can be understood in twofold ways (discussed above).

Further, this also raises the question of explainability patterns. In practice, under this approach, AI systems, including ML models, are acknowledged to be explainable once their reasoning is "understood by humans through an external, simplified representation".[59] This problem is thus analyzed from both IT and legal perspectives. Even though the law itself does not provide a uniform definition of explainability, there is a consensus over rendering decisions that is well justified and reasoned. Such decisions should be based on the facts, legal provisions, and arguments raised by the parties concerned. In this light, the AI system should be designed to provide both decisions along with the legal rules and arguments relevant in view of the particular case.[60]

Moreover, it is worthwhile to note that the quality of the explanation is equally important as transparency. Therefore, explanations provided must be clear, appropriate, and sufficiently elaborated to meet these requirements. Following Tasioulas,

> even if an explanation exists and is accessible to a minimally adequate degree, there is still a further question as to whether it is an explanation of the right kind, in the sense of being one that justifies the decision that has been made. A clear explanation leaves no doubt as to the real reason behind the decision, while an appropriate and sufficient explanation is tailored to specific facts on which the decision was based.[61]

On the other hand, Bordt et al. represent a different standpoint. They believe that "explanations do not work especially in adversarial relationships because different algorithms have the potential to produce inconsistent explanations or because there is inherent ambiguity in explanations".[62]

Overall, even if the requirements for transparency and explainability of the AI applications are crucial in their operation, their enforcement may be a challenge and even may hinder AI developments. In this light, these requirements may play a crucial role in limiting the design flexibility of AI systems and thus result in the reduction of their effectiveness. Against this background, Adadi and Berrada stress that:

> explainability is an essential property; however, it is not always a necessity. In fact, requiring every AI system to explain every decision could result in less efficient systems, forced design choices, and a bias towards explainable, but less capable and versatile outcomes. Furthermore, making AI systems explainable is undoubtedly expensive; they require considerable resources

58 B. Brożek, M. Furman, M. Jakubiec, B. Kucharczyk, *The black box revisited...*, p. 428.

59 *Ibidem*.

60 *Ibidem*, pp. 428–429.

61 A. Kouroutakis, *Rule of law...*, p. 5.

62 *Ibidem*. See more: S. Bordt, M. Finck, E. Raidl, U. von Luxburg, *Post-hoc explanations fail to achieve their purpose in adversarial contexts*, "FAcc" 2022, pp. 891–905.

> both in the development of the AI system and in the way it is interrogated in practice.[63]

This view thus considers two sides of a coin and explains both advantages and challenges of such a solution. In this context, it is also crucial to remember that the theoretical framework of AI systems' operations may differ from their practical dimension. Therefore, it is advised to find a consensus on how to properly balance both extremes. Currently, this situation is commonly considered a policy challenge. It is thus difficult to find the proper balance between transparency and explainability of AI systems, and thus to comply with the rule of law. This is particularly important from the perspective of the individuals who would like to receive decisions in respect to their due process rights. To address these challenges, one possible solution stresses the importance of human agency. In this regard, human oversight could be seen as a response to this challenging problem and a way to counter the risks resulting from the lack of both transparency and explainability in government algorithms.[64]

On the other hand, Green represents a different view and thus argues that

> evidence suggests individuals are often unable to fulfill the necessary oversight functions effectively. As a result, policies that rely on human oversight to mitigate these risks may legitimize such AI Applications without the necessary safeguards. In line with the above, it is argued that human oversight monitoring complex AI systems is ineffective as it is not possible to have meaningful control.[65]

Lastly, the "black boxes" also result in a lack of interpretability. In this view, there is no transparency in the algorithm's operation. Given that, it is difficult, if not impossible, to outline the critical elements necessary to make autonomous decisions. As such, humans may have some difficulties in identifying both the internal workings of an algorithm and the decision-making process. In fact, without the proper understanding of the algorithm's operation, many new challenges arise, including those associated with the rule of law. This entails that the decisions rendered based on the "black boxes" may be biased and thus lack transparency and accountability in the decision-making process.[66]

To address this challenging problem, the so-called "white boxes" have been developed in the form of "explainable AI movement" (X.AI). In practice, they reflect the assumption that "AI algorithms already perform tasks [...] that are transparent not only to their creators but also to end-users (or anyone who may

63 A. Kouroutakis, *Rule of law...*, p. 5. See more: A. Adadi, M. Berrada, *Peeking inside the black box: a survey on explainable artificial intelligence (XAI)*, "IEEE 2018", vol. 6, pp. 52138–52160, https://ieeexplore.ieee.org/stamp/stamp.jsp?tp=&arnumber=8466590. Accessed on June 23, 2025.

64 A. Kouroutakis, *Rule of law...*, p. 5.

65 B. Green, *The flaws of policies requiring human oversight of government algorithms*, "Computer Law Security Review" 2022, vol. 45, https://doi.org/10.1016/j.clsr.2022.105681.

66 A. Kouroutakis, *Rule of law...*, p. 3.

be affected by the algorithm's decision)".[67] Further, the US National Institute of Standards and Technology elaborated four principles related to the Explainable Artificial Intelligence that could be summarized as follows:

1. Explanation: A system delivers or contains accompanying evidence or reason(s) for outputs and/or processes.
2. Meaningful: A system provides explanations that are understandable to the intended consumer(s).
3. Explanation Accuracy: An explanation correctly reflects the reason for generating the output and/or accurately reflects the system's process.
4. Knowledge Limits: A system only operates under conditions for which it was designed and when it reaches sufficient confidence in its output.[68]

This concept reflects a twofold approach that considers the significance of both process-based and outcome-based explanations along with the role of explanation purpose and style of delivering such an output. In this context, it is worthwhile to remember that developers and designers of AI tools may differ from policymakers and end users in terms of explanation needs.[69] The scrutiny of an AI tool through the lens of these four principles may be useful in avoiding the "black box" dilemma in the decision-making process. The core of this analysis lies in the proper understanding of terms such as explanation, output, and process.

The first one, explanation means "the evidence, support, or reasoning related to a system's output or process".[70] Second, the output is defined as "the outcome from or the action taken by a machine or system performing a task".[71] In practice, there are different outputs depending on the tasks. To illustrate, in the case of a grammar checking system, the output is represented by the list of grammatical errors and proposed corrections. In the context of classification systems, such an output is understood as an object identifier or a spam detector. The last term, namely process, concerns "the procedures, design, and system workflow that underlie the system. This includes documentation about the system, information on data used for system development or data stored, and related knowledge about the system".[72]

The explanation principle does not assess the correctness, accuracy, or usefulness which fall within the scope of meaningful and explanation accuracy principles. In practice, explanations will differ depending on the given system or scenario.

67 B. Brożek, M. Furman, M. Jakubiec, B. Kucharczyk, *The black box revisited...*, p. 429.

68 P. Jonathon Philips et al., *Four principles of explainable Artificial Intelligence*, "National Institute of Standards and Technology" 2021, p. ii, https://nvlpubs.nist.gov/nistpubs/ir/2021/NIST.IR.8312.pdf. Accessed on May 2, 2025.

69 *Ibidem*, p. 2.

70 *Ibidem*.

71 *Ibidem*.

72 *Ibidem*.

Such a broad understanding of this term aims to accommodate a wide variety of AI applications.[73]

Under the meaningful principle, "the intended recipient understands the system's explanation(s)".[74] This principle thus focuses on explaining why a system behaved in a particular way. There are various factors that result in considering an explanation as a "good" one. These factors relate to the person's prior knowledge, past experiences alongside psychological differences existing between people. In addition, it is worthwhile to remember that the significance of the term "meaningful" will also evolve because of the new experience with a task or system. Likewise, different groups will also have different expectations concerning the explanations provided by the system. In this light, it is natural that developers of the system will expect different explanations than an end user. Equally, beyond audience features, the explanation's purpose also influences what type of information should be transferred. Given that, "meeting the meaningful principle will be accomplished by understanding the audience's needs, level of expertise, and relevancy to the question or query at hand".[75]

Both the explanation and meaningful principles have the aim to provide that a system's explanations can be understood by the intended audience. In this context, according to these two principles, there is no need to provide a truthful explanation of how a system processes in order to generate its content. In contrast, that responsibility results from the explanation accuracy principle, which focuses on the actual veracity of a system's explanation. This concept also differs from decision accuracy, which reflects either correct or incorrect system judgment. Despite the system's decision accuracy, it is possible that the corresponding explanation is far from describing the real process of how this system has reached a decision or an action. Currently, AI researchers use standardized measures of algorithm and system accuracy. To address these challenges, there is still an ongoing process of developing more accurate metrics for explanation accuracy.[76]

The last principle, namely knowledge limits, stresses that systems should identify and explicitly indicate when they are working outside their scope or when their outputs may not be reliable. Through understanding of knowledge limits, systems may refrain from providing inappropriate or inaccurate answers and thus a judgment is also not provided. Such transparency may result in enhancing the users' trust and thus prevent generating misleading, dangerous, or even unjust content. In practice, a system may reach or exceed its own knowledge limits in two different ways. First, the system may process an operation or query that is mainly outside its area of expertise and thus cannot provide an answer. Second, "the confidence

73 *Ibidem*, p. 3.
74 *Ibidem*.
75 *Ibidem*, p. 4.
76 *Ibidem*.

of the most likely answer may be too low, depending on an internal confidence threshold".[77]

Overall, in order to enhance the rule of law in the decision-making process, there is a need to ensure human involvement. In addition, it is also recommended to provide both the reason and explainability of a particular decision.[78]

### *4.2.2 Multi-Agents AI*

At the outset, it is worthwhile to define the term "Multi-Agent Systems" (MAS)[79], which has become a paradigm for addressing complex tasks that typically exceed the capabilities of a single agent. Therefore, this term can be understood as follows:

> A Multi-Agent System consists of several agents, which interact with one another using a communication language. In such systems, agents can negotiate, collaborate or even compete with one another to achieve common system delegated goals. Each agent has a local view of the environment; generally it has been provided by specific operational goals, and it is known that the agent is unable to solve the system tasks alone, at least with the quality, efficiency, resources, and other constraints defined by the problem.[80]

The MAS concept is based on interdisciplinary research. In this context, game theory has played a key role in shaping formal frameworks. These frameworks are necessary for analyzing interactions between rational agents. Information theory is necessary for the proper application of mechanisms driven by seminal works in order to conduct encoding, transmission, and signal interpretation between MAS.[81] In fact, MAS[82] were created to enhance adaptability and provide greater robustness. This is based on the assumption that the MAS would be more effective than single-agent systems.[83]

77 *Ibidem*, p. 5.

78 A. Kouroutakis, *Rule of law...*, p. 3.

79 See also: K. Gal, B.J. Grosz, *Multi-agent systems: Technical & ethical challenges of functioning in a mixed group*, "Daedalus" 2022; vol. 151, issue 2, pp. 114–126, doi: https://doi.org/10.1162/daed_a_01904; B. ASbrahams, E. Belluci, J. Zeleznikow, *Incorporating fairness into development of an integrated multi-agent online dispute resolution rnvironment*, "Group Decis Negot" 2012, vol. 21, pp. 3–28, https://doi.org/10.1007/s10726-010-9189-3; Xie Jing, C.C. Liu, *Multi-agent systems and their applications*, "Journal of International Council on Electrical Engineering" 2017, vol. 7, issue 1, pp. 188–197, https://doi.org/10.1080/22348972.2017.1348890.

80 K.M. Khalil et al., *Intelligent techniques for resolving conflicts of knowledge in multi-agent decision support systems*, "arXiv" 2014, https://arxiv.org/pdf/1401.4381. Accessed on June 25, 2025.

81 Tian Fangqiao et al., *An outlook on the opportunities and challenges of multi-agent AI systems*, "arXiv" 2025, p. 1, https://arxiv.org/pdf/2505.18397.

82 See more: Feng Zhaohan et al., *Multi-agent embodied AI: Advances and future directions*, "arXiv" 2025, https://arxiv.org/pdf/2505.05108.

83 *Ibidem*, p. 4.

It should be noted that MAS are trained to address various limitations related to the "divide-and-conquer" rule. Therefore, these agents can promptly adjust their task allocations based on real-time feedback and environmental changes. This means that, rather than being confined to fixed task partitions, these MAS can adapt the distribution of workloads based on the current situation among different agents. In practice, this refers to self-organized task allocation beyond human-specified decompositions. For example, in traditional systems, humans are responsible for deciding how to properly divide complex tasks into smaller, more detailed subtasks and assign them to various agents. In contrast, MAS are trained to adapt to a changing and unpredictable environment based on real-time feedback. Accordingly, MAS self-organize to complete a particular task. While this feature is interesting, it is also associated with risks, most notably error amplification in self-organizing task allocation. If an error occurs within the dynamic structure of the MAS, it can easily spread throughout the entire system.[84]

In this light, the autonomous agent primarily has two tasks to complete. The first relates to "deliberation". In this context, the agent decides what to achieve, which refers to its goal. The second task focuses on "means-end reasoning" and involves planning how to achieve the goal.[85]

In practice, the MAS could be applied to the procedural stages of international arbitration as follows. First, the claimant's submission could be reviewed by the MAS for correctness. Then, the MAS could automatically forward it to the respondent and appoint the arbitrator, as well as schedule the preliminary meeting or case management conference. Thus, rather than applying different AI models, the MAS could manage the entire arbitration process. This is currently just a theoretical concept, but it may become more relevant as AI technology develops. The key issue is providing a human-in-the-loop to comply with well-established international arbitration standards. For this reason, human-AI hybrid models are highly recommended.

### *4.2.3 Human-AI hybrid models*

Alongside the rapid development of new technologies, the human-AI hybrid models seem to be a reasonable response. Importantly, there is a considerable number of AI systems that cannot be classified as fully autonomous. Instead, they are recognized as hybrids of computer and human responsible for the decision-making process.[86]

84 *Ibidem*, p. 5.

85 N. Maudet, S. Parsons, I. Rahwan, *Argumentation in Multi-Agent Systems: Context and Recent Developments* [in:] *Argumentation in Multi-Agent Systems*, ed. N. Maudet, S. Parsons, I. Rahwan, "ArgMAS 2006. Lecture Notes in Computer Science", Springer 2007, vol 4766, p. 4, https://doi.org/10.1007/978-3-540-75526-5_1.

86 H. Surden, *Artificial Intelligence and law: An overview*, "Georgia State University Law Review" 2019, vol. 35, issue 4, p. 1320.

Under this concept, the human arbitrator would still be still responsible for rendering a reasoned and enforceable arbitral award with the support of AI-powered tools. Indeed, this solution would properly balance both human and technology factors to fit the best practices in international arbitration.

Currently, while rendering an arbitral award, an arbitrator is required to go through a four-level steps process and thus he must:

1. consider, weigh, and hear the evidence from both parties, including witness testimonies, documents, and other relevant information;
2. consider the legal framework governing the dispute, including contractual agreements, relevant laws, and any applicable rules of arbitration;
3. understand the nuances of the case and evaluate the strength of each party's position; and
4. issue a written award outlining their findings, the legal reasoning behind the decision, and any remedies or damages awarded to the prevailing party.[87]

At the current status of development, the AI-powered tools have been designed to summarize the large sets of documents, evidence, and case-related information. Even though some emotion AI-related tools have been developed, they are rather seen as a supporting tool, instead of being fully able to conduct sentiment analysis. In fact, such AI tools lack the ability to evaluate evidence in a more nuanced way. Therefore, they cannot fully act like human arbitrators. This feature is crucial in assessing the witness's credibility or assessing the reliability of documents.[88]

Finally, looking into the future, there are more in-depth discussions concerning the concept of "Arbitration Bot" (ArbBot) as an alternative digital substitute for human arbitrators. From scratch, under this idea, ArbBot would be responsible for maintaining procedural fairness along with upholding the principle of equality between the parties. Thanks to access to well-developed and extensive case law databases, the possibility to analyze outcomes and the application of precedent-based logic, the ArbBot could be potentially programmed in order to deliver arbitral awards. Even though such a theoretical model could be implemented in view of the technological advancements, it raises questions about the legitimacy of such awards under the 1958 New York Convention. In fact, they may not be recognized and enforced under the currently binding legal framework. Supporters of this concept suggest a more pro-technology approach that should be incorporated by the

87 E. Chan, K.N. Gore, E. Jiang, *Harnessing Artificial Intelligence in international arbitration practice*, "Contemporary Asia Arbitration Journal" 2023, vol. 16, issue 2, pp. 292–293.

88 *Ibidem*, p. 293.

New York Convention.[89] Given the above, it is thus recommended to implement a human-AI hybrid model which will support the work of the human arbitrator.[90]

89 E. Treacy, *The effectiveness of Artificial Intelligence in simplification of arbitration proceedings: Fiction or seventh seal in the world of arbitrators?*, "International Journal of Law, Ethics and Technology" 2022, vol. 137, pp. 144–145.

90 See also: M. De'Shazer, *Advancing legal reasoning: The integration of AI to navigate complexities and biases in global jurisprudence with semi-automated arbitration processes (SAAPs)*, "arXiv" 2024, https://arxiv.org/pdf/2402.04140; R. Alnaber, *An "A-eye" to the future of arbitration: a new world or a better world?*, "International Journal of Law and Information Technology" 2025, Vol. 33, https://doi.org/10.1093/ijlit/eaaf006; G.I. Zekos, *Advanced Artificial Intelligence and Robot-Justice*, Springer 2022; C.I. Florescu, *The interaction between AI (Artificial Intelligence) and IA (International Arbitration): technology as the new partner of arbitration*, "Romanian Arbitration Journal Revista Romana de Arbitraj" 2024, vol. 18, issue 1, pp. 42–73.

# Conclusions and recommendations

AI-powered tools are fundamentally changing the landscape of dispute resolution. Against this backdrop, all actors in the arbitral process are adopting a pro-technology approach, seeking to maximize the benefits of these new technologies while preserving the right to a fair trial, due process, and privacy. This is done, *inter alia*, to improve efficiency, accuracy, and accessibility.

It should be noted, however, that in addition to the positive aspects of the use of AI in arbitration, there are many legal issues and challenges that need to be addressed, including ethical issues, the regulatory framework, and transparency. This analysis leads us to conclude that the use of AI in arbitration is not a fundamental revolution but a gradual evolution. Arbitral institutions are aware of the potential challenges, which is why they mainly limit their use of AI tools to administrative tasks.

In addition, it is worthwhile to note that there is a significant distinction between ad hoc and institutional arbitrations. The former refers to the broader responsibility of an arbitrator who manages the entire arbitral proceedings by himself. This means that an arbitrator should also be equipped with technological competence to the best extent to fulfill his duties in a digital environment. The latter, in turn, provides support by an arbitral institution. In fact, such an institution may be responsible for some technical use of AI-powered tools, including case management and the checking of arbitral awards in view of their spelling and mistakes. In this light, the arbitrator can delegate some technical work to such an institution. However, in the context of CIArb Guidelines on the Use of AI in International Arbitration, the arbitrator himself should also understand the functionality, limitations, and risks related with employing different types of AI-supported tools in arbitral proceedings and even guide the parties of the dispute. In fact, both ad hoc and institutional arbitration introduce a new paradigm in handling disputes with the use of AI tools. This will certainly require new competencies of arbitrators – not only in using such tools but also in providing the parties with reliable information on their potential impact on the arbitral proceedings.

The arbitrators' abuse or misuse of AI-powered tools without proper disclosure may have negative ramifications on their reputation in the future. Importantly, it may even impact their appointments as arbitrators in the next proceedings. Whether the lack of disclosure will have an influence on the panel of arbitrators and potential removal from the panel of arbitrators still remains a question to be addressed.

DOI: 10.4324/9781003667834-6

Despite these unknown directions, there is no doubt that arbitrators are highly encouraged to enhance their technical skills to avoid any troublesome situations in rendering binding and enforceable arbitral awards. In the longer perspective, such an approach may even be helpful to preserve a good name of arbitrator and reflect its flexibility in adjusting to new trends in international arbitration.

By contrast, in practice, it will be difficult to assess whether the parties have used AI tools in arbitral proceedings, if not even impossible to prove so in certain situations. This also relates to the problem of not strictly using AI but being inspired by AI-generated outcomes. Indeed, the rapid advancement in AI will shift the paradigm in international arbitration.

In terms of AI ethics, the UNESCO Recommendation provides a broad framework. Importantly, these recommendations can be applied to international arbitration as well. The key issue is thus to raise awareness of these ethical guidelines and enhance training for arbitrators, legal practitioners, and arbitral institutions. These actions are necessary to ensure that AI tools comply with well-established ethical standards.

To sum up, the rapid development of AI and advancements in this field will definitely change standards in conducting arbitral proceedings. The increasing number of administrative tasks will be constantly delegated to AI-powered tools to enhance efficiency and reduce costs and time. Even though there is nothing wrong in AI itself, it is advised to first understand both advantages and challenges resulting from these new technologies and their impact on arbitral proceedings.

Importantly, we should look for a "golden mean" to incorporate AI tools into arbitration while respecting the fundamental principles of international arbitration. Therefore, the future of arbitration is likely to be shaped in the form of a human-AI hybrid model, which would combine AI-based tools with human oversight and expertise. Such a balance is necessary to ensure optimal outcomes in arbitration.

The analysis of the current status of AI-powered tools in international arbitration led to the formulation of the following recommendations that are divided into short- and long-term solutions to these challenging problems.

The short-term solutions provide relatively easy adaptable tools that could fill the legal gap in using AI-powered tools in arbitration. These recommendations could be summarized as follows:

First, each actor of the arbitral proceedings should be equipped with technological knowledge on AI. Both the legal counsels who prepare documents along with the arbitral institutions and arbitrators will have to represent a deeper understanding of advantages along with limitations and risks in using AI in international arbitration. It will be crucial in view of arbitrators who will have to comply with this new trend. In this light, it is recommended that arbitrators enhance their technological competence and improve their skills in using AI tools through special training. This begs the question of who should be responsible for providing such courses on AI and how to verify the technological skills of arbitrators. In this context, it is probable that well-known arbitral institutions such as the Chartered Institute of Arbitrators (CIArb) might introduce specialized training for arbitrators to comply with the new digital era.

On the other hand, it also begs the question of whether such technological skills should be verified prior to listing on the panel of arbitrators or even require some updates on the current lists to reflect this new trend. As for now, it seems that the arbitrators should be aware by themselves that such competencies are needed in view of their duty to render binding and enforceable arbitral awards. This is also crucial given the recent case of LaPaglia, which has already raised the question of using AI tools by arbitrators without proper disclosure to the parties of the dispute. Even though there is no judgment in this case so far, it is also interesting whether the court in California will consider the specificity of arbitral institutions. In the LaPaglia case, the AAA-ICDR institution was responsible for handling the arbitral proceedings. Indeed, this institution is commonly known for its pro-technology approach, and the examples of issued "Principles Supporting the Use of AI in Alternative Dispute Resolution" and "Guidance on Arbitrators' Use of AI Tools" by AAA-ICDR confirm this standpoint.

Second, in light of above, the amendment of the rules of arbitral proceedings, which would specify permitted use of AI, could also be seen as a solution to this problem. In spite of this recommendation, this does not compromise the need to avoid hallucinations, errors, and mistakes in arbitral awards. Arbitrators not only are, but should always be responsible for rendering binding and enforceable awards under the 1958 New York Convention.

Third, the close cooperation between IT and arbitral institutions is recommended to provide services fulfilling their obligations in terms of confidentiality and data protection. In the future, it is possible that arbitral institutions will develop their own chatbots to provide the best quality of their services with respect to fundamental principles of arbitration itself. As such, the arbitral institutions could create their own AI-powered tools like platforms for e-filing of a case, remote hearings, and submission of documents in cooperation with IT companies.

Fourth, special codes of conduct reflecting ethics of using AI in the digital environment are needed to guide arbitrators on potential risks and limitations of different tools. Arbitrators are deemed to be responsible for the integrity of arbitral proceedings and thus they should be aware of all possible ramifications of inappropriate application of AI in international arbitration. In fact, it may relate even to violations of due process and thus impact the recognition and enforcement of arbitral awards under the 1958 New York Convention.

Fifth, the use of AI in arbitration should focus on upholding the fundamental principles of arbitration. Therefore, both arbitral institutions and arbitrators personally will play a crucial role in the whole process. It is therefore recommended to introduce a global standardization of AI in arbitration. Cooperation between arbitral institutions would make it much easier to develop global standards and best practices to ensure the uniformity and reliability of arbitral proceedings.

Under the last, sixth recommendation, it is advised to create a legal framework that defines how arbitrators can use AI in their daily work, providing solutions similar to the IBA Guidelines on Conflicts of Interest in International Arbitration. Therefore, this recommendation considers the practical dimensions of using AI-powered tools by all stakeholders of the arbitration process. Importantly, the

*Table 1* Disclosure Guidelines on Using AI Tools

| ***RED LIST (Non-waivable)*** *Prohibited use of AI* | ***RED LIST (waivable)*** *Allowed use of AI upon the consent of the parties (and arbitral tribunal)* | ***ORANGE LIST*** *Use of AI may give rise to justifiable doubts and disclosure is recommended* | ***GREEN LIST*** *No obligation to disclose the use of AI* |
|---|---|---|---|
| AI trained on confidential data | Using AI for legal reasoning | Preparing documents (submissions and evidence) | ClauseBuilder AI |
| AI fully renders an arbitral award without the human oversight and supervision (arbitrator does not review the outcome generated by AI-powered tool) | Analysis of the AI-based evidence | Making case summaries | Document review and contract analysis |
| Assessment of witness credibility only by AI tools without human involvement (Emotion AI) | Machine translation tools for parties' submissions | Appointing arbitrators | AI-powered legal research tools (i.e. Jus Mundi AI) and analysis of case precedents |
| | AI-based translations to interpret witness testimony | Legal analysis and case summaries | AI-based document search and tags |
| | Emotion AI for parties' and arbitrator's behaviors | Drafting procedural orders | Case management of arbitral proceedings, including scheduling hearings, witness examinations, and experts |
| | Drafting an arbitral award (with human oversight and review by arbitrator prior to publication) | AI-powered transcription tools | Spelling, grammar, and style checking of arbitral awards and submitted documents |

complex rules on what types of AI-assisted tools are allowed would prevent any violations and undesirable behaviors in both the arbitral proceedings and the process of rendering an arbitral award. Similarly, the distinction between a green, orange, and red list would also indicate which of the AI-based tools could lead to a challenge or even the setting aside of an arbitral award (see Table 1).

On the other hand, it is always recommended to implement human oversight when using AI-powered tools, regardless of the proposed classification on the green, orange, or red list.

Considering the long-term solution, there is a need for more intense international cooperation to create a legal framework covering the use of AI-powered tools in arbitration at an international level. Importantly, the UNCITRAL could play a significant role in this field. In this light, this recommendation opts for regulating these issues by international "soft law" akin to the UNCITRAL Model Law. This "soft law" framework would provide greater flexibility and adaptability compared to traditional "hard law" instruments such as international conventions. It could lay down the legal foundation for future implementation by individual states through their domestic legislation. This solution aims to harmonize legal, ethical, and technological considerations related to the use of AI-powered tools in international arbitration with respect to promoting both innovation and adaptability in arbitration practices globally.

To support this idea, it is worth recalling the definition of "soft law" norms which "are generally understood to be those that cannot be enforced through public force. These norms can emanate from State actors, be they legislators, governments or international organizations. They can also emanate from non-State actors, such as private institutions and professionals or trade associations".[1] One may ask, however, what are the practical dimensions of "soft law" regulations. Even though such "soft law" does not possess a normative power, it carries the so-called "soft normativity". This means that it represents a recognized standard-setting function which has far-reaching consequences. Such "soft law" shapes behaviors instead of creating strict obligations. In spite of having a non-binding effect, "soft law" represents an efficient tool in addressing challenging problems.[2] It also results in upholding respect and voluntary compliance between different stakeholders. It has already been proven by the UNCITRAL Model law, albeit not a formally binding instrument, which played a significant role in shaping national legal arbitration systems. In addition, the UNCITRAL fulfills its obligations in harmonizing arbitration standards globally.

1 G. Kaufmann-Kohler, *Soft law in international arbitration: Codification and normativity*, "Journal of International Dispute Settlement" 2010, vol. 1, issue 2, pp. 283–284.

2 *Ibidem*, p. 295. See more: J.S. Reddy, V. Singh, *Soft law, hard justice: Regulating Artificial Intelligence in arbitration*, "Contemporary Asia Arbitration Journal" 2024, vol. 17, issue 2, pp. 191–236.

# Index

Made in the USA
Las Vegas, NV
19 September 2026

5b26b19d-6ca3-4e00-a898-98e8ef14ebd8R01